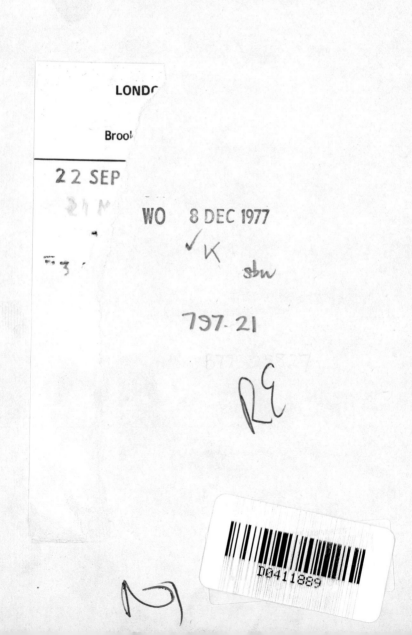

D0411889

HARRY GALLAGHER ON SWIMMING

Harry Gallagher
on Swimming

(REVISED EDITION)

PELHAM BOOKS

First published in Great Britain by
PELHAM BOOKS LTD
52 Bedford Square
London WC1B 3EF
1970
REVISED EDITION 1976 ✓

ISBN 0 7207 0335 2

Printed in Great Britain by
Hollen Street Press Ltd at Slough
and bound by James Burn at Esher, Surrey

To all those swimmers who tried hard
but never quite made the grade –
I dips me lid

CONTENTS

ILLUSTRATIONS

LINE DRAWINGS

ACKNOWLEDGEMENTS

My thanks to P.S. Harburger, U.S.A. Swim Records Officer, for his assistance.

FOREWORD

by Sir Edgar S. Tanner, C.B.E., E.D., M.P.

To write the foreword to this excellent book by my friend Harry Gallagher, is indeed a pleasure.

Coach of Australian Olympic Swimming teams, of 46 world record holders in Freestyle, Back and Butterfly strokes, of winners of 9 Gold, 10 Silver, and 5 Bronze Medals at Olympic Games, of 12 Gold, 6 Silver, and 3 Bronze Medals at British Commonwealth Games, and winners of 146 Australian Championships during the past few years is enough, alone, to stamp the author as a coach who not only knows the science of, and the practical sides of swimming, but also how to impart and demonstrate that knowledge.

The 'Fox' of Australian swimming, now coaching at the London 'Y' Aquatic Club, Ontario, Canada, fashions his pupils in a graceful style that brings speed, beauty of action, and develops determination and the will to win, governed always by the true spirit of sportsmanship.

I recommend this book, written by one of the greatest and most successful swimming coaches of all time.

1 *Modern History of Sprint Swimming in the U.S.A. and Australia.*

The United States of America and Australia have provided between them practically all the great sprinters over the last 20 years. Certainly all the Olympic sprint winners in freestyle in recent years have come from these two nations. Australia can provide from time to time an outstanding individual, but the United States overwhelms us by depth of numbers. Australia has no male superstars on the horizon but the U.S.A. is very strong at present. The reason the United States is pre-eminent in speed swimming can be attributed in part to the very extensive high-school and college swim programmes. It is estimated that there are 100,000 students participating in high-school swimming and up to 80,000 at the N.C.A.A. level. One of the unique events, common to both programmes, is the 50 yards freestyle. No other country or swim programme has this short, all out sprint for swimmers in the 15 to 22 years age range.

The evolution of both the 50 and 100 yards distances has been virtually parallel since the 1920s. Only twice has a younger high-school swimmer surpassed the collegiate men. This was in 1960 when Steve Clark bettered both the 50 and 100 yards records, and in 1975 when Andy Coan clipped the national record. The rate of improvement in both these distances has been very similar – 24·5 per cent for the 50 yards and 26·4 per cent for the 100 yards. Early this century, records for both distances were set by Harry Lemoyne, with times of 27·2 and 61·4 in 1904. This 27·2 for the 50 yards proved very vulnerable, for within the following 9 years, the mark improved 14 per cent. The 100 yards record tumbled to 57·0. Lemoyne's 27·2 was lowered to 26·6 by Lawrence in 1905, to 25·2 by Charlie Daniels in 1906, then to 24·8 by Harry Hebner in 1911 and then the dual Olympic sprint champion, Duke Kahanamoku, finally lowered it to 23·4, a time that lasted for 9 years.

In August, 1922, another dual Olympic sprint champion, Johnny Weissmuller, moved the record lower to 22·8 seconds. 'The Duke' then staged a great comeback taking the mark down to 22·6 seconds, a time that was not to be beaten for nearly 20 years, this time being the longest any record has remained unbroken in the history of the U.S. short course programme. Finally, in March, 1943, Henry Kozlowski from North Western University, chopped half a second from the old mark, with a time of 22·1 seconds. This record stood for 11 years.

Dick Cleveland, Ohio State's great sprinter, equalled Kozlowski's record in 1952, but had to wait 2 years before he could lower it to 21·9. During the next 7 years this record was equalled by Fred Westphal of the University of Wisconsin, and Harvard's Bruce Hunter. Finally, in 1961, Cleveland's mark was passed by Frank Legacki and Steve Jackman with a 21·4. Jackman lowered this to 21·1 in 1962 and to 21·0 a year later. Neither of these two great sprinters made an Olympic team, indicating that the world's fastest swimmers need a little endurance to help them survive the 100 metres long course jungle. Steve Clark was the first to break 21 seconds for the 50 metres, when he hit a 20·9 whilst swimming for Yale in 1964, a mark that was equalled by Zac Zorn in 1968. Dan Frawley moved the record down to 20·7 in 1969 and then the following year, Dave Edgar of Tennessee, listed a 20·5. April 1975 saw Joe Bottom cover the distance in 20·11, so the time is fast approaching when man will swim faster than 2½ yards a second.

In the 100 yards event, the standard sprint distance in the U.S.A., at the turn of this century, Harry Lemoyne set a 61·4 but Charlie Daniels lowered this mark dramatically to 56·0 (1906), 55·4 (1907) and 54·8 (1910). Charles M. Daniels was the first great American 100 metres man, winning the sprint title at Athens in the 1906 Olympics and then again at London, in 1908. His 100 yards record of 54·8 stood for 11 years. During the latter part of Daniels' career, Duke Kahanamoku came into prominence and broke the record down to 54·6 in 1913. Gradually, he further reduced this to 53·0 seconds in 1917. 'The Duke's' times were set in a 50 yards pool and they became the long course records. Daniels' 54·8 remained the short course record until the arrival of that giant of sprinters, Johnny Weissmuller.

September 1921 saw Weissmuller set a time of 53·2 over the 25 yards course, and after many races and 4 years, he whittled this time to 52·4, then to 52·0 in 1925. Finally, in 1927 at Ann Arbor's Michigan Union pool he swam his historic 51·0 flat, beating Buck Sampson. Weissmuller's record was the most durable of all time in the sprint in the U.S.A. It lasted alone for 9 years and was not bettered for 16 years.

Peter Fick equalled the 51·0 in 1936 as a warm-up to his Berlin Olympic win. In 1942, Howard Johnson of Yale, William Prew of Wayne and Alan Ford also of Yale, all equalled this time, but the record lingered until January 1943, when Ford swam 50·7, then 50·6 in February. The next year Ford dropped the time to 50·1 and eventually he became the first man under '50' with a 49·7 performance in March, 1944. This record remained for 8 years. Dick Cleveland of Ohio State University went a 49·3 and then a 49·2 in 1952, and this record lasted for 4 years until Robin Moore, a Stanford football player, hit a 48·9 in 1956. This record remained on the books for the remainder of the decade.

With the advent of the 1960's Jeff Farrell of the New Haven swim club recorded 48·2. Then in 1961 at Yale, a schoolboy from Los Altos, California, Steve Clark, electrified the capacity crowd at the Payne Whitney Exhibition Pool by taking 1·4 seconds from the old mark. His time was 46·8. During the next 5 years, Clark, now a student at Yale, and Steve Jackman of the University of Minnesota, see-sawed the record. Jackman went 46·5 in 1963, Clark went 46·3 in 1964 and eventually 45·6 in 1965. Ken Walsh of Michigan came on the scene in 1967 and equalled the old mark, and the following year, Zacary Zorn of U.C.L.A., registered a 45·3 in the N.C.A.A. championships at Hanover, New Hampshire.

Into the 'seventies, David Edgar of Tennessee swam a 45·1 during the A.A.U. championships at Cinncinati. In 1971, David lowered it again to 44·5. Andy Coan, a 16 year-old Pine Crest Prep. Junior, became the fastest man or boy afloat on February 22nd, 1975, when he went an incredible 43·9 at the Lawrenceville Invitational.

Australia has no comparable record lists over the 50 or 100 yards. One hundred yards events have not been held since 1935. Fifty yards events have never been recognised. There are no competition pools of 25 or 50 yards and until only a few years ago, the pools were 55 yards long, thereby placing an unnecessary handicap on competitors who had to swim further than the 100 metres in order to put up a record.

U.S.A. Record Progression 50 Yards Freestyle

High School		N.C.A.A.	
25·2 Bill Wright	1921	25·2 S. E. Hoadley	1914
24·0 Pau Kealoha	1923	25·0 Edwin Binney	1919
24·0 Arthur Lindgren	1932	24·4 Edwin Binney	1920
24·0 Mat Chrostowski	1934	24·0 Edwin Binney	1921
23·8 Mat Chrostowski	1934	23·9 Arthur Rule	1924
23·6 Mat Chrostowski	1935	23·8 Harry Lewis	1925
23·5 Robert Delozier	1940	23·6 James Bronson	1926
23·5 Edward Garst	1947	23·2 John Howland	1930
23·4 Edward Garst	1947	23·1 Ray Thompson	1931
23·4 Ray Lemaire	1949	22·9 Charles Flackman	1935
23·3 Ronald Gora	1950	22·9 Waldemar Tomski	1939
23·2 Kenneth Gest	1954	22·8 Alan Ford	1943
22·9 Kenneth Gest	1954	22·6 Henry Kozlowski	1943
22·9 Bruce Hunter	1957	22·1 Henry Kozlowski	1943
22·6 William Baker	1958	22·1 Richard Cleveland	1954
22·6 Lance Larson	1958	22·1 Donald Hill	1954
22·6 Steve Jackman	1959	22·1 Robin Moore	1956
22·5 William McGinty	1960	22·0 Robin Moore	1956
22·5 Marty Hull	1960	21·9 Fred Westphal	1959
22·3 Marty Hull	1960	21·9 Bruce Hunter	1960
22·3 Steve Clark	1960	21·4 Stephen Jackman	1961
21·8 Steve Clark	1960	21·4 Frank Legacki	1961
21·6 Steve Clark	1961	21·1 Stephen Jackman	1962
21·4 Louis Janos	1966	21·0 Stephen Jackman	1963
21·2 David Edgar	1968	20·9 Steve Clark	1964
20·7 John Trembley	1970	20·9 Zacary Zorn	1968
20·7 Dave Fairbank	1972	20·7 Dan Frawley	1969
		20·5 Dave Edgar	1970
		20·2 Dave Edgar	1971
		20.11 Joseph Bottom	1975

U.S.A. Record Progression 100 Yards Freestyle

High School		N.C.A.A.	
56·8 L. A. Handy	1916	56·4 Hal Vollmer	1916
55·4 Pau Kealoha	1923	55·6 D. L. Jones	1921
54·4 George Kojac	1927	54·8 D. L. Jones	1923
54·3 Baker Bryant	1933	54·6 James Bronson	1925
54·2 Baker Bryant	1933	53·4 James Bronson	1926

54·0 Mat Chrostowski	1934	53·2 Albert Schwartz	1929
53·9 Mat Chrostowski	1934	52·8 George Kojac	1930
53·4 Mat Chrostowski	1935	52·4 George Kojac	1931
53·2 Mat Chrostowski	1935	51·6 Walter Spence	1933
52·6 Henry Kozlowski	1941	51·6 Walter Spence	1934
51·5 Ronald Gora	1950	51·6 William Prew	1941
51·2 Richard Hanley	1955	51·6 Howard Johnson	1942
50·9 Elton Follett	1957	51·1 Edward Hall	1942
50·7 Fred Rounds	1957	50·7 Alan Ford	1943
50·4 Peter Sintz	1958	49·7 Alan Ford	1944
50·2 Lance Larson	1958	49·3 Richard Cleveland	1952
50·1 William McGinty	1959	49·2 Richard Cleveland	1954
49·6 William McGinty	1959	49·0 Rex Aubrey	1956
48·9 Steve Clark	1960	48·9 Robin Moore	1956
48·4 Steve Clark	1960	48·6 Bruce Hunter	1960
47·8 Steve Clark	1961	47·9 Ray Padovan	1961
47·7 Steve Clark	1961	47·0 Michael Austin	1962
47·7 Robert Jamison	1966	46·3 Steve Clark	1964
47·6 Robert Jamison	1967	46·1 Steve Clark	1965
47·6 Rick Eagleston	1967	45·6 Ken Walsh	1967
47·4 Rick Eagleston	1967	45·3 Zacary Zorn	1968
47·0 Robert Jamison	1967	44·5 Dave Edgar	1971
46·6 Robert Jamison	1967		
46·0 Mark Spitz	1968		
45·6 Mark Spitz	1968		
43·9 Andy Coan	1975		

If you have glossed over the preceding lists of U.S. record holders, please examine it a little more closely. There are some magnificent sprinters in the lists. Ford, Cleveland, Clark, Austin, Walsh, Zorn in the latter years, and Kojac, Kealoha, Schwartz and Spence in the 1920s and 1930s. These men in their time were the fastest freestyle sprinters in the world and yet an absolutely amazing fact emerges from the list: of all the swimmers on the list *only one* has ever won an Olympic 100 metres freestyle title – Mark Spitz. Many have placed and some have assisted in winning relays, but only Spitz has placed first as an individual. Kealoha placed second in 1920 at Antwerp, Kojac placed fourth in 1928 at Amsterdam, Schwartz managed a third in 1932 at Los Angeles and Thompson came in sixth. Alan Ford swam a second at London in 1948 and Richard Hanley a sixth in 1956. Lance Larson was the closest of seconds at Rome in that disputed finish in 1960, and Hunter finished fourth in the same race.

Mike Austin managed a sixth in 1964 at Tokyo and in 1968 at Mexico, Spitz finished third, Walsh second. Mark Spitz placed first at Munich. If these great stars have only managed a placing now and then, where have the winners come from and, just as important, why have the high-school and N.C.A.A. champions failed to produce winning form at the Olympics?

The Americans who have won the 100 metres freestyle event at the Olympics, have, in the main, emerged from swim clubs and swim teams controlled by professional coaches. A similar situation applies in Australia and Canada. This book portrays in part, aspects of the full-time coaching schools.

The list below shows what has happened on the American sprint scene since 1905. It is estimated that by 1985, the record for the 100 yards freestyle will be approaching 42 seconds, but from this point on the improvement will slow dramatically. The 100 metres mark should be in the 49s. The average improvement over the past 60 years is close to 1·8 seconds a decade, or point 2 of a second each year, for the 100 yards.

Improvement in Seconds for the 100 yards Men's Freestyle in 10-yearly periods

Year	Record	Swimmer	Improvement	Some Technical Additions
1905	61·4 secs	Lemoyne	—	—
1915	54·8 secs	Daniels	6·6 secs	rope lanes
1925	52·0 secs	Weissmuller	2·8 secs	first modern crawl stroke
1935	51·0 secs	Weissmuller	1·0 sec	refined crawl stroke
1945	49·7 secs	Ford	1·3 secs	weight training
1955	49·2 secs	Cleveland	·5 sec	tumble turns, pool improvement
1965	46·1 secs	Clark	3·1 secs	sloping blocks, better lanes
1975	43·9 secs	Coan	2·2 secs	improved swim suits, grab start
1985	42·0 secs(predicted time)		1·9 secs	

The Australian sprint record lists cannot be validly compared with the American short course marks, since most of their swims have been made over the long course (either 50 yards, 50 metres or 55 yards) in cold, open pools. Sprint specialisation does not exist at coaching level and there are no exclusive sprint meets. In the earliest days, Australia did have a 100 yards event in state and national open titles and their records were ahead of the U.S.A. In 1894, Thomas Meadham from New South Wales, won the title in 69·8 and in 1896, John Hellings took this mark down to 65·8, times that were well ahead of the Americans'. In 1901, Fred Lane, our first Olympic sprint winner, swam 60·6 and later he became the first Australian under the 60 seconds mark. In 1903 we can make our first real comparison. 'Tums' Cavill covered the 100 yards in 59·7 in Sydney, whilst in the U.S.A. Harry Lemoyne swam 61·4. For the next 20 years the United States swimmers slowly forged ahead while Australia hardly moved at all. In 1921 the American fastest was 53·2 and the best Australia could muster was 57·1.

Progression of Australian 110 yards or 100 metres Freestyle Records Either in or outside Australia.

Men		Women	
66·0 C. Healy	1909	1·13·0 J. Cocks	1929
65·4 C. Healy	1910	1·12·4 E. Stockley	1932
65·0 W. Longworth	1911	1·11·6 K. McKay	1934
64·8 A. W. Barry	1913	1·10·6 P. Norton	1935
59·6 F. O'Neill	1949	69·0 K. McKay	1936
57·2 J. Henricks	1953	69·0 E. De Lacy	1937
56·2 J. Henricks	1954	68·5 M. McQuade	1949
55·4 J. Henricks	1956	65·5 L. Crapp	1955
54·6 J. Devitt	1957	65·0 F. Leech	1956
54·4 M. Wenden	1966	64·5 D. Fraser	1956
54·2 D. Dickson	1966	63·2 L. Crapp	1956
54·2 N. Ryan	1966	62·0 D. Fraser	1956
53·8 M. Wenden	1966	61·5 D. Fraser	1958
53·7 M. Wenden	1968	61·4 D. Fraser	1959
52·2 M. Wenden	1968	60·2 D. Fraser	1960
		59·9 D. Fraser	1962
		58·9 D. Fraser	1964
		58·9 S. Gould	1971
		58·5 S. Gould	1972
		58·2 S. Gray	1975

To be able to swim 100 yards in 42 seconds or less, a new and truly specific approach will have to be undertaken. Super-swimmers will have to be selected by testing and by elimination. They will eventually train for distances up to 100 yards and very little else.

2 *Something to Think About*

All things being equal the more miles you swim, the younger you start, the greater your chances of becoming a real champion. The world's leading swim schools have the six- and seven-year-olds covering 4, 5 or 6 miles a day in hard training. There have been no detrimental effects on these real water babies in health or in mental advancement. Actually the scales have tilted the other way. Children in hard training are fitter, stronger, less susceptible to infection and more intelligent than their non-exercising contemporaries. One thing that is hard to measure, but is becoming increasingly evident, is the stronger line of character that the well-disciplined trainee develops.

Slogging along, mile after weary mile, unable to hear, except the rushing of the water, unable to see, except for a few feet down into the haze, the swimmer can experience a real sense of loneliness. The desire to succeed or improve drives him on. Every stroke is slowly but surely building within him, the tenacity to 'hang on', a determination to be a little better than the next.

Have you ever noticed that within top training teams is an absence of undesirables? The going is too tough, the discipline too demanding for the weaker. Our sport attracts the better type of boy and girl, and further develops their good points.

One thing we can prove is that children in hard training improve their position in class. It is a proud claim of mine that one in every three of our senior team members in Australia is either a State or Commonwealth Scholarship winner. Furthermore, look at our Olympic swim champions – up to 90 per cent of the male winners are University students or graduates. Who could be a better example than Australian David Thiele. In 1956 he won the Olympic 100 metres backstroke title. He had just started Medical School. During

1957–58 he broke world records. In 1960 he duplicated his Melbourne feat with a win at the Rome Games. A year or so after this he graduated 'Top of the State' in Medicine. Here was a boy capable of combining sport and study in just the right amounts. Chester Jastremski (U.S.A.) had an almost similar career. He specialised in world records.

A simple principle worth remembering when combining sport and study is this. When you leave the pool turn the swimming tap ('hot' physical) off, and turn the study tap ('cool' mental) on, and vice versa. If you have both running at once you will only get luke-warm results in both fields. In other words do not think swimming when you study and vice versa.

Swimming and sport generally opens many doors that would otherwise remain closed in business and life generally.

Australia's failure to reach the top is not pool shortages or crowded pool conditions as some coaches suggest. The reason is the shortage of coaches – good coaches. It is well known in Australian swimming circles that this drastic shortage exists. Would I be unjust in saying that there are only four coaches of international standing in this country? This is bad. If there were forty top coaches much more improvization, inventiveness and original thought would circulate through the sport. Imagine six Arthur Cusacks in Queensland, six Don Talbots and six Forbes Carliles in N.S.W., etc., etc. Can you imagine the competition, the number of champions being produced, the exchange of ideas. We would be so far in front of the rest of the world, our main danger would be complacency.

Since 1956 when we did lead the world, our population has increased by about one million people but our swimming generals have decreased.

This is one reason why Aussie coaches are continually sifting the teachings of other swim nations to supplement their knowledge. This is why Aussie coaches continually travel abroad to widen their knowledge of their sport.

Coaches and swimmers do not grumble because your facilities for training are not what you desire. Make the best of what you have. Many a world champion has been developed under circumstances inferior to the nation's best. Having second rate facilities should be a challenge to the coach to use his ingenuity and to make do. No need for me to tell you that one hour of superior training in a 20 metre pool is better than several hours of 'sloppy' work in the best swimming pool in the world. I sincerely believe that the enthusiasm of the squad can overcome any shortcomings in the training facilities.

Swimmers are getting younger. This in turn is creating new problems for the coach. The coach must be continually adjusting his attitude towards the squad. The coach is getting older and every four years the swimmers are getting younger. The coach cannot stagnate. I have often thought that one reason why great swimmers rarely turn out to be great coaches is because they tend to say, 'This is the way I did it when I got my world record,' etc. forgetting, of course, that this may have been five or ten years ago. A quick survey of the world's top coaches seems to underline the fact that they were only mediocre competitors. A Melbourne contemporary coach Ray Kemp recently said, 'My best young girl is Bryn Illingworth (50 metres in 37·0 seconds, U/8); she has often brought her dolls to the pool while she trains.' Yes, swimmers are getting younger.

Parents and swimmers often fail to put things in their true perspective. They should keep in mind that for the young pupil a time improvement is really the most important thing. I have often said to a dissatisfied parent, 'If your son, John, had swum the 100 metres in 65 seconds would you have been satisfied?' Knowing this would be an improvement of about 5 seconds, the parent beams, 'Certainly!' I then say, 'But what if all his other swimming friends had swum 63 seconds and your boy had come last. Would you still be satisfied?' There is usually no answer. Parents should not become over-emotionally involved. The child is not swimming for the parents' self-gratification or to make up for a shortcoming in the parents' youth or present life. The child should primarily be swimming to become a faster swimmer, for an insurance in good health in later years, for the friendship that exists in a training squad, for the fact that training will 'keep him off the streets' and develop his character. If they have a win or make the touring team, this is a bonus as far as I am concerned. Certainly they should strive for it.

In the older pupil his position in the event usually is more important. Understandably the tactics to win an event need not necessarily be the tactics which would produce a personal best time. Australian distance star Robert Windle came to me after the final of the Men's 200 metres freestyle at Mexico City. In this event he finished fifth. He was very disheartened, saying, 'If only I had broken 2 minutes, that was all I wanted to do.' I explained that he had finished fifth in what was possibly the fastest and best 200 metres race in the history of swimming and this on a limited preparation at altitude. Bob then realized that finishing fifth under these circumstances was certainly better than breaking 2 minutes.

Also at Mexico during casual conversation with 'Pokey' Watson I remarked, 'Well Pokey, you have had a long and a wonderful career, I suppose you will be retiring after these Olympics?' Her reply was one that others should consider before making decisions of quitting the game. She said, 'I have trained harder this season than ever before. If I am beaten I will not retire because of this; if I do not improve upon my best times I shall retire.' You know the rest of the story, she went on to win a gold medal. Far too many swimmers quit the game prematurely fearing that the up-and-coming younger swimmers will beat them, causing embarrassment and loss of face. Season after season I have seen that the younger swimmers often do not improve as predicted and overseas trips have been missed because of a hasty decision by the older swimmers.

Coaches and swimmers can learn from each other. It is true that a high percentage of swimming 'experts' can watch a squad or a champion work out and not learn a thing. Some cannot see what is going on right under their noses. Every swimmer, every coach has at least one facet of stroke, conditioning or tactics that could be included in an inquisitive coach's programme to advantage. Often things that other people do can put the observant coach on to a new train of thought.

We must always be ready to modify, improve or change those sections of our work where we are weak. Certain axiomatic principles must not be interfered with. There is nobility in simplicity. The hard facts of the stroke and conditioning will reduce the swimmer's time to say 53 seconds. The 'frills' will further reduce it to 52·9 seconds.

We are certainly out of the kindergarten of swimming, possibly through junior school, but by no means through high school, let alone University. 'Where will it all end? Every day somewhere a record is broken. Can it go on much longer? These are the sentences most coaches are asked by press men and others. One thing is certain, we have travelled little more than half way towards the ultimate in world records since the inception of speed swimming at the beginning of the century. Today's times are terrible. The improvement is phenomenal. For example, in 1956 5 minutes was bettered for 400 metres for the first time by a woman. Since then it has been bettered a thousand times. Just 19 years ago it was considered phenomenal. Today it is not even considered good. I am rather glad that I am coaching now when the results can be so rewarding. One hundred years from now it will be a much harder job, but just as exciting.

3 The Layman's Scientific Approach

As you climb the ladder, from week-end club events towards State or National levels, it becomes increasingly evident that your training must be infused with a greater knowledge of the functions of the body; a more scientific approach. Less than 1 per cent of participating athletes have superior ability, but even this 1 per cent can be aided by science and physics. By observation and extracts from important literature certain basic facts are worth recording. These points can be discussed, dissected and included in your training if they are applicable.

1. *Top fitness.* Top condition is that physiological status of the human body that enables it to perform the best job with the least amount of effort and least amount of subsequent fatigue. Observance of all body mechanical laws, knowledge of how to perform a movement for any particular event, etc., all fall by the wayside if the swimmer does not possess a human machine that can convert energy into action and reduce the accumulation of fatigue substances by both *elimination* and *neutralisation*. An excellent swimmer with perfect technique for 200 metres isn't worth his salt if he runs out of conditioning at the 100 metres marks.

2. *Weight Zone Classification.* Classify according to Normal and Danger Zone, 5 per cent Underweight and 5 per cent Overweight fall in the danger zones for speed swimming. Remember tissue in good condition weighs more than similar quantity of soft and flabby tissue. Under normal health conditions, the body usually replaces lost weight in 24 hours. Expect the weekly weight to drop during

the conditioning pre-season training and to either gain during the season or at least to maintain a seemingly level plateau. Drops during the season usually indicate over-exertion. (*See the section on* Notes from my Olympic Notebook.)

3. *Get the muscle groups involved into preparatory condition*, if you wish maximum and best results. This includes increasing the temperature, making supple the joints and stretching of the important muscle groups involved. Increased temperature in some varies between 98·6 and 102 degrees. Stretching is an instinctive preparatory self-defence reflex, i.e. before making a group of muscles contract, stretch them. The time for this preparatory conditioning is from 5 to 15 minutes, depending upon the age group (less time for youths) and the severity of the exertion expected. Some Americans, swimmers and of course divers, adhere to this important rule. A large percentage of Australian and American swimmers exercise on Exogenie or similar machines prior to competition.

4. *Prepare for the 'effort' by taking deep breathing exercises* (not to the point of beginning symptoms of dizziness) both before and after exertion. In the former case, increased storage of oxygen is a result and in the latter case, the increased heart action and respiration is returned to normal sooner. Generally 4 to 6 breaths is enough.

5. *Concentration on your event.* How many times do you see a coach impress final racing instructions on a pupil 10 minutes before the event and the pupil is very serious and determined. Then on his way to the starter well-wishers, friends and other competitors *break this concentration* by slapping him on the back, shouting out to him, etc. When you have been given final race instructions, concentrate on them and do not break your concentration until the race is over.

6. *Concentrate the mind on the performance of action.* Have the nervous system alert for the starter's gun. Think of these sound waves hitting your ear drum. If your ear drum, middle ear, or other hearing conduction apparatus has experienced ear and nasal 'cold' infections remember you have been desensitized. Thus, keep colds away if you expect to get off the mark before your opponent does, other factors being equal.

7. *Eliminate all muscle contractions not essential* to execution of the movement. A skilled person can do this. Skill means execution of a movement involving the least amount of effort with the attainment of a large amount of work or muscular effort results. A 'beginner' brings all sorts of extra muscle groups into play. That is why he looks awkward. Skill in any activity also involves the transition from mass movement to movement of finer muscles. This has its basis in the first movements of the child which are mass movements in character. As he becomes older and growth takes place, the smaller muscles replace mass movement with less expenditure of energy.

8. *A straight line is the shortest distance between two points.* We learn this from geometry. Hence, have recoveries, pulls, extensions, flexions, abductions, adductions, etc., performed in 'short-cut' distances, and save energy.

9. *'Taper off' severe cardiac exertion.* After a severe race, whenever possible continue to swim until the pulse, respiration and general feeling seems to be normal. This will also aid in elimination of waste products.

10. *Stressing agents.* Here are a few factors that will drain the physical resources of the swimmer resulting in poor performances:
(a) Unusual activities in the days prior to the event (other sports, long car drives, etc.)
(b) Inadequate rest or an altered sleeping pattern.
(c) Inadequate diet or an altered eating pattern.
(d) The mental stress associated with 'poor form', school activities, emotional disturbances.
(e) Inoculations, sulphur drugs.
(f) Sudden body weight increase.
(g) Extremes of temperature and/or humidity.
(h) Chronic constipation or diarrhoea.
(i) Inflamed tonsils, defective teeth.

11. *Stress signs and symptoms.* The experienced coach and swimmer will be on the alert for signs of prolonged stress. The observable signs could be:
(a) Muscle soreness (not at the beginning of the season).
(b) Continual body weight loss.

(c) One nostril blocked or rhinitis (morning head cold).

(d) Swollen and tender lymph glands.

(e) Skin eruptions and rashes (sometimes due to the water).

(f) Pouches under the eyes.

(g) Loss of appetite or frequent stomach upsets.

(h) Irritability feeling of depression.

(i) General lassitude (watch for the swimmer who is slow to leave the locker rooms, and takes 5 minutes to get his track suit off).

(j) Unusually high early morning heart rates and/or slow recovery rates after effort.

(k) Loss of 'stroke' for no apparent reason.

(l) Inability to hold 'repeat' times.

(m) Crying at workouts (girls).

(n) Shortness of breath.

(o) Swollen liver.

Clinical Signs

(a) A falling haemoglobin level.

(b) Disturbances in the E.C.G. chart (flattening of the T wave).

(c) Protein and/or excessive red and white blood cells in the urine.

(d) Marked changes in the white cell count, disappearance of the eosinophil because of physical stress.

(e) Increase of eosinophils (asthma, hay fever).

(f) Increase of ketosteroids in blood stream.

13. *Even Pace Swimming*. In 1953, my tutor in physiology, Professor Frank Cotton, said, 'the day will come when the second half of middle distance and distance events will be swum faster than the first half.' This is now becoming evident, from the way top swimmers, especially the Americans 'kick on hard' after the half-way mark. An even distribution of effort over a given period of time is less stressing on the performer and allows for a fast time. The time-worn example of a motor vehicle that goes over a given distance with sudden spurts and acceleration changes using up more fuel than the even speed vehicle, is well worth quoting to young team members.

14. *Warm up swimming*. Some eminent physiologists claim there is no benefit from pre-race warm-ups, but swimmers generally do

warm up before all competitions, although it is not strictly necessary to warm up for training swims.

At Olympic level, the world's best swimmers have a full and hard warm-up. Here is the warm-up I gave Lyn McClements before she won her Gold Medal in the 100 metres Butterfly:

1. 300 metres of swimming freestyle, 1 lap fast, 1 lap slow, but non-stop.
2. 6 × 25 kick sprints without a kickboard, one every minute.
3. 6 × 25 dive butterfly sprints, each one becoming harder than the previous one, e.g. 15·8, 15·3, 15·0, 14·6, 14·2, 13·8 seconds.
4. 100 metre cool down.

50 MINUTES BEFORE THE EVENT

This is the warm-up I gave Mike Wenden before he won his two Gold Medals:

1. 500 metres for style, relaxing.
2. 4 × 50's each one harder until the last – 26·6, 25·9, 25·3, 27·5 from push.
3. 200 metre slow and some turns.

45 MINUTES BEFORE EVENTS

That the warm-up is beneficial is emphasized by swimmers often perform their best on their second or third event of the meet. A fine example was the performance of Michael Wenden in the medley relay at Mexico. His freestyle (the world's fastest time) leg was 51·4 seconds, just minutes after beating Don Schollander in the final of the 200 metre event in the fastest time of Wenden's career. *Warm-Up:* A warm-up may also be beneficial because it:

(a) Relieves pre-race TENSION. Some American swimmers were observed to have two warm-up sessions before their first event at Mexico.

(b) Allows swimmers to adjust to the starting blocks, turns and finish.

(c) Allows swimmers generally to get the 'feel of the water'.

Here is an extract from my 'Instructions' for the Championships, which our team are now using with success:

'*About* 40 *minutes before your event, swim from* –

1. 400 to 600 metres at a medium pace, but with some short bursts in your racing lane. Think about technique.

2. Pull 100 metres, 50 metres fast, 50 metres steady.

3. Then kick 100 metres, 50 metres fast, 50 metres steady.

4. From push sprint 2 or 3 times 25 metres at race pace on your stroke.

5. Sprint 50 metres from push or drive at race pace (timed by coach).

6. Race into your turn 6 to 8 times at exactly race pace.

7. Try a few finishes at race pace to judge the touch.

8. 200 metres medley as a relaxer.

9. Hot shower for a minute, but finish with a 10 second cool spray.

10. Then put on your racing costumes, track suit, shoes and socks.

11. Report to coach for final race instructions.

4 Practical Psychology in Coaching

Evidently very little has been written about the psychology of coaching swimmers, from a practical point of view. This chapter will be an attempt to break new ground in this field – a field which is becoming ever-increasingly important. We know that the human body is capable of swimming feats far in excess of those being made today. The body is capable, but very little advancement has been made into breaking down the mind's resistance, and allowing the body to become an unshackled unit. I have often told my team, that in five or ten years time, swimmers will be producing times unthought of today. There will be very little change in swimming pools, coaching methods, food and physique, yet I ask my pupils why it will be, that ten years from now, all the average swimmers will be breaking today's world records. It is obvious, I explain, that the mind will be the deciding factor. You will notice advancement, just as happened with the number of athletes who ran sub-four minute miles after Bannister had accomplished the feat.

Motivation and psychology in sport are so closely allied, that for the purposes of this exercise we will treat them in the same chapter. Psychology, after all, is common sense, but it is the applied common sense that is important to us. From my observations, today's swimming coach is a highly intelligent, energetic, field psychologist.

The success of a coach will depend largely upon his under-standing of the psychology of coaching. Most of our knowledge in this field has been developed from experience built up over the years, and I feel the best way to become knowledgeable about psychology in coaching, is to expose yourself to a successful model; a top flight coach who has proved his successes over the years.

33

Sell yourself, then sell your product. The coach must be exemplary at poolside and in private life. His manner and morals must be above reproach. His dress, his speech, his sense of fair play must make him a highly respected person. Gone for good are the days when overweight coaches with cigarettes dangling from their mouths, screamed abusive instructions across the pool. Today's coach sets a fine image. Once he has sold himself to his pupils, it is an easy job to sell his product; speed swimming.

Coach–pupil relationship. This is of vital importance. Without it there will be no success. There are all sorts of techniques to develop champions, and all sorts of coach–pupil relationships. Here are some of the fundamental points. It is virtually impossible today to reach championship level without a coach. That intangible something that a coach gives his pupil, is extremely valuable. Despite the wide variety of different coaching techniques, they all have this in common. There must be a very special, close bond between them. I can think of Rose and Herford. I can think of Lydiard and Snell, Cerutty and Elliot, Counsilman and Jastremski, Talbot and the Konrads, and myself and Fraser and Henricks.

Some coaches are of the stinging, abusive type, while others are more gentle and encouraging. They all evoke a positive response in their pupils.

I have observed, that in young swimmers, there has occurred a transferring of their affection from their homes and people within them, to outsiders, such as ministers, coaches, scout masters, teachers. If every coach knows that swimmers have undying faith in his ability and creed, (usually between the ages of 10 and 16 years) swimmers will place the teachings of the coach above all else. This transitional object is a very precious gift, and once given to the coach, should be nurtured. It is the time when the pupil is most susceptible to suggestion. This is the birthplace of the close friendship that will endure for the rest of the pupil's swimming life. The coach has his greatest opportunity to break down the mental reservations in his pupil.

You can motivate your pupil by word, inference or actions. When and how you do this is of utmost importance. First of all, your suggestions must be logical and believable. Do not make great claims that in the competitions, the swimmer will better his best performance by an unbelievable margin. Be logical. When motivating a pupil for a particular performance I often refer back to a member of a previous team. I say: 'Do you remember so and so? Well, his time for this distance was 60 seconds. You work better than he did, you have a better technique, you have done more hard mileage than he ever did, and yet in this meet he reduced his time by a full second. If he could do it, how obvious it is that you can do it even more so?'

Suggestions like this are believable, but it is not only important for the pupil to believe, the coach must sincerely believe it himself.

The power of suggestion: I do not think it is recognized how powerful suggestions can be as a coaching technique. Hitler was an example of the power of suggestion. Suggestibility is the quality of youth. If a young person is told a thing often enough, then he tends to believe it; whereas one of the qualities of adulthood is that we are critical. We do not believe everything we are told, we tend to evaluate things for ourselves. The essence of suggestibility is to absorb uncritically the thoughts, feelings and actions that are suggested to us. However, we are all suggestible to varying degrees, and there are certain situations which make us more suggestible, and these are important to the coaches.

Your suggestions must be given with firmness and intensity. It is of no value just mumbling a few ill-chosen words that you may have often repeated before. Your attack must be something that has been well thought out; it must be given with firmness and must instil confidence.

The place and the time: Never make your motivating suggestions to your individual pupil in front of the whole team. Your suggestions will have more impact if sitting over a cup of coffee. You are able to make the pupil feel that he is a special case. One particular method I have used with success is to telephone the pupil at home after the workout. I explain to him that it would be quite the wrong thing to show him special favours in front of the team, but in the privacy of our telephone conversation, I can motivate him very strongly with his special plans, his special instructions. I have always believed that you can motivate individuals, to greater intensity, away from the pool. I recall one particular exception, prior to the commencement of the Olympic swimming events at the 1956 Olympic Games. One night I took Jon Henricks and Dawn Fraser, and we sat at the highest point of the stand, long after everyone else had gone. I explained to them that after so many years in the doldrums, they were the two swimmers who were to launch

Australia into its Golden Era. Sitting there with only a few under-water lights on, and the rest of the giant stadium in darkness, my words obviously had tremendous impact. I had capitalized on the environment.

The time: Motivating suggestions are useless if given too close to the event. As the swimmer walks to the block he is usually pre-occupied with his racing plans. To be fruitful, your suggestions should have been made sometime previous, when his mind was in a receptive mood. The next point illustrates what I mean. Whilst preparing the Australian team for the 1968 Olympics, I had purposely had my stop-watches doctored, to read 3/10 of a second faster in every minute. Therefore in all the efforts the team carried out in our three months preparation, I was actually cheating on the team; but the doctored stop-watches were doing the job I wanted them to do. Disappointed at their relatively slow times, the team tried harder and harder to reach respectable training times. The night before Michael Wenden was due to go out and swim in the heats of the Men's 100 metres freestyle event, I took him to one side and asked him to manipulate the stop-watches against an accurate stop-watch. I then told him what I had done. I explained that every time he swam a 60 second sprint, actually it was 59·7. I told him this was the 3/10 of a second I had been looking for. The narrow margin it would be necessary to have to win the Olympic title. He went to bed that night extremely happy and full of con-fidence, knowing that over the last thirteen weeks, his swims, even though they had been great, were actually greater. I had kept my secret until the eve of the Olympic heats. This I feel was the right time. Psychologically lifting your pupil can have the reverse effect on the opposition. It is a well known fact that top swimmers shave their legs before competing in international competition. I pur-posely stopped Michael Wenden from shaving his legs until after he had swum in his Olympic 100 metres heats. After he had won his heat in the fastest time of the day, I then made sure that the opposition coaches knew that we had not yet shaven, thereby holding an ace up our sleeves. I feel we timed this nicely. Of course you can have a long range plan, in which you gradually motivate the swimmer to reach targets that will get him to his desired objective, but I personally feel that motivate suggestions made within the last 48 hours tend to bring the pupil to concert pitch.

Repetition. Psychologists know that by repeating a thing often

enough, the subject tends to believe it. I used this form of attack
when trying to get Dawn Fraser to break 60 seconds for the 100
metres for the first time. I repeated the suggestion strongly and
convincingly, just often enough to make her believe. I had the
number plate of her automobile changed to 59·999, a symbolic
suggestion that must have sunk into her mind thousands of times.
The coach is put on his metal by often repeating suggestions,
because it is wise to repeat them with a different punch line each
time.

Anxiety. Anxiety makes us much more suggestible. When we are
anxious or fearful we tend to slip back into the habits of childhood,
and we look around for someone to lean on; someone to give us a
lead. A swimmer before his event is extremely anxious, and in this
state they are highly suggestible.

The age of the pupil determines the method of motivation. In the
very young, the promise of a gift by the parents is enough to make
the swimmer produce his best time; and of course, James Counsilman
of Indiana can get his boys to produce their best training session,
just on the promise of a bag of jelly beans. We need the motivating
factors to be their strongest possibly between the ages of 16 and 22,
when the pupil is likely to be exposed to international competition.
Therefore it is important at this age level to treat the pupil as your
equal when speaking to him. Above all use a positive approach in
your suggestions. I knew of an Australian swimming coach who told
his top pupil, just prior to the National titles, that if she did not win
this particular event, he would give up coaching for good. To me
this is a negative approach. It is self-pity, and certainly not the right
approach for an intelligent teenager. Dawn Fraser's main motivating
factor for wanting to win her third Olympic sprint medal at Tokyo,
was two-fold. For years she had been inspired with the idea of
making swimming history, by becoming the first swimmer to
perform such a feat. This had been the matrix of all her swimming
desires. Her number one motivating factor at Tokyo was however,
her desire to swim to win this race for her mother, who had died
just previously in an automobile accident, because her mother had
planned to be at the games to see Dawn win.

There are numerous means of motivating a team, whether it be in
performances, in training targets. There are many valuable gimmicks that can be employed, such as graphs, special badges, group
pep talks, special incentives; but when it is all boiled down, the

success of the scheme usually depends on the coach's ability to talk to his team, with strength and conviction, enthusing them to do things a little better than previous teams. At our training camp in Scarborough in Queensland, Australia, I imbued the 24 swimmers with the desire to train longer and harder than any other Australian team had ever done. I set a target of 200 miles of intensive work, for the six weeks preparation. I motivated our team, by daily putting up our target mileage, our achieved mileage, and the mileage of the previous team at this stage of the preparation. The whole team took up the challenge and consequently we passed the target with ease. Team targets successfully reached, bring a sense of pride to the group, and so it snowballs. The prouder they are to be a group, the more chance there is for them to achieve greater heights. It is noteworthy that the world's greatest swimmers come from the world's greatest training camps. I know of no individual that won at Mexico. Every winner was part of a team, a training team held together and motivated by the coach.

Most coaches stop motivating once the race is over, but the sensible coach can take advantage of a successful climax to his plans, by following through motivating suggestions. On the 'plane trip home from Mexico City, I made sure I took full advantage of our successful climb to be the world's number two swimming nation. I gently reminded the pupils individually, how we had been correct in doing this or that, etc. I was mentally preparing the subjects for future international competition.

5 *Food, Facts and Fallacies*

In the following pages my aim is to acquaint you with the Australian meal pattern. They may or may not suit your particular conditions. Recently I discovered, after conducting a survey, that:

1. The breakfast was usually adequate in calories, but very low in protein which is so necessary for growing children.

2. Lunch was usually all carbohydrate (sandwiches, rolls, meat pies, etc.). In most cases the pupils were given money to buy their lunch and it often consisted of coca-cola, rolls, ice-creams or chips (french fries). Again little or no protein.

3. Dinner in the evening was adequate.

What led me to do the survey was the fact that the afternoon training sessions were poor. The swimmer could do a few good efforts, but usually the quality dropped off quickly. This no doubt was due to a lower blood-sugar level.

Such food additions as 'Sustagen' and 'Peak' are helping to overcome this blood-sugar problem.

It is a fact that the nations that consume the most food per capita, have the highest Olympic representation. Australia has great diversification of natural foods, mainly fruit, dairy products and meats. Swimming parents need guidance in such matters as natural foods, blood-sugar levels, pre-race meals and balanced diets. The weekly meal pattern I have set out in this chapter should not be slavishly followed, but should be used as a guide to form the meal pattern. Emphasis has been placed on natural foods.

Natural Foods

Whenever possible it is advisable to substitute natural foods in a fresh state into the diet in preference to processed foods. Mineral and

39

vitamin content is higher especially against foods that have been cooked or preserved by additives.

Murray Rose, triple Gold Medal winner, has a diet consisting of fresh natural foods. Since this fact was published an ever-increasing number of top line swimmers and athletes have duplicated his diet. These are the foods that constitute the diet, and it is advisable to include them in your weekly meal pattern. Advice on the preparation of the natural foods is readily available from the health food stores.

Murray Rose's Basic Foods

Eggs, cheese, brown lentils, soya beans, lima beans, nuts and nut products, millet, sesame, sunflower seed, 100 per cent wholemeal bread, porridge, scones, cakes, etc., made from soya bean flour millet 'flour, rye, bran and any grain which has not been processed or refined. Honey, dried fruits, such as raisins, dates, figs, raw brown sugar, fruit juices, vegetable juices. Unpasteurised milk (preferably goat's milk), and a predominance of raw fruits and raw vegetables of every type.

A weekly meal pattern

This meal is built on natural foods and a predominance of offal meats. It is reasonably balanced and the average person would notice a slight weight gain. Individual preferences for other items should be respected as long as they do not include copious amounts of white breads, cakes, jams and condiments.

MONDAY

Breakfast Weet-bix, wheat-germ, fresh or stewed fruit, oatmeal, raw sugar, ½ pint milk, lamb's fry, bacon, egg, 100 per cent wholemeal bread, honey, pure fruit juice, dates.

Lunch Clear vegetable soup, cheese and egg salad including grated carrot, celery, lettuce, tomato, orange, cabbage, eggs, 100 per cent wholemeal bread, honey, glass of Bonox or pure fruit juice, or ½ pint milk, dried prunes.

Dinner Soup if desired, steak, braised with pressure-cooked vegetables (carrots, potatoes, peas or beans) and always a green leaf (cabbage, celery tops, silverbeet, etc.). Fresh fruit salad with ice-cream, fruit juice, or Milo or Akta-vite, dried figs.

TUESDAY

Breakfast Rice, raw sugar, prunes, ½ pint milk, or oatmeal, lamb chops, egg, fresh tomatoes, 100 per cent wholemeal bread, honey, pure fruit juice, sultanas.

Lunch Vegetable soup or beef extract if required, a garden salad to include fresh lettuce, tomato, pineapple, apple, orange, grated carrot, celery, cabbage, etc., cheese, eggs, raisins, sultanas, etc., 100 per cent wholemeal bread, honey, pure fruit juice or ½ pint milk, nuts.

Dinner Soup if desired, kidneys in an onion dumpling or braised kidneys, pressure-cooked vegetables, apricots and custard, prunes, fruit juice, Milo or Akta-vite.

WEDNESDAY

Breakfast Weet-bix, wheat-germ or oatmeal, fresh or stewed fruit, raw sugar, ½ pint milk, steak grilled, tomato, egg, 100 per cent wholemeal bread, honey, dried figs, pure fruit juice.

Lunch Beef extract soup if desired, mixed meat salad but plenty of fresh green and yellow vegetables included, 100 per cent wholemeal bread, vegemite or honey, pure fruit juice or ½ pint milk, nuts, dried apricots.

Dinner Soup if desired, roast lamb with mint sauce, potato, beans or peas, cauliflower or cabbage, carrots or grilled, whole tomatoes, stewed prunes and cream, fruit juice, Milo or Akta-vite, sunflower seeds, sultanas.

THURSDAY

Breakfast Cereal, wheat-germ, Enertone, fresh or stewed fruit, oatmeal, raw sugar, ½ pint milk, bran cakes and grilled tomatoes, 100 per cent wholemeal bread, honey, pure fruit juice, dates.

Lunch Vegetable soup if desired, egg salad with plenty of green and yellow vegetables and fruits, 100 per cent wholemeal bread, vegemite or honey.

Dinner Soup if desired, sweet bread croustade, with pressure-cooked carrots, potato, brussels sprouts, beans, steamed honey pudding and ice-cream, fruit juice, Milo or Akta-vite, dried figs.

FRIDAY

Breakfast Cereal, All-bran, wheat-germ, fresh or stewed fruit, raw sugar, ½ pint milk, grilled kidneys (or a kidney dish), tomato, egg,

100 per cent wholemeal bread, dried fruits, honey, pure fruit juice, dried apricots.

Lunch Soup if desired, grilled whiting and garden salad, 100 per cent wholemeal bread, vegemite, honey, fruit slices, pure fruit juice or vegetable juice, or ½ pint milk, sunflower seeds.

Dinner Soup if desired, cutlets in bread-crumbs (substitute wheat-harts for bread-crumbs), boiled onion, carrots, parsnips and brussels sprouts, jellied fruit and cream or fresh fruit, fruit juice, Milo or Akta-vite, handful of mixed dried fruits.

SATURDAY

Breakfast Boiled rice and stewed fruit or cereal, All-Bran, wheat-harts, Enertone, raw sugar, ½ pint milk, poached or scrambled eggs with parsley sprigs or a cheese omelette, 100 per cent wholemeal bread, honey, dried fruits, pure fruit juice, prunes.

Lunch Vegetable soup if desired, grilled steak and garden salad or grilled tomatoes and mince, 100 per cent wholemeal bread, honey, vegemite, carrot juice, fruit juice or ½ pint milk.

Dinner Soup or tomato juice if desired, meat and potato pie with cauliflower and white sauce, apple pie and cream or fresh fruit, fruit juice, Milo or Akta-vite.

SUNDAY

Breakfast Millet and wheat porridge or cereal, All Bran, wheat-germ, Enertone, fresh or stewed fruit, raw sugar, ½ pint milk, eggs and bacon or baked beans on toasted wholemeal bread, or baked liver patties, 100 per cent wholemeal bread, dried fruits, honey, pure fruit or vegetable juice, sultanas.

Lunch Soup if desired, baked dinner (traditional) or lamb cutlets with garden salad, 100 per cent wholemeal bread, vegemite, honey, fresh fruit or fruit juices, fruit slices and cream, vegetable juice, or ½ pint milk.

Dinner Soup or tomato juice or carrot juice, braised kidneys entree with onion gravy or small grilled whiting, fried rice, first-class steak with mushroom sauce or braised steak and onions with pressure cooked or fresh vegetables, fruit salad and cream or ice-cream, fruit juice, Milo or Akta-vite, dates.

The following recipes are given in order to make the swimmers' meals more appetising. The offal meats, namely – liver, kidneys, brains, tripe and tongues provide the blood stream with essential blood-forming and oxygen-carrying components. Offal meats, as a rule, have a strong taste and smell and are not liked by all. They should constitute one-third of the meat intake of competitive swimmers.

It is important to prepare offal meats well before cooking. Here are some of the things you should do:

For brains. Wash under running water, then soak in cold or tepid salted water (1 teaspoon to 1 pint water) for 1 hour, changing the water three times during soaking.

Separate the lobes of the brain carefully with a knife and then with the fingers, gently remove the skin which covers them.

Place in cold water until required – then blanch by putting the brains into a saucepan, covering with cold water to which a teaspoon of vinegar or lemon juice has been added. Bring to boil and strain immediately.

How to remove strong flavour

For kidneys. Soak in warm water with a tablespoon of vinegar for 40 minutes to remove strong flavour, then remove skin and core.

For liver. Dip quickly into boiling water, take out, dry, then carefully remove the thin skin. The quick dip in boiling water seals the juices in, and when the liver is properly cooked, it should be tender and juicy. Do not soak in water as this decreases its nutritive value.

For tripe. Wash tripe with three-quarters teaspoon bi-carbonate of soda in water and then wash again. Scrape the inner side free from all fat and soak in cold water for half an hour. Blanch by putting into a saucepan, covering with cold water, and bringing to the boil to whiten and remove any strong smell. Drain water off and repeat the process twice more if necessary.

Note: There is no need to present offal meats in recognisable form – mince them up and make them look like something else. For variety it is suggested that a large croustade be made; this can be filled with creamed brains, tripe or tongues.

Grilled Sheep's Tongues

Wash 4 sheeps tongues, cover them with cold water and bring to the boil. Simmer with 3 carrots for 3 hours, or until tender. Place the tongues in cold water, remove the skins, cut in half lengthwise and trim the roots.

Make a batter by beating 2 eggs with quarter of a cup milk and 1 teaspoon of mixed flour, then adding 1 teaspoon mixed mustard, salt, pinch of cayenne pepper.

Dip halved tongues in the batter and fry in a deep frier until golden brown. Drain and arrange in two rows on a hot dish. Slice the carrots and fry till just brown in a little of the frying oil, then drain and place in the centre of the two rows of tongues. Garnish with parsley sprigs.

Parsley Sauce

Sheep's tongues are just as delicious if served in parsley or tomato sauce.

Cook by simmering until tender, then remove the skin and cut in half lengthwise.

Put the tongues in hot white sauce which has been flavoured with tomato.

Heat through and serve with mashed potato.

Kidney in an Onion Dumpling

Cut a large onion in half and scoop out enough of the middle to contain a sheep's kidney cut in four. Season with salt and pepper, put the onion halves together again, and enclose the whole in suet or pastry crust. Bake in a moderate oven for about 1 hour and serve at once. It must be baked long enough to cook the onion, which could be slightly boiled first, and then cooled. Do not attempt to boil the dumpling. It MUST be BAKED.

Baked Liver Patties

1½ lb. lamb's fry	⅓ cup tomato juice or puree
small ½ cup breadcrumbs	1 beaten egg
1 teaspoon salt	1 small minced onion
¼ teaspoon pepper	8 slices streaky bacon
	2 tablespoon's bacon fat

Method. Wash the lamb's fry, cut in thick slices and soak 15 minutes in salted water, mince and combine with other ingredients, except the bacon, and form into patties about 1 inch thick and 2½ inches in diameter. Wrap slice of bacon around each, and fix with a toothpick. Place in a well-greased pan and bake 1 hour in a slow oven. Serve for supper with spring onions, radishes and young greens.

Brain Cakes

Chop finely 2 or 3 sets of cooked sheep's brains. Mix with white breadcrumbs. Add the yolk of 1 egg, season with pepper and salt. Roll in flour, pepper and salt, and then in beaten egg white reduced with a tablespoon of milk.

Roll in fine white breadcrumbs and shape into round cakes, balls, into short bars, a cutlet shape or like a small carrot. Shake off all loose crumbs and fry in smoking fat until a golden brown. Drain and serve garnished with parsley.

Brains au Gratin

Season 1 cup bechamel sauce with a little pepper and salt. Cut in dice 3 sets of sheep's brains and add to the sauce with one teaspoon finely chopped parsley. Place in buttered pie dish or scallop shells. Sprinkle lightly with brown breadcrumbs. Place in oven to heat for about 20 minutes. Garnish with parsley before serving.

Honey

Honey, a natural food, predigested by the bee, is a very readily available source of energy. It is recommended in the diet in preference to sugar, and where possible should be used as a substitute; e.g. in tea, on bread, on cereals. Honey is not damaging to the teeth and, unless taken in excess, aids digestion. It is converted into energy within 20 minutes and therefore is a good pick-up between races.

The following recipes can be included in the diet because they are carbohydrate loaded and provide quick energy:

Honey Fruit Cake

½ cup honey	1 large tablespoon butter
¼ cup milk	1 breakfast cup plain flour
1 egg	½ cup chopped walnuts or mixed nuts
pinch salt	½ cup sultanas or raisins
	1 heaped teaspoon baking powder

Method. Cream butter and honey: add well-beaten egg, beat again, add milk and flour (sifted with baking powder and salt), then fruit and nuts. Bake in a moderate oven in an oblong tin for between 45 minutes and 1 hour. When cold, slice and serve plain or buttered.

Honeyed Fruit Jellies

3 tablespoons honey	¾ cup lemon juice
⅔ cup orange juice	sliced fruit such as bananas
⅔ cup hot water	oranges and whole strawberries
1 dessertspoon gelatine	

Method. Dissolve gelatine in hot water. Add fruit juices and honey, pour into a mould. Sliced fruit may be set in jelly and/or served with jelly. Serve with cream or custard.

Honey Pep Cocktail

1 teaspoon honey	juice of 1 lemon
juice of 1 orange	raw yolk of 1 egg (not white)

Method. Shake together well. This cocktail is marvellous for restoring energy.

Honey for Sleep

To sleep soundly and wake refreshed – 1 tablespoon of honey in a glass of milk before retiring.

Salads

1. *Energy Salad.* Grated apples, carrots, chopped celery, grated beets, sliced tomatoes, finely chopped mint or parsley. Mix lightly together, arrange on a bed of lettuce, squeeze orange juice over all, and serve.

2. *Apple and Lettuce.* Grate ripe apples on a coarse grater, chop celery finely, mix lightly together and arrange on lettuce leaves. Add one tablespoon finely grated almonds to each portion.

3. *Pineapple and Cheese.* Put slices of fresh pineapple on a large lettuce leaf, add cottage cheese. Decorate with grated carrot, finely grated lemon rind and one dessertspoon raisins.

4. *Nerve Salad.* Finely shredded pumpkin or swede, mixed with cream and 1 dessertspoon stabilised wheat-germ, serve on lettuce leaves.

5. *Vitamin Salad.* One lettuce, one heart of white cabbage, bunch

of watercress, one large carrot grated, one stick of chopped celery, one finely sliced leek, one grated parsnip, quarter cucumber, one tablespoon raw, grated beetroot, large tomato finely sliced, chopped parsley and mint. Mix all together, add grated cheese or nuts, serve with cream dressing.

6. *Honey Fruit Salad.* Chop finely one ripe apple, dice half a banana, cut up two sweet navel oranges, slice two ripe mellow bananas. Mix all together, and the juice of half a lemon and the pulp of six passion-fruit. Add two dessertspoons clear honey and leave to stand for one hour. Serve on lettuce leaves with grated almonds or whipped cream.

Soups

1. *Energy Broth*

4 large carrots	1 bunch spinach
4 sticks celery	2 large tomatoes
1 bunch parsley	

Cut up all vegetables, which should make three cups carrot, three cups celery, one cup spinach, quarter cup parsley. Add these to two quarts of water and simmer slowly for thirty minutes. Season with vegetable salt and serve.

2. *Vegetable Soup*

3 cups diced carrots	1 bunch spinach
3 cups chopped celery	2 large tomatoes
2 large potatoes (unpeeled)	1 cup chopped spinach

Cut up all the vegetables finely, cover with water, simmer slowly for 30 minutes. Add the finely chopped parsley and leave to draw. Flavour with vegetable salt.

3. *Stock Soup*

1 quart vegetable stock	1 cup sliced onion
1 cup diced carrots	3 ripe tomatoes
1 cup diced turnips	chopped parsley
1 cup diced celery	

Cut all the vegetables very finely and simmer in the stock until tender. Slice the tomatoes, add to the soup, simmer another five minutes. Season with vegetable salt and add finely chopped parsley just before serving.

Cold savouries

1. *Vegetable Rolls.* Mix together one cup cooked lentils, one cup each of chopped celery and parsley, half cup grated carrot, three

teaspoons stabilised wheat-germ, two tablespoons melted butter, juice of one lemon, vegetable salt to taste. Place heaps of the mixture on lettuce leaves, roll up and hold together with a ring of sliced cucumber, removing the centre for the purpose.

2. *Agar Vegetable Mould.* Cook slowly for 15 minutes half pound diced vegetables, such as carrots, turnips, celery, parsnips, with green peas or chopped green beans, in one and a half pints vegetable stock. Add one teaspoon Vegemite extract and one tablespoon finely chopped Agar and cook another 10 minutes. Fill moulds and allow to set. Place on lettuce leaves and garnish with sliced tomatoes and chopped watercress or parsley.

Desserts

1. *Apples and Wheat-Germ.* Butter a pie dish, line it with Life Force Wheat-Germ, then place layers of sliced apples, seedless raisins and Wheat-Germ, till the dish is full. Add a little honey and hot water, cover the top with Life Force Bran, dot with butter and bake in the oven till brown.

2. *Dried Apricots or Peaches.* Wash in boiling water, then in cold, soak overnight, add a little honey and steam for 10 minutes. Serve with cream or grated almonds. Dried nectarines, pears or apples may also be used.

RETAINING NUTRITIVE VALUES

Fruit and vegetables are quickly damaged nutritionally. A lot of this damage is not within the purchaser's control. Picking, packing, transporting and storing can rob the items of much of their goodness.

Vegetables and fruits lose much of their 'freshness' if left in a warm position, especially loose, leafy vegetables. At home the vegetables should be washed and placed in an airtight vegetable bin. Cold storage is acceptable – at a temperature of 43° F. seems satisfactory. In all instances fruit and vegetables should be left in their natural coverings; e.g. corn in their husks, peas in their pods.

These salient points should be borne in mind:

(a) Boil or steam vegetables in their skins; this reduces loss of water soluble nutrients into the cooking water.

(b) When peeling or scraping vegetables before cooking, cut off as thinly as possible.

(c) Chopped salads can lose their vitamin C content if left standing. Prepare at the last possible moment.

(d) To retain vitamin potency, vegetables should be added to vigorously boiling water and heated rapidly under cover.

(e) Soda should never be added to the cooking of vegetables, because of the destruction of vitamins B and C.

(f) Cover during cooking wherever possible.

(g) Avoid vigorous boiling or stirring over long periods.

(h) Serve vegetables with their cooking waters where possible.

(i) Cook beef, lamb and veal at low temperatures to avoid shrinkage.

(j) Wherever possible use stainless steel cooking utensils.

(k) The following foods have the highest iron content (blood):

	Mgs		Mgs
Dried Brewer's yeast	18·1	Oysters	7·1
Fresh liver	12·1	Fresh tongue	6·9
Wheat-Germ	8·1	Molasses	6·7
Soya beans, soya flour	8·0	Fresh heart	6·2
Egg yolk	7·2	Carrots	5·9

(l) The following foods have the highest phosphorus content (nerve).

	Mgs		Mgs
Dried Brewer's yeast	1,893	Dry whole milk	728
Wheat-Germ	1,096	Cocoa	709
Dry skim milk	1,030	Fat	623
Processed canned cheese	831	Cheddar or all	
Eggs, whole, dried	800	other types	610
		Yeast compressed	605

PRE-COMPETITION MEALS

The pre-race meal will not cancel out months of poor eating habits by the ill-advised swimmer. They will complement a good diet and assure the swimmer that his fuel intake in the last 24 hours is as good as science can provide. I suggest a predominance of carbohydrate, with a little fat, and some protein. Here are the meal patterns of three of Australia's best performers at Mexico City:

LYN McCLEMENTS (17 years) 100 metres Butterfly in 1 minute 05·5 seconds to gain the gold medal:

8.30 a.m. Fruit juice, breakfast cereal, bacon and eggs, toast and coffee.

1.00 p.m. Steak, chip potatoes, peas, lemon meringue pie and coffee.

3.30 p.m. 1½ glasses of sustagen.

4.30 p.m. Warm up swim.

5.30 p.m. Olympic gold medal.

JUDY PLAYFAIR (15 years) 100 metres Breaststroke in 1 minute 15·9 seconds to gain a silver medal in the Medley Relay:

8.00 a.m. Scrambled eggs, pancakes, fruit juice, coffee, toast, four vitamin E's.

12.30 p.m. Steak, mashed potatoes, beans, jelly, fruit juice, coffee, honey.

3.00 p.m. Two glasses of sustagen, mixed with the juice from tinned fruits, a few milk arrowroot biscuits, four vitamin E tablets.

4.30 p.m. Warm up. Swim.

5.00 p.m. Best time ever by an Australian.

MIKE WENDEN had ten hard swims in eleven days at Mexico, all world-class efforts. Here is what we did on the day he broke the world record for 100 metres:

8.00 a.m. Arose – Laevulose drink mixture.

8.30 a.m. Grilled fish, mashed potatoes, ham, fruit juice, two pieces of toast, coffee, five vitamin E's.

9.30 a.m. to 11.30 a.m. Walked around the village and generally kept alert.

12.30 p.m. Lunch: Two pieces of scotch fillet, chip potatoes, jelly and ice-cream, coffee, five vitamin E's, Laevulose drink.

1.00 p.m. to 3.00 p.m. Sleep.

3.30 p.m. Sustagen, 1½ glasses mixed with milo, Laevulose drink.

4.50 p.m. Swim.

5.30 p.m. World record for 100 metres.

I suggest you alter the time segments to suit your time of racing for the day and see if these diets suit you.

Pre-race Additives

In some instances, where maximum effort is required, I have found the inclusion of pre-race additives of great importance. These drug-free substances often have a double-barrelled beneficial effect – psychological and chemical. Some are to increase the blood-sugar level over a long period, others act as catalysts, and another group delay fatigue and help neutralize lactic acid.

Sustagen. A liquid pre-race meal, to be used also before training sessions. Sustagen has proven itself over the years to be a real aid to swimmers who usually get 'nausea' stomachs pre-race. It is an almost complete food and can be taken up to two hours before your race. We use it extensively for the afternoon training session when pupils arrive at the pool usually 'tired out' and hungry after school work.

Laevulose. Glucose has difficulty in penetrating the muscle cells, it requires insulin to do this effectively. Laevulose on the other hand can enter the muscle cell easily and is metabolized immediately, yielding energy during its oxidization cycle. There is a lower urinary loss of Laevulose than glucose, pointing out that it has better utilization. Furthermore there is much evidence to prove that Laevulose can be used directly by the muscles when the body's reserves fall low, making it a wonderful 'pick-up' between events.

Dosage. Our team have one tablespoonful mixed with fruit juice three times on the day of the event.

Direct Metabolic Pathway of Laevulose. Following extensive experimental and clinical research which has been carried out within recent years it has become very apparent that Laevulose, as a carbohydrate supportive therapy, offers many advantages.

Laevulose follows a more direct metabolic pathway into the energy yielding system than glucose, details of which have recently been established by Lamprecht and set out in the following scheme:

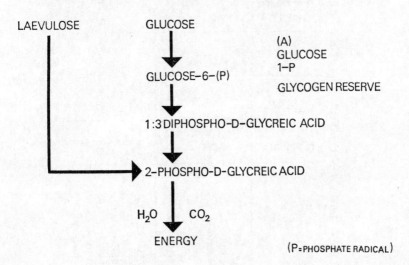

Fig. 1. Direct Metabolic pathway of Laevulose

COMPARISON OF THE SUSTAGEN PRE-GAME DIET WITH THE NORMAL STEAK MEAL

	Vitamin C mg.	Protein G	Fat G	Carbo-Hydrate G	Calories	Calcium mg.	Iron mg.	Carotene mg.	Vitamin A mg.	Thiamine mg.	Ribo-flavin mg.	Niacin mg.
STEAK MEAL 8 oz. steak 3 oz. potatoes 2 oz. pumpkin 3 oz. peas 8 oz. orange juice	147	53.1	43.5	49.3	680	74	5.7	1447	0	471	.4	8.4
SUSTAGEN MEAL 8 oz. Sustagen 4 oz. apricots syrup 2 oz. honey 2 slices toast 8 oz. orange juice	192	30.5	5.3	190.1	888	766	5.7	2212	1102	304.2	2.36	24.4

483

1839

Phosphates. Phosphates furnish the energy for muscular contraction and function as buffers in the blood. It is a well-known fact that hard workers on phosphates substantially increase their output. The substance can be taken over long periods, even years, without side effects. Phosphates are a mild laxative and produce a feeling of well-being. It is also possible that phosphates aid in the 'recovery' period after effort, shortening it somewhat.

Only small doses are suggested, large doses being a possible cause of insomnia.

The two leading swim squads in Australia have one teaspoonful of Disodium Phosphate daily. Dennigs mixture has also been used with apparently good results.

6 Interval Training

As the pioneer of interval training in Australia I feel that it has been a major training reason for Australia's twenty-one Olympic swimming gold medals since 1956. For the imaginative coach, there will be many avenues open to improve the system. Interval training can be described simply as the repetition of high quality speed work dove-tailed with controlled resting periods.

I am now modelling our pre-season land exercise programmes upon an interval training system. Since the average age of the Australian trainee is twelve years I feel continual motivation but changing interest patterns are a pre-requisite for long range success.

Major advantages of this type of work-out are that:

(i) The pupil trains faster than he would on a non-interval training schedule.

(ii) The coach can use the rest segments to discuss stroking, etc.

(iii) The short rest periods enable the body to adjust physiologically and chemically to a level conducive to carry out more hard work.

(iv) Team members, irrespective of stroke, sex, age or ability can do the same schedule. It consolidates a 'Team'.

(v) Better use is made of the pool space.

(vi) A swimmer has more chance of holding good stroke form over the shorter distances usually involved.

Major disadvantages are:

(i) Turns are often neglected or 'scruffy'.

(ii) Breaststrokers can be 'pulled along' by swimming too close behind a faster breaststroker.

(iii) Two timing clocks are required.

(iv) It is hard to control the short rest periods accurately at the far end of the pool with only one training clock.

(v) The tail end swimmers in a 'chain' system tend to ease up on the last few strokes into the wall.

(vi) Shortsighted swimmers are at a disadvantage.

For group training I use a system we call the chain-gang. A continuous chain of say eight to ten swimmers, each swimming 5 seconds apart in a lane of a 50 metre pool.

In one form or another interval training constitutes 60 per cent of our work-outs.

For motivation reasons, in our training parlance we differentiate between the short 'repeats' (50 and 100 metres) and the longer 'repeats' (200 and 400 metres). The former are known as 'scorchers', the latter 'grinders'.

Milestones in Interval Training

On our notice board I have set down the milestones of interval training as targets for our young 'hopefuls'. They tell the story of interval training clearly.

John Konrads (1958) set a very high pattern in interval training in 1958–1960 when he included in his daily schedule 32 × 50 metres with 10 seconds rest intervals. He would aim for 34 seconds for the first 800 metres then on the *last* 800 *metres aim to get as low as 32 seconds*. At this period he was World Record Holder and Olympic Champion.

Murray Rose (1960). In his preparation for 1960 Olympic Games, Murray swam 10 × 400 metres in 60 minutes (one every 6 minutes) at an average time of 4 minutes 45 seconds. He won the 1960 400 metres Olympic title.

Kevin Berry (1960). Training for the 1960 Olympics Kevin covered sixteen consecutive 200 metre sprints at an average of 2 minutes 51 seconds going off 'every 4 minutes'. He was at this stage fifteen years old.

Dawn Fraser (1962). In her preparation to break 60 seconds for 100 metres Dawn in 1962 swam 8 × 100 metres 'on the next minute' sprints an average of 68·5 seconds from push-off.

Dawn Fraser (1964). Covered a 'broken' 400 metres in 4·26 seconds she also carried out 8 × 100 metres, averaging 67·7 seconds from push-off, departing every 2 minutes. This was prior to the success at Tokyo Olympics.

Julie McDonald (1966). 16 × 100 metres from push averaging 69·1 seconds departing every 90 seconds (in sets of four).

Graham White (1968). 16 × 50 metres averaging 30·9 seconds with ten-second rest intervals, 16 × 100 metres averaging 65·0 seconds with ten-second rest intervals. (Mexico)

Karen Moras (1968). 30 × 50 metres averaging 36·9 seconds with ten-second rest intervals, 6 × 400 metres, 5·07, 5·03, 5·00, 4·55, 4·51, 4·49, departing every 10 minutes.

Robert Windle (1968). 16 × 50 metres averaging 30·1 seconds going every 60 seconds.

Michael Wenden (1968). 16 × 50 metres averaging 29·0 seconds going every 60 seconds.

Stephen Holland (1974). 20 × 100 metres averaging 63·5 seconds and departing every 1 minute 20 seconds.

The mileage of the Australian trainee has settled down now to about 9 miles daily in two equal sessions, or about 45 miles a week. The seasonal total of champion-type trainees varies between 500 and 600 miles. During the years 1956–1959, coaches pushed their pupils up to 12 miles a day, but the work was, in the main, low quality long-distance training without much sprinting or variation. Interval training has completely changed this system.

My system of Timed Interval Training

I use special stop-watches (Huer 30 second run-on or Omega split stop-watches) for training which have a run-on action. By this I mean that when I stop the watch at the end of the first sprint, it has recorded say 30 seconds for the 50 metres, I *do not* 'zero' the watch. Then, when next I start the watch, it now reads say 62 seconds and so on.

I find that my swimmers appreciate that at the end of 8 × 50 metres sprints the time recorded on the watch is say 4 minutes 30 seconds for the 400 metres or *'broken quarters'* as we call them. This time motivates them more than if I were to say 'you swam those sprints at an average of 34 seconds', because 4 minutes 30 seconds is synonymous with 400 metres.

For further motivation I might say to Brad Cooper, 'I want you to swim four broken 400 metres breaking the World Record (3 minutes 52 seconds) on each swim.' With my special run-on system of timing, I call his times at the end of each 100 metres in *training*, but this limits the coach's output and time.

Self Timing

When swimming 'broken' 400 metres the squad starts off when the large synchronized pool clocks are on the 50 seconds mark. They then swim their 8 × 50 metre sprints with ten-second rest intervals. At the end of the eight sprints the clock hand will be on say 30 seconds. They know the swimming time could not be 3 minutes 30 seconds and very unlikely to be 5 minutes 30 seconds so their time must be 4 minutes 30 seconds for the 'broken' quarter. By starting on the 50 second mark, all they do is actually cancel out 70 seconds of rest intervals.

This method is accurate enough for group training. It depends of course on the swimmer having *exactly* 10 *seconds rest* between sprints. If the second swimmer comes in on the 40 seconds mark and the third on the 50 seconds mark, their times for the 'broken' 400 metres would be 4 minutes 40 seconds and 4 minutes 50 seconds respectively, *providing they take exactly* 10 *seconds rest intervals.*

Accuracy in Timing Rest Intervals

Because of poor eyesight, parallax errors, sore 'training eyes' and steamy pool conditions, rest intervals can become 'ragged' and inaccurate. To overcome this I have made 10 second, 15 second, 20 second and 30 second 'hour glasses'. These are placed at the ends of the swimmer's lanes. They are of various colours for quick identification. As soon as the swimmer sprints in, he flicks over his hourglass and then when the sand runs through, he sprints off again. I dislike being snowed under by unnecessary equipment, but for short-sighted swimmers these 'timers' are ideal.

Sprint and Stroke

Another training exercise I incorporate is called *Sprint and Stroke* which I consider a segment of interval training.

On the blast of my whistle the squad sprints down the pool, say 30 metres, until I blow the whistle again, which could be a rest interval of say 10 or 15 seconds, and then they all swim slowly aiming for *perfect stroke*, until I blow the whistle once more when they sprint, and so on until they cover 400 metres.

The object of this exercise is to combine *sprinting and ideal stroking* and impress it in the swimmer's mind that the two are inseparable in racing. Done correctly it is very tiring.

The Australian athletes also use this training system for track work.

Turns

Turns tend to become neglected during interval training sessions. To counteract this, I have devised an interval training segment with fast tumble turns.

The swimmer stands up in our shallow pool at the 40 metre mark facing the 50 metre end. He then sprints 100 metres executing tumbles at the 50 metres and 100 metres ends and finishes up at the 40 metres mark again where a mark is set on the pool floor. He then goes 'on the next minute' for his next 100 metres sprint. We usually do these in sets of eight.

My Favourite Interval Training Segments

(a) Three sets of 10 × 50 metres with 10 seconds rest intervals, each set becoming faster and with 3 minutes rest between each set.

(b) Four sets of 4 × 100 metres departing every 90 seconds and with 3 minutes rest between each set.

(c) Two sets of 3 × 200 metres departing every 3 minutes with 6 minutes rest between the sets.

(d) 4 × 400 metres departing every $7\frac{1}{2}$ minutes, OR, 8 × 400 metres in 60 minutes.

(e) 4 × 'broken' 400 metres with approximately 3 minutes between each 400 metres.

(f) 2 × 'broken' 400 metres medley departing every 50 seconds.

(g) 20 × 50 metres with 5 seconds rests.

(h) 20 × 100 metres with 5 seconds rest intervals.

7 Team Tit-bits

'No pain no gain' is a phrase I often throw to the team, and for at least two-thirds of the work-out it applies. Nevertheless, a training programme should keep the interest of the pupil, must be finely balanced between stroke, effort, speed and diversion. When I started coaching in 1952, one of the first experiments I undertook was to set a small group of swimmers working at full capacity, at every session. I carefully recorded times, counted heart-rates to assess percentage of effort in each sprint, and looked for signs of the stress concept. For a while the swimmers swam faster and harder than they had ever swum before, but by the end of the week it was amost impossible for them to get within 4 seconds of their best 100 metres time. This lesson has indelibly inscribed itself on my training schedules, because no matter how much I feel like pushing the team at full pressure all the time, I desist a little.

Far too many swimmers go to the starting blocks for their major annual events with 'flattened batteries', consequently a year's hard work is lost because the coach was over-zealous. Plautus said, 'In all things the middle course is best.' This certainly applies to swimming, the hard sessions to be hard, the sessions for stroke to be relatively easy, the sessions for heart tone to be long and gradually fatiguing. I have found that a juxtaposition of these principles most rewarding. Training has now become 10 or 11 months of the year job. It is much more important to have great variety of the work-outs. My team programmes change daily, but they are cyclic. In other words, every few weeks we revert back to the original programme, and as previous training times have been recorded the team are expected to show an improvement. The clever coach can include small interesting variations in the work-outs, but these must be hard sections. I will outline a few of the variations I include in my programme:

1. 10 × 100 *metres medley sprints*. 1 sprint every 1 minute 45 seconds. This item can be done in a 50 or 25 metre pool, and if you push the swimmers right out in this section, you will find it very rewarding. All groups are worked to capacity, the stroke variation makes this section interesting, and since each section is only 25 metres, the weaker swimmers on some sections don't mind pushing through. I often use this as a warm up to the main programme.

2. 800 *metres as a lungbuster, timed*. In this segment, the swimmer does the first 50 metres bilateral, then comes back the second 50 breathing every four strokes, then bilateral, then every six strokes, then bilateral, then every eight strokes, until the end of the 800 metres, when the swimmer is swimming the last length breathing every 18 strokes. In some ten years of using this practice, no more than six swimmers have managed to do this work-out correctly and at a satisfactory speed. It was one segment that we used often in our preparation for the altitude at Mexico City.

3. 8 × 50 *metres sprints with the legs crossed, one sprint every 60 seconds*. You will not believe how hard it is to swim with your legs crossed, until you try it. Not just trailing behind, but locked together at the ankles. The extra stress thrown upon the upper body is tremendous. I prefer these in sets of eight.

4. 400 *metres legs tied, with weighted bands, weighing 2½ ounces*. This I like the team to do as a long endurance type exercise, in which the muscles are gradually stressed.

5. 8 × 50 *metres polo sprints, one every 60 seconds*. In this exercise the swimmer imitates the body position of the sprinter, that is high arched back, head extremely high and very little turning of the head for the breathing. We call these sprints 'Weissmuller sprints'. They have the second advantage of placing great stress upon the leg drive. A short session on this type of work, and your team will be complaining of weary muscles and aching backs.

6. '*Back-to-back medleys*.' In this segment I have the swimmer swim a straight medley, then at the end of the medley continue on with another medley in reverse order, such as butterfly, backstroke, breaststroke, freestyle, freestyle, breaststroke, backstroke, butterfly. Four such medleys in 30 minutes makes for good variation to the training programme. The fact that you finished the medley with a butterfly sprint, enhances its value as a toughening up action.

7. *Stroke rate 50's.* In this exercise 16 × 50 metres sprints, one every 50 seconds, aiming to keep the stroke rate at a low level. For example, a swimmer may be asked to keep each of the 50 metres at less than 40 strokes. If he fails to do this he comes back and starts all over again. He must also keep his time at a normal training standard, such as 33 or 34 seconds for the length. This exercise has double-barrel efficiency in as much as it impresses on the swimmer the desirability of having a low stroke rate, and secondly it emphasizes the push through that so many swimmers and coaches neglect.

8. *The underwater relays.* I assemble three-man relay teams, and we race across the pool underwater. Once a team member has to come up for a breath before he reaches the end of the pool, that team is automatically disqualified, and so the teams eventually eliminate themselves until only one team is left.

9. *Across and back sprints against time, on an elimination basis.* The coach lines the whole team up alongside the pool, he then pre-determines a time, for example 30 seconds for the 40 metres across the pool and back. At the blast of his whistle, the team departs, and if they have not stopped swimming by the time the whistle blasts again they are eliminated. The coach drops the time slot by 0·5 seconds each sprint, until you get down to the last ten swimmers. It then becomes an elimination on placings, the last swimmer each time retiring. For this exercise I like to separate the girls from the boys, to give each section an equal chance.

10. *Plus or minus time trials.* I sometimes like to vary my weekly time trials, by having the swimmers swim against the National records. However, instead of swimming the full distance of say 100 metres, a swimmer swims a solo attempt on say the National record of 53 seconds for the 100 metres. When 53 seconds has elapsed, a chalk mark is made at the side of the pool, and we measure off the number of feet he is short of the Australian record. I have found this invaluable in motivating swimmers, especially the young, to greater efforts. They seem to appreciate the fact that they are 6 or 8 or 10 feet short of the record, whereas 219 or 311 seconds is not so readily understood.

8 Training Schedules

PART ONE

One thing about preparing work schedules in Australia is that there is always something new to include each season, or to delete, or modify. This in turn makes it hard to prepare a schedule that will stand the test of time. I have an overriding principle when setting down a programme and it is simply this – the schedule to be superior in every way to the previous season.

The schedules of leading coaches carry a lot more influence than is realized. Amateur coaches, country club coaches, group leaders often use the schedules of the 'Top six' to fill their own requirements. Stroke work can be imitated, for better or for worse, but the complete schedule remains a mystery to most students of swimming. Of course it is no secret that the top coaches lean heavily upon the schedules of each other to fortify their programmes. This is a good system as long as there is originality continually being fed into the national complex.

A brief history of Australian training methods reveals that in the past we have often disposed of certain training procedures only to re-include them in later years. The total annual mileage has fluctuated violently, weight training has been in and then out, seasons have lengthened from 5 months to 10 months, in fact there are now two distinct seasons.

In 1924 Andrew 'Boy' Charlton put up a world record for 440 yards in 5 minutes 11·8 seconds. 'Boy' was a 'natural' for all his training consisted of surfing and long surf swims. Sometimes he would have lunchtime swims at the old Domain Baths but organized training was not a regular feature. Coach Harry Hay was active in the 1930s and 1940s in Sydney and his training methods produced a spate of National Champions. His training was well organized for those days and pupils would often swim up to 2 miles in a day.

Typical training of the day was:

(a) 880 yards at a steady pace.

(b) 880 yards on the kick board.

(c) A special sprint or two over the race distance.

(d) Several 55 yard sprints.

(e) A long cool down swim or some of the secondary stroke.

A little callisthenics were included in the winter months but weight training had not been introduced.

The exodus of John Marshall to Yale University in 1949 and the reports he sent back of his schedules and in particular his land exercises influenced the Australian coaches tremendously. Most conscientious trainee of this era would without a doubt be Judy Joy Davies of Victoria. Her career spanned three decades and included world and national records. She placed third at the London Olympics of 1948 in the 100 metres backstroke. The fact that Miss Davies broke the world record for the mile by 20 seconds indicates that the training she used was at least up with the world's best of those days.

Here is a schedule set by Forbes Carlile for Miss Davies. Training had been increased to twice a day, but mileage rarely went beyond 1½ miles each session.

(a) 440 yards loosening up.

(b) 440 yards at 80 per cent effort.

(c) 440 yards 'basic' swimming (backstroke).

(d) 440 yards at 85 per cent or at 90 per cent effort.

(e) 440 yards 'basic' swimming or 440 yards kicking.

(f) 440 yards at 80 per cent effort.

Miss Davies alternated every second session on backstroke work. Arms-only work was not included at this stage. Emphasis was upon stroke mechanics and even pace swimming. Carlile introduced the 'hot bath' warm up system.

The change in the training system is dramatically shown in the 1953–56 era by this extract from the log books of Dawn Fraser and Jon Henricks, both sprint winners at the Melbourne Olympics:

September 7, 1956. Townsville, Queensland.

(a) 440 yards stroke – warm up.

(b) 440 yards effort (D.F. 5·15, J.H. 4·51).

(c) 440 yards kick at 80 per cent.

(d) 2 × 220 yards effort (D.F. 2·27, 2·25, J.H. 2·14·1, 2·11·8).

(e) 440 yards with legs tied at 80 per cent.

(f) 2 × 110 yards sprints (D.F. 68·3, 67·5, J.H. 59·9, 59·1).

(g) 16 walk back sprints at 95 per cent effort. E.g. D.F. 31·5, 31·3, 30·7, etc. J.H. 28·8, 28·6, 27·7, etc.

(h) 440 yards bilateral warm down.

Moderate weight training, calisthenics, 'partner' exercises and a long afternoon sleep were all part of the routine. The distance swimmers and the sprinters did completely different programmes. E.g. Murray Rose's schedule about this time was:

(a) 440 yards loosening up swim.

(b) 10 × 440 yards efforts all within one hour, with an average time of 4·45.

(c) 440 yards kick as a cool down.

Here is a schedule of John Konrads set by Don Talbot in 1957.

(a) 32 × 55 yards sprints with 10 second rest intervals, the first 16 at about 35–34 seconds and the final 16 at as low as 33 or 32 seconds.

(b) 440 yards kicking in 7 minutes (Ilsa Konrads 6·40·0).

(c) 440 yards swimming with legs tied in less than 5·30·0.

(d) 4 × 440 yards efforts at between 4·40·0 and 4·50·0. (Ilsa Konrads 5·00·0 to 5·11·0.) One effort every 10 minutes or less.

(e) 440 yards cool down on stroke. (Ilsa Konrads bilateral.)

This was the 1957 era. At this point large doses of weight training and calisthenics were supplementing the training and the seasons were October to March in the water, July to September heavy weight and allied land training. 'Legs tied' or arms only work had become an essential part of the schedule. Swimmers now slept between sessions, with vitamin supplementation being advised.

By the mid '60s great diversification of the strokes were being included in the schedules. Heavy weights had been eliminated and the influence of Wenden's isometrics and Carlile and Gathercole's resistance machines have had tremendous impact on the forming of today's schedules. Coaches realize that all the strokes 'help each other'. Here are two examples of schedules using all strokes from leading swim schools of the world.

Coach Peter Daland (U.S.A.) gives a different work-out for male and female team members. Here is an extract from the boys' schedule:

Monday. A.M. May 3.

(a) 3 × 200 metres kicking with 1 minute rest.

(b) 3 × 200 metres arms only, with 1 minute rest.

(c) 3 × 200 metres kicking in the four strokes, with 1 minute rest.

(d) 2 × 200 metres arms only, with 1 minute rest.

P.M.

(a) 4 × 400 metres with 2 minutes rest.

(b) 2 × 200 metres medley, with 2 minutes rest.

Tuesday. A.M. May 4.

(a) 4 × 100 metres kicking, with 45 seconds rest.

(b) 4 × 100 metres arms only, with 45 seconds rest.

(c) 4 × 100 metres kicking, with 45 seconds rest.

(d) 4 × 100 metres arms only, with 45 seconds rest.

P.M.

(a) 3 × 800 metres with 2 minutes 30 seconds rest.

(b) 400 metres medley.

Wednesday. A.M. May 5.

(a) 3 × 200 metres kicking, with 1 minute rest.

(b) 3 × 200 metres arms only, with 1 minute rest.

(c) 2 × 100 metres kicking, with 30 seconds rest.

(d) 2 × 100 metres arms only, with 30 seconds rest.

P.M.

(a) 12 × 200 metres with 1 minute rest.

(b) 2 × 200 metres medley, with 45 seconds rest.

Thursday. A.M. May 6.

(a) 2,000 metres.

P.M.

(a) 16 × 100 metres alternating 100 metres arms only, 100 metres kicking, with very short time for recuperation.

Friday. A.M. May 7.

(a) 4 × 100 metres with styles other than crawl, with 30 seconds rest.

(b) 400 metres kicking.

(c) 400 metres arms only.

P.M.

(a) 3 × 800 metres with 3 minutes rest.

Saturday. A.M. May 8.

(a) 16 × 50 metres with 30 seconds rest.

(b) 8 × 100 metres with 30 seconds rest.

Complete rest until Monday

Monday. A.M. May 10.

(a) 3 × 200 metres kicking, with 10 seconds rest.

(b) 3 × 200 metres arms only, with 10 seconds rest.

(c) 2 × 200 metres kicking, with 10 seconds rest.

(d) 2 × 200 metres arms only, with 10 seconds rest.

P.M.

(a) 3 × 800 metres with 3 minutes rest.

Tuesday. A.M. May 11.

(a) 4 × 100 metres kicking with practically no rest.

(b) 4 × 100 metres arms only with practically no rest.

(c) 4 × 100 metres kicking with practically no rest.

(d) 4 × 100 metres arms only with practically no rest.

P.M.

(a) 10 × 200 metres with 2 minutes 30 seconds rest.

Wednesday. A.M. May 12.

(a) 3,000 metres.

P.M.

(a) 3 × 200 metres kicking.

(b) 3 × 200 metres arms only.

(c) 3 × 200 metres kicking.

(d) 400 metres arms only.

Thursday. A.M. May 13.

(a) 400 metres kicking.

(b) 400 metres arms only.

(c) 400 metres kicking, dolphin and back.

(d) 400 metres arms only medley.

P.M.

(a) 7 × 200 metres medley.

Friday. A.M. May 14.

(a) 8 × 50 metres butterfly, breaststroke, backstroke, crawl; the series of choice.

(b) 5 × 50 metres sprint with 3 minutes rest.

Here is a sample of general training from Forbes Carlile Swim School. (Ryde, N.S.W.) 1969.

2 × 50 metres butterfly kick.

4 × 200 metres freestyle.

3 × 100 metres freestyle.

2 × 100 metres butterfly.

2 × 100 metres breaststroke.

2 × 100 metres backstroke.

2 × 100 metres freestyle.
400 metres freestyle.
2 × 400 metres freestyle.
4 × 50 metres butterfly.
4 × 50 metres backstroke.
4 × 50 metres breaststroke.
4 × 50 metres freestyle.
200 metres freestyle kick.
200 metres butterfly kick.
200 metres breaststroke kick.
200 metres backstroke kick.
All the above programme to be done as sprints or 'stroke' work.
Sessions when there was racing the next day were as under:
400 metres freestyle kick.
400 metres freestyle.
2 × 50 metres freestyle – dive.
400 metres backstroke.
4 × 25 metres freestyle.
8 × 50 metres butterfly.
400 metres kick (100 metres of each).
8 × 25 metres freestyle sprint.

2 × 400 metres freestyle (30 seconds between).
4 × 50 metres butterfly.
200 metres backstroke.
200 metres breaststroke.
200 metres freestyle.
2 × 100 metres freestyle kick.
1 × 100 metres breaststroke kick.
1 × 100 metres butterfly kick.

200 metres backstroke.
400 metres breaststroke.
4 × 50 metres butterfly.
4 × 100 metres freestyle.
4 × 50 metres backstroke.
2 × 100 metres breaststroke.
4 × 50 metres freestyle kick.

2 × 100 metres breaststroke kick.

2 × 50 metres butterfly.

2 × 50 metres backstroke.

2 × 50 metres breaststroke.

2 × 50 metres freestyle.

400 metres freestyle.

A normal work-out

6 × 400 metres freestyle.

8 × 50 metres butterfly.

4 × 100 metres breaststroke.

4 × 100 metres breaststroke kick.

4 × 100 metres backstroke kick.

4 × 50 metres freestyle.

Graham White is the fastest 1500 metre swimmer and Michael Wenden is the fastest 100 metre swimmer ever produced in Australia. Here is an extract from their 1968 preparation for the Mexico Olympics:

GRAHAM WHITE (17 years) September 11, 1968. Scarborough, Queensland.

A.M.

(a) 500 metres warm up.

(b) 4 × 800 metres efforts (5 minutes rest) 9·45·0 to 9·10·0.

(c) 3 × 400 metres efforts (2 minutes rest) 4·39·0 to 4·35·0.

(d) 4 × 200 metres efforts (1 minutes rest) 2·18·0 to 2·19·0.

(e) 3 × 100 metres efforts (1 minutes rest) 64·0 to 63·0.

Here are KAREN MORAS's (14 years) times for the same schedule which incidentally is based upon the Olympic 1500 metre champion Michael Burton's work-outs.

(a) 500 metres warm up.

(b) 11·10, 10·25, 10·50, 10·35.

(c) 5·20, 5·15, 5·15.

(d) 2·27, 2·31, 2·34, 2·32.

(e) 1·14, 1·12, 1·09.

On the same morning MICHAEL WENDEN did this work-out.

(a) Swim 400 metres steady.

(b) 10 × 25 metres sprints.

(c) 10 × 100 metres sprints departing every 5 minutes and trying to better 60 seconds from push.

(d) 3 × 200 metres kick sprints hard.

(e) 3 × 200 metres pull with kick board held between legs.

(f) 8 × 25 metres from push, hard.

(g) 16 × 50 metres every 2 minutes trying to better 30 seconds from push.

Michael's times were:

(c) 61·3, 60·6, 59·9, 59·3, 60·0, 59·9, 59·8, 58·8, 58·0, 57·7.

(g) 31·1, down to 26·8, seconds.

This programme has overtones of the type of work-out of Steve Clark (U.S.A.) former world record holder.

PART TWO

Since the present trend is to allot copious amounts of all four strokes it means that sprinters, medley and distance swimmers can follow the same programme early in the season, at least. I will now present sections from the training schedule I used this season, which incidentally paid off with many records. Space makes it impossible to place every training session down, but you will get an idea of the type of work, the system, etc. from the following extracts.

First Month, June. Build up period
  Calisthenics: 1 hour weekly.
  Dynastatics (resistance machine): 15 minutes daily. (Every day.)
  Weight training: 3 sessions of 45 minutes weekly.
  Bush running: 1 × 9 miles and 1 × 11 miles.
  Water mileage (weekly): 8, 10, 12, 12, 14. (Total 56 miles)
  A mid-June programme is as below:
  1st day 6 A.M.   (a) 4 × 200 metres medleys at 70 per cent effort.
                         (b) 4 × 200 metres kick medleys at 70 per cent effort.
                         (c) 4 × 100 metres butterfly every 2½ minutes at 70 per cent effort.
                         (d) 4 × 100 metres backstroke every 2 minutes at 70 per cent effort.
                         (e) 8 × 100 metres medleys every 2 minutes at 70 per cent effort.
           4 P.M.   (a) 2 × 400 metres medleys at 70 per cent effort.
                         (b) 2 × 400 metres kick medleys at 70 per cent effort.
                         (c) 4 × 100 metres breaststroke every 2½ minutes at 70 per cent effort.
                         (d) 4 × 100 metres freestyle every 2 minutes at 70 per cent effort.
                         (e) 8 × 100 metres medleys (in reverse) every 2 minutes at 70 per cent effort.
  2nd day 6 A.M.   Swim rest. Do dynastatics and/or weight training.

4 P.M.   (a) 400 metres bilateral freestyle loosen up.

(b) 400 metres kick under 8 minutes.

(c) 400 metres pull (legs tied) non-stop.

(d) 400 metres of secondary stroke at 70 per cent effort.

(e) 32 × 50 metres of all strokes (follow the leader of each lane) departing every 60 seconds.

3rd day 6 A.M.   Swim rest. Do dynastatics and/or weight training.

4 P.M.   (a) 8 × 100 metres kick medleys every 2½ minutes.

(b) 8 × 100 metres medleys every 2½ minutes.

(c) 16 × 50 metres sprints every 60 seconds (main stroke).

(d) 8 × 50 metres sprints every 60 seconds (second stroke).

(e) 8 × 50 metres sprints every 60 seconds (third stroke).

4th day 6 A.M.   (a) 4 × 100 metres butterfly every 2½ minutes at 70 per cent effort.

(b) 4 × 100 metres backstroke every 2 minutes at 70 per cent effort.

(c) 4 × 100 metres breaststroke every 2½ minutes at 70 per cent effort.

(d) 4 × 100 metres freestyle every 2 minutes at 70 per cent effort.

(e) 8 × 100 metres mixed kick sprints every 2½ minutes.

(f) 8 × 100 metres medley sprints every 2½ minutes.

4 P.M.   Swim rest. Do dynastatics and/or weight training.

5th day 6 A.M.   Swim rest. Do dynastatics and/or weight training.

4 P.M.   (Long day)

(a) 800 metres freestyle at 80 per cent effort.

(b) 2 × 400 metres medleys, one every 8 minutes.

(c) 400 metres kick in under 8 minutes.

(d) 400 metres arms only (legs tied) in under 7 minutes.

(e) Relays (to total 800 metres in sprints).

Remarks

The first month is 'shake down' month. The coach should have ample time to do stroke work. Swimmers should become more proficient on their poorer strokes, e.g. 'that breaststroke kick', 'that bent-arm backstroke push', 'those lifted elbows on the butterfly and freestyle'. No pressure is applied to the work-out. Keen swimmers will now start recording heart rates, body weights and other pertinent details. A time trial is conducted once a fortnight and it should be over a 400 metres or 200 metres medley. June is winter in Australia and vitamin supplementation is taken in the form of vitamin C (250 mgs daily) and/or one multi-vitamin capsule, 'Minacon'. Not too much attention is given to starts or turns at this stage, all work being done from 'push'. Other sports are carried on at school, basketball, golf, tennis, trampolining and gymnastics being advocated. Some swimmers have influenza injections and teeth attended to.

Second Month, July. Work increase period

Calisthenics: 30 minutes weekly.

Dynastatics: 15 minutes daily.

Weight training: 3 sessions of 45 minutes weekly.

Bush running: 1 × 13 miles.

Water mileage (weekly): 14, 14, 16, 16. (Total 60 miles, progressive total 116 miles.)

A mid-July programme is as below:

1st day 6 A.M.   (a) 8 × 100 metres medleys every 2 minutes at 75 per cent effort.

(b) 4 × 100 metres kick every 2¼ minutes at 1 minute 45 seconds.

(c) 4 × 100 'pulls' at 1 minute 30 seconds every 2 minutes.

(d) 4 × 100 metres backstroke at 1 minute 30 seconds every 2 minutes.

(e) 4 × 100 metres breaststroke at 1 minute 45 seconds every 2¼ minutes.

(f) 8 × 100 metres freestyle at 1 minute 20 seconds every 2 minutes.

(g) 8 × 50 metres butterfly at 40 seconds every 1 minute.

4 P.M. (a) 1500 metres non-stop.

(b) 8 × 100 metres kick sprints every 2½ minutes at 90 per cent.

(c) 2 × 400 metres medleys at 90 per cent. Timed.

2nd day 6 A.M. Swim rest. Do dynastatics and/or weight training.

4 P.M. (a) 400 metres medley loosen up.

(b) 32 × 50 metres 'on the minute' at 80 per cent (all strokes).

(c) 200 metres dolphin kick at 75 per cent.

(d) 200 metres breaststroke kick at 75 per cent.

(e) 16 × 50 metres 'polo' sprints every 1¼ to 1½ minutes.

(f) 800 metres effort at 80 per cent. Timed.

3rd day 6 A.M. (a) 200 metres butterfly.

(b) 200 metres medley.

(c) 6 × 200 metres efforts every 3½ minutes at 80 per cent.

(d) 16 × 50 metres 'pull' sprints every 60 seconds at 80 per cent.

(e) 16 × 50 metres kick sprints every 60 seconds at 80 per cent.

(f) 8 × 50 metres butterfly sprints at 85 per cent (walk backs).

4 P.M. Swim rest. Do dynastatics and/or weight training.

4th day 6 A.M. (a) 2,400 metres non-stop. (70–90 per cent)

(b) 16 × 25 metres sprints, all strokes.

(c) 800 metres medley non-stop.

4 P.M. (a) 4 × 100 metres kick every 2 minutes at 75 per cent.

(b) 4 × 100 metres 'pulls' every 2 minutes at 75 per cent.

(c) 4 × 100 metres butterfly every 2 minutes at 75 per cent.

(d) 4 × 100 metres breaststroke every 2 minutes at 75 per cent.

(e) 4 × 100 metres **backstroke** every 2 minutes at 75 per cent.

(f) 4 × 100 metres freestyle every 2 minutes at 75 per cent.

(g) 2 × 400 metres efforts (or medleys) at 85 per cent.

5*th day* 6 A.M.   Swim rest. Do dynastatics and/or weight training.

4 P.M.   (a) 200 metres medley, loosen up.

(b) 1,500 metres timed and recorded at 85–90 per cent.

(c) Relay teams to cover 800 metres.

(d) 3 × 200 metres medleys or 3 × 200 metres 'pulls'.

Remarks

The pattern of the first month is repeated and intensified. Long swims are introduced to increase cardio-respiratory fitness and general endurance. Interval training becomes a regular feature. All strokes receive equal attention. Time trials are now held weekly but not on a training day. Trials are held over 800 metres and 400 metres. The form strokers also trial on freestyle. July is a build-up to August which actually is the first heavy month. June and July will allow the pupil to keep up with school commitments, whereas August will cause students to completely reorganize their daily living schedules. Strokes should now be starting to take upon a polished appearance. Swimmers should be starting to rise a little higher in the water due to muscle adaptation. During June most swimmers will be very low in the water especially the breaststroke and butterfly swimmers. Muscle soreness will be diminishing by the end of July. The swimmer will now be over the shock stage and moving towards the fatigue zone. This is one reason I like to hasten slowly in the first weeks of the new season, to give the pupils time to adjust physically, mentally and socially. Weight should be steady, as should be haemoglobin levels.

Third Month, August

Calisthenics: 30 minutes weekly, e.g. ankle flexibility exercises.

Dynastatics: Increased to 20 minutes daily.

Weight training: 3 sessions of 30 minutes weekly.

Bush running: 1 × 15 miles.

Water mileage (weekly): 20, 22, 24, 26. (Total 92 miles, progressive total 208 miles.)

A mid-August programme is listed below:

1st day 6 A.M.   (a) 8 × 50 metres kicks, one every 60 seconds.

(b) 8 × 50 metres 'pulls' one every 60 seconds.

(c) 6 × 400 metres efforts, one every 8 minutes at 80 per cent.

(d) 8 × 50 metres breaststroke one every 60 seconds.

(e) 8 × 50 metres backstroke 'pull', one every 1½ minutes.

(f) 4 × 200 metres medleys, one every 4 minutes.

4 P.M.   (a) 8 × 100 metres medley loosen up, one every 2 minutes.

(b) 8 × 100 metres main stroke, every 2 minutes at 75–80 per cent effort. (Distance men try for race pace.)

(c) 8 × 100 metres kicks every 2½ minutes at 80 per cent effort.

(d) 8 × 100 metres 'pulls' every 2 minutes at 75 per cent effort.

(e) 32 × 50 metres with 10 seconds rest intervals. (Variety of strokes.)

2nd day 6 A.M.   (a) 8 × 50 metres butterfly, one every 60 seconds.

(b) 8 × 50 metres breaststroke, one every 60 seconds.

(c) 32 × 50 metres with 10 seconds rest intervals (main stroke).

(d) 32 × 25 metres from push, one every 30 seconds.

4 P.M.   (a) 8 × 50 metres backstroke kicks, one every 1½ minutes.

(b) 8 × 50 metres breastroke 'pulls', one every 1½ minutes.

(c) 8 × 50 metres dolphin kick, one every 1½ minutes.

(d) 8 × 50 metres freestyle 'pulls', one every 1½ minutes.

(e) 32 × 50 metres push with 7 seconds rest intervals.

3rd day 6 A.M.   (a) 8 × 100 metres medleys (in reverse order) one every 2 minutes.

(b) 8 × 200 metres efforts, one every $3\frac{1}{2}$ minutes at 85 per cent effort.

(c) 400 metres kick. Timed and recorded.

(d) 400 metres stroking for relaxation.

(e) 800 metres 'pull', 1 lap fast, 1 lap steady throughout.

(f) 16 × 25 metres sprints from push, all strokes.

4 P.M.   (a) 400 metres loosen up.

(b) 3,000 metres timed and recorded, the second 1,500 metres to be of higher quality than the previous 1,500 metres, e.g. 18 minutes 20 seconds and 17 minutes 45 seconds.

4th day 6 A.M.   Complete rest.

4 P.M.   (a) 2 × 200 metres medleys as a warm up.

(b) 10 × 150 metres sprints, one every 3 minutes at 90 per cent. (5 efforts on the main stroke and 5 efforts on the secondary stroke.)

(c) 8 × 50 metres backstroke sprints, one every 60 seconds from push.

(d) 8 × 50 metres butterfly sprints, one every 60 seconds from push.

(e) 8 × 50 metres breaststroke sprints, one every $1\frac{1}{4}$ minutes from push.

(f) 8 × 100 metres kick sprints, one every $2\frac{1}{4}$ minutes at 80 per cent, all strokes.

5th day 6 A.M.   (a) 8 × 100 metres medleys as a loosen up, one every 2 minutes.

(b) 40 × 50 metres sprints in sets of ten, going on the 60, each set slightly faster than the previous set, with 4 minutes rest between sets.

(c) 8 × 100 metres legs tied sprints, one every 2 minutes at 80–85 per cent.

(d) 16 × 50 metres kick sprints, one every $1\frac{1}{4}$ minutes all strokes.

(e) 16 × 25 metres butterfly walk back sprints.

6th day 6 A.M.   Swim rest. Do dynastatics or special exercises.

4 P.M.   (a) 400 metres medleys loosen up.

(b) 3 × 800 metres efforts in 45 minutes, each effort becoming harder than the previous, e.g. 9·30·0, 9·20·0, 9·05·0.

(c) 400 metres kick for relax.

(d) 8 × 50 metres 'polo' sprints, every $1\frac{1}{4}$ minutes.

(e) 400 metres backstroke/breaststroke for relax.

(f) 16 × 50 metres sprints every $1\frac{1}{2}$ minutes (high quality).

Remarks

Towards the end of August, State Winter Championships are held. Most pupils do not taper off severely for these meets and coaches should use the titles to 'blood' their young hopefuls. National Winter Titles will soon be held in Australia and this then will make it necessary for two distinct seasons so far as coaching is concerned. Therefore at the end of August a ten day or even two weeks break from all water work is recommended, this to occur immediately after the Winter Titles. The break, although taken begrudgingly by some, is well worth it. Teams and coaches come back anxious to hit the water again whereas I have found that teams who train continually from June to March or April tend to slacken in drive and purpose from January on.

Other sport activities as well as pulleys, weight training, etc. can be maintained. The August schedule still keeps the squad working as one unit, all swimmers, except in very special circumstances, doing the same work-out. The variety of 'other strokes' and 'other kicks' is not so great during this month, the reason being that time is at a minimum, especially in the mornings where swimmers are short on pool time. By August weekly pennant competition has started at State level and therefore swimmers are exposed to weekly relays and individual events. Important school examinations occur in early September and the compulsory two weeks rest previously mentioned allows swimmers to concentrate upon their grades. The winter titles and pennant races allow the coach and swimmer to assess the stroke and conditioning standard to this point.

PART THREE

Fourth Month, September

Calisthenics and Dynastatics: Combined, 6 sessions of 20 minutes weekly.

Weight training: 2 sessions of 40 minutes weekly.

Water mileage (weekly): rest, 28, 28, 30, 30. (Grand total 324.)

The third week's programme is listed.

1st day 6 A.M.
(a) 400 metres kick loosen up.

(b) 8 × 50 metres kick, one every 60 seconds.

(c) 5 × 100 metres freestyle, one every 2 minutes at 85 per cent.

(d) 3 × 100 metres breaststroke, one every 2 minutes at 80 per cent.

(e) 5 × 100 metres backstroke, one every 2 minutes at 85 per cent.

(f) 3 × 100 metres butterfly, one every 2 minutes at 80 per cent.

(g) 400 metres pull (legs tied) non-stop.

(h) 8 × 50 metres pull sprints at 90 per cent, every 60 seconds.

(i) 4 sets of 8 × 50 metres with 10-second rest intervals, each set becoming faster than the previous set, 3 minutes rest between each set.

4 P.M.
(a) 8 × 100 metres medleys or secondary stroke as a loosen up.

(b) 400 metres kick at minus 7 minutes 30 seconds.

(c) 400 metres pull (legs tied) at minus 6 minutes.

(d) 8 × 200 metres efforts departing every $3\frac{1}{2}$ minutes at 90 per cent.

(e) 8 broken 200 metres, one every $3\frac{1}{2}$ minutes.

2nd day 6 A.M.
(a) 400 metres butterfly and backstroke as a loosen up.

(b) 20 × 100 metres departing every 2 minutes and having a 2 minutes rest after the first ten, at 85 per cent.

(c) 8 × 50 metres kick (all styles) every 75 seconds. 8 × 50 metres pull (all styles) every 75 seconds.

(d) 32 × 50 metres with 10 seconds rest intervals at 85–90 per cent non-stop.

4 P.M.　(a) 8 × 100 metres medleys one every 2 minutes as a loosen up.

(b) 8 × 400 metres efforts one every 8 minutes, every second effort to be at 90 per cent, every other one at 80 per cent.

(c) 800 metres kick, going up the pool hard and coming down the pool at a steady speed.

(d) 16 walk back or hard push 50 metre sprints, one sprint about every 1½–2 minutes.

3rd day 6 A.M.　Rest morning.

4 P.M.　(a) 400 metres slow swim loosen up for stroke.

(b) 400 metres medley loosen up for stroke.

(c) 3,000 metres non-stop (timed and recorded).

(d) 16 × 50 metres kick sprints one every 75 seconds.

4th day 6 A.M.　(a) 8 × 100 metres medleys one every 2 minutes as a loosen up.

(b) 20 minutes of relays across the diving pool (20 metres), i.e. each swimmer would cover up to 800 metres at 95 per cent in 20 metres or 40 metres bursts.

(c) a circuit of

　(i) 800 metres bilateral freestyle.

　(ii) 400 metres kick.

　(iii) 400 metres pull (legs tied).

　(iv) 200 metres backstroke.

　(v) 200 metres breaststroke.

　(vi) 200 metres butterfly.

　(vii) 200 metres medley.

Timed and recorded, the boys trying to better 40 minutes and the girls 42 minutes.

(d) 16 × 50 metres walk backs sprints or hard push 50 metres, departing every 1½ minutes.

4 P.M.　Team leaders are asked to compile the afternoon's work-out to cover 3 miles. I have

observed that on this day the team leaders select segments of 400 metres, e.g. 400 metres kick, 400 metres back, 400 metres pull, 400 metres kick, etc.

5*th day* 6 A.M.   (a) 400 metres medley loosen up, or 2 × 200 metres medley.

(b) 10 × 150 metres sprints, one every 3 minutes at 85–90 per cent (strokes can be varied).

(c) 4 × 200 metres kick sprints one every 5 minutes.

(d) 4 × 200 metres pull sprints one every 5 minutes.

(e) 4 × 200 metres medley one every 5 minutes, at 90 per cent.

(f) 16 × 25 metres sprints at 95 per cent.

4 P.M.   (a) 8 × 100 metres medley, one every 2 minutes, as a loosen up.

(b) 8 × 100 metres kick sprints, one every $2\frac{1}{2}$ minutes at 80 per cent.

(c) 8 × 100 metres mainstroke sprints, one every $1\frac{1}{2}$ minutes at 85–90 per cent.

(d) 8 × 100 metres pull (secondary stroke) sprints, one every $2\frac{1}{2}$ minutes at 80 per cent.

(e) 8 × 100 metres secondary stroke sprints, one every 2 minutes at 85 per cent.

(f) 800 metres 'lungbuster' or 400 metres 'polo' and 400 metres medleys.

6*th day* 6 A.M.   Rest morning.

4 P.M.   (a) 800 metres medley as a loosen up.

(b) 4 × 100 metres kicks one every $2\frac{1}{2}$ minutes, at 95, 90, 85 and 80 per cent.

(c) 4 × 100 metres pulls (legs tied) one every $2\frac{1}{2}$ minutes at 95, 90, 85 and 80 per cent.

(d) 200 metres medley as a stroke exercise.

(e) 5 × 300 metres efforts one every 5 minutes.

(f) 32 × 25 metres sprints (push) with 15 seconds rest intervals.

(g) 600 metres of stroke mechanics on the mainstroke.

Remarks

By the end of the fourth month (September) the team is now ready to move into two groups, i.e. distance and 400 metre medley performers in group one, the sprinters of all strokes in the second group. At this point the coach definitely needs at least one assistant, if not two – depending upon the size of the squad, because the schedules are so different, especially the rest intervals. The team has a very critical haemoglobin count taken at this point. School examinations are very close and the specialized swim work is about to commence, care must be taken not to overload a run-down trainee. The coach must now be alert to observe early stress signs and make the necessary adjustments. Body weight especially should be controlled. The overweights will still have time to pare off their surplus, but I advocate no more than a pound a week. Those on or near correct racing weight, should, by judicious eating habits and a balancing work output, stay there.

Fifth Month, October

Calisthenics: Now cut to a minimum, special exercises for 'your' stroke to be carried out, e.g. ankle flexibility exercises for breast-strokers; shoulder flexibility movements for 'fly swimmers; etc.

Dynastatics, Rubbers, etc.: These now assume greater importance. Two 12 to 15 minute sessions daily, if possible before the swim work-out, and if time is short concentrate on the exercises of your stroke.

Weight training: Two sessions of 30 to 40 minutes, or 4 sessions of 20 to 25 minutes weekly.

Water mileage: Distance and medley swimmers, 30, 30, 30, 30. (Total 120, grand total 444 miles.) Sprinters, 30, 28, 26, 25. (Total 109, grand total 433 miles.)

A mid-October programme is as below:

Sprint Swimmers
1st *day* 6 A.M.
(a) 8 × 100 metres medley as a warm up.
(b) 8 × 100 metres kick sprints every 2 minutes at 85 per cent.
(c) 8 × 100 metres, sprints every 90 seconds at 85 per cent, emphasizing even lapping.

Distance and Medley swimmers

(a) 400 metres medley loosen up.

(b) 4 × 500 metres efforts, one every 10 minutes at 85, 90, 85 and 90 per cent.
(c) 4 × 200 metres, kick efforts, one every 4½ minutes at 85 per cent.

Sprint swimmers

(d) 8 × 50 metres, 'polo' sprints, every 75 seconds.

(e) 8 × 50 metres secondary stroke sprints every 75 seconds at 85 per cent effort.

(f) 16 × 50 metres sprints, dive, at best time plus 2·5 seconds every 2 minutes or thereabouts.

4 P.M.

(a) 200 metres kick loosen up.

(b) 200 metres medley.

(c) 1 × 400 metres at 80 per cent.

(d) 2 × 200 metres at 85 per cent with 5 minutes rest between each effort.

(e) 4 × 100 metres at 90 per cent with 3 minutes between each sprint.

(f) 8 × 50 metres at 95 per cent departing every 2 minutes from push.

(g) 16 × 25 metres at 95 per cent from push every 30 seconds.

(h) 4 × 100 metres kick every 2 2 minutes at 85 per cent.

(i) 4 × 100 metres pull (legs tied) every 2 minutes at 85 per cent.

(j) 800 metres of continuous swimming, mixing up all strokes.

2nd day 6 A.M.

(a) 400 metres of general loosening up (any style, varying speeds).

(b) 24 × 100 metres in sets of 6, every 90 seconds with 3 minutes rest between sets, aiming for best time plus 10 seconds from push.

(c) 400 metres of general kicking (any style, varying speed)

(d) 32 × 25 metres sprints from

Distance and medley swimmers

(d) 16 × 100 metres, 'repeats' every 90 seconds aiming for race pace, eg. a distance swimmer whose best time for 1500 metres is 18 minutes 45 seconds would aim for repeats of 1 minute 15 seconds.

4 P.M.

(a) 200 metres kick loosen up.

(b) 200 metres medley.

(c) 3 × 1,000 metres efforts at 80, 85 and 88 per cent with 10 minutes rest between each.

(d) 400 metres kick as a hard effort, approaching best recorded time.

(e) 400 metres pulling a small float (plastic bottle) at an even pace.

(f) 8 × 50 metres sprints from push every 90 seconds.

6 A.M.

(a) 400 metres of general loosening up (any style, varying speeds).

(b) 16 × 200 metres every 4 minutes aiming for a steady speed of, say, best time plus 12 seconds from push.

(c) 400 metres of general kicking (any style, varying speeds).

(d) 32 × 25 metres sprints from

Sprint swimmers
dive at maximum speed with no more than 30 seconds between each sprint.

Distance and medley swimmers
push at maximum speed, one every 30 seconds.

4 P.M.
(a) 4 × 100 metres medley as a loosen up.
(b) 16 × 100 metres in sets of 4, every 90 seconds, with 3 minutes rest between each set, aiming for best time plus 7 seconds.
(c) 400 metres medley (or any other stroke as a relaxer).
(d) 32 × 25 metres, sprints from push at near maximum speed, on every 30 seconds.
(e) 400 metres of free choice in less than 7 minutes.

4 P.M.
(a) 4 × 100 metres medleys as a loosen up.
(b) 2 × 1500 metres efforts at 88 per cent then 90 per cent, with a 10 minute rest between each effort.
(c) 8 × 50 metres kick sprints every 90 seconds at 85 per cent.
(d) 8 × 50 metres secondary stroke sprints every 90 seconds at 85 per cent.
(e) 400 metres pull (legs tied) effort approaching best personal time.

3rd day 6 A.M.
(a) 400 metres of own choice loosen up.
(b) 16 × 50 metres very hard kick sprints, one every 90 seconds.

(c) 400 metres medley to loosen up leg muscles.
(d) 32 × 50 metres sprints with 10 seconds rest intervals (actually joining in with the distance men and setting a hard pace for them)
(e) 8 × 50 metres secondary stroke sprints, one every 90 seconds at 90 per cent.

(f) 32 × 25 metres sprints from push on all strokes but with a predominance of butterfly stroke.

4 P.M.
(a) 400 metres of own choice as a loosen up.
(b) 64 × 50 metres with 10 seconds rest intervals, starting off at a medium effort (say, 36 seconds) and building up to maximum effort (say, 32 seconds) towards the end.
(c) 200 metres kick of own choice.

(d) 200 metres pull of own choice.

(e) 800 metres pull (legs tied) at best time for distance (stroke) plus 90 seconds, e.g. a 9:00:0 minute swimmer would be expected to swim a 10:30 pull.

4 P.M.
(a) 400 metres medley kick loosen up.
(b) 6 × 200 metres efforts on main-stroke varying the efforts between

4 P.M.
(a) 4 × 100 metres medleys as a loosen up.
(b) 3,000 metres as a hard but even paced effort, picking up the last 400

Sprint swimmers

80 and 90 per cent, every 5 minutes, e.g. 2·12, 2·08, 2·10, 2·06, 2·10, 2·05.

(c) 3 × 200 metres kick, one every 4 minutes at 75 per cent (main and secondary stroke kick).

(d) 3 × 200 metres pull, one every 3½ minutes at 85 per cent.

(e) 8 × 100 metres medleys as sprints one every 2 minutes.

4th day 6 A.M.

(a) 8 × 100 metres medleys but in reverse order as a warm up, one every 2 minutes.

(b) 10 × 150 metres sprints, one every 3 minutes between 85 and 90 per cent.

(c) 16 × 50 metres kick sprints at one every 2 minutes at maximum speed, e.g. minus 40 seconds.

(d) 800 metres of steady legs trail (not tied).

4 P.M. *Relay day*

(a) 4 × 200 metres medleys, one every 4 minutes on each medley to concentrate on a different stroke, e.g. the first one concentrate on a hard butterfly section, the second one concentrate on a hard backstroke section, etc.

(b) The sprinters now combine with the distance men and form 3-man relays and race non-stop for 30 minutes over 50 metres, i.e. approximately 1,000 metres each man.

(c) 400 metres kick going up fast and coming back steady.

(d) 400 metres pull (legs tied) going up fast and coming back steady.

(e) Teams now combine again and swim across the pool (20 metres) in teams of 3 (use the medley order of

Distance and medley swimmers

metres to almost maximum speed (timed and recorded).

(c) 400 metres kick or 400 metres medley (no time).

(d) 16 × 25 metres hard sprints, from push one every 30 seconds.

(e) 200 metres backstroke.

(f) 200 metres breaststroke.

6 A.M.

(a) 800 metres of steady legs trail (not tied) as a warm up.

(b) 8 × 400 metres efforts to be completed in 60 minutes in the following manner, e.g. 4·50, 4·40, 4·48, 4·38, 4·46, 4·36, 4·44, 4·34 (for a 4.20 man).

(c) 16 × 50 metres kick sprints one every 75 seconds at 90 per cent effort.

4 P.M. *Relay day*

(a) 4 × 200 metres medleys, one every 4 minutes on each medley to concentrate on a different stroke, e.g. the first one concentrates on a hard butterfly section, the second one concentrates on a hard backstroke section, etc.

(b) The distance and medley swimmers now combine with the sprinters and form 3-man relays and race non-stop for 30 minutes over 50 metres, i.e. approximately 1,000 metres each man.

(c) 400 metres kick going up fast and coming back steady.

(d) 400 metres pull (legs tied) going up fast and coming back steady.

(e) Teams now combine again and swim across the pool (20 metres) in teams of 3 (use the medley order of

Sprint swimmers

strokes). Swim non-stop for 15 minutes, i.e. approximately 400 metres each swimmer.

(f) 400 metres 'polo' swimming.

(g) 400 metres controlled breathing non-stop, i.e. in this breathing order for the 8 lengths of the pool bilateral, every 4 strokes, bilateral, every 6 strokes, bilateral, every 8 strokes, bilateral, every 10 strokes.

5th day 6 A.M.
Rest morning.

4 P.M.
(a) 400 metres loosen up on any stroke.
(b) 10 sprints of 75 metres at 93 per cent effort for 50 metres then 98 per cent for last 25. One every 3 or 4 minutes.
(c) 400 metres kicking motivating the whole team to better 7 minutes.
(d) 20 × 25 metres sprints from push, with 10 seconds rest between each sprint.
(e) 12 × 25 metres 'fly sprints from dive.

6th day A.M.
Rest morning.

4 P.M.
(a) 400 metres back to back medley as a warm up.
(b) 4 special 100 metres from dive, one every 4 minutes at 90 per cent effort.

Distance and medley swimmers

strokes). Swim non-stop for 15 minutes, i.e. approximately 400 metres each swimmer.

(f) 400 metres of pull (legs tied) with a 2 oz. weighted band around the ankles.

(g) 400 metres controlled breathing non-stop, i.e. in this breathing order for the 8 lengths of the pool, bilateral, every 4 strokes, bilateral, every 6 strokes, bilateral, every 8 strokes, bilateral, every 10 strokes.

6 A.M.
Rest morning.

4 P.M.
(a) 400 metres loosen up on any stroke.
(b) 800 metres at 85 per cent effort.

(c) 400 metres kick (steady).

(d) 5 minutes rest.

(e) 800 metres at 90 per cent.
(f) 400 metres medley (steady).
(g) 5 minutes rest.
(h) 800 metres at 95 per cent.
(i) 20 × 25 metres from push with 10 seconds rest between each sprint.
(j) 12 × 25 metres 'fly sprints from dive.

A.M.
Rest morning.

4 P.M.
(a) 400 metres back to back medley as a warm up.
(b) 3 special 200 metres from dive, one every 7 minutes at 90 per cent effort.

Sprint swimmers

(c) 400 metres steady secondary stroke.

(d) 4 special 100 metres from dive, one every 4 minutes at 92 per cent effort.

(e) 400 metres of steady kick.

(f) 4 special 100 metres from dive, one every 4 minutes at 95 per cent effort.

(g) 400 metres of medley strokes at a steady speed.

(h) 16 'walk back' 50 metre sprints aiming for best time plus 2·5 seconds.

Distance and medley swimmers

(c) 400 metres steady secondary stroke.

(d) 3 special 200 metres from dive, one every 7 minutes at 92 per cent effort.

(e) 400 metres of steady kick.

(f) 3 special 200 metres from dive, one every 7 minutes at 95 per cent effort.

(g) 400 metres of medley strokes at a steady speed.

(h) Up to 800 metres of stroke work, or timed turns, etc.

Remarks

By October you will start to consolidate a fit team which will be approaching very fast times, only the fact that there are so many 'repeats' will delay the team from reaching its peak. In other words the work load is still high, the quality of the work is good but not excellent, the rest periods are not too long. Under this system we will put down a very solid foundation of condition, the type of conditioning that is necessary to eventually reach 100 per cent fitness. Some sessions can be extremely demanding if done correctly, for example the 'relay days' or the 'dive programme days'.

I advocate one full rest day weekly – actually I organize the individual's programme, especially the older pupils, in such a way, that as long as the target mileage for the week (say 30 miles) is completed, it does not matter which sessions the pupil attends. With heavy schooling commitments and other aspects of living, all pupils cannot attend the set training times, since pupils go to different schools and universities with different timetables. This is the reason I keep the daily mileage constant, at 5 or 6 miles, if a pupil misses one session, he knows he has 2½ or 3 miles to catch up. Most pupils have their target mileage completed by the Saturday morning and therefore have the week-end free. I do not believe as some of my contemporaries do, that the pupil loses touch by having a day away from the pool. The system that some American coaches adopt of training seven days a week is, in my opinion, wrong. Sensible programming during the week can be set down to offset any shortcomings. An exception of course, can be a crash programme, when only weeks are available to 'peak'.

The short (usually 50 metres) 'polo' sprints now assume a greater importance. Arching the back, and lifting the head helps sprinters develop a strong leg drive and a good sprint position.

The days when 3 × 800 metres efforts are programmed for the distance swimmers are the real backbone of their week. The medley swimmers concentrating on 200 metre events can now work with the sprinters from October on. The 400 metres medley performers remain with the distance swimmers, mixing their strokes at the coach's direction. For example on the days when 8 × 400 metres efforts are listed the medley swimmers would do 4 × 400 metres medleys, then 400 metres of each of the four strokes, except perhaps for the butterfly section where they would do a mixture of butterfly and backstroke.

During October weekly time trials are maintained. I prefer to conduct trials at the end of the week, when the swimmer is not fresh.

Sixth Month, November

Calisthenics: Same exercises as for last month, i.e. special exercises for 'your' stroke only.

Dynastatics, Rubbers, etc.: A percentage of swimmers tend to drop these special and important exercises when the swim load increases and they become tired or pressed for time. The coach should, by weekly log book checks or other means, insist on the maintaining of two 15-minute sessions daily, five times a week. Some pupils take advantage of the lunch break at school and attach their exercising units to playground seats and doors.

Weight training: Two sessions weekly of 30 to 40 minutes or, if more convenient, shorter sessions of 20 minutes three or four times a week. Weight sessions can be carried out at week-ends when swimming sessions are at a minimum.

Water mileage: Distance and 400 metres medley swimmers, 30, 30, 30, 30. (Total 120, grand total 564 miles.) Sprinters and 200 metres medley swimmers, 25, 25, 25, 25. (Total 100, grand total 533 miles.)

The programme taken from the third week is typical of the month.

Sprint swimmers

1st day   6 A.M.

(a) 800 metres of steady non-stop swimming as a loosen up.

(b) 8 × 100 metres pulls sprints (legs tied) every 2 minutes, at 85–90 per cent.

(c) 8 × 100 metres kick sprints, every 2 minutes at 85–90 per cent.

(d) 8 × 100 metres sprints on the mainstroke, every 1½ minutes at 90 per cent.

(e) 16 × 50 metres repeats with 15 seconds rests at 90 per cent.

4 P.M.

(a) 8 × 50 metres kick one every 60 seconds at 75 per cent as a loosen up.

(b) 8 × 50 metres kick sprints, one every 90 seconds at 90–95 per cent.

(c) 8 × 50 metres pull (legs tied) at a steady pace.

(d) 8 × 50 metres pull (legs tied) sprints, one every 90 seconds at 95 per cent.

(e) 8 × 50 metres mainstroke sprints at a steady pace, one every 45 seconds.

(f) 8 × 50 metres sprints, one every 60 seconds at 95 per cent.

(g) 16 × 50 metres sprints as walk backs at 95 per cent.

(h) 32 × 25 metres from dive at maximum speed.

2nd day   6 A.M.

(a) 400 metres swimming any style as a loosen up.

(b) 16 × 50 metres sprints, one every 60 seconds at 95 per cent.

(c) 4 'broken' 200 metres kick efforts, i.e. 4 × 50 metres kick sprints with 10 seconds between

Distance swimmers

6 A.M.

(a) 800 metres of steady non-stop swimming as a loosen up.

(b) 8 × 100 metres pulls sprints (legs tied) every 2 minutes, at 85–90 per cent.

(c) 8 × 100 metres kick sprints, every 2 minutes at 85–90 per cent.

(d) 8 × 100 metres sprints on the mainstroke, every 1½ minutes at 90 per cent.

(e) 32 × 50 metres repeats with 7 seconds rest intervals non-stop at 85–90 per cent.

4 P.M.

(a) 400 metres medley as a loosen up.

(b) 4 efforts of 800 metres in the following manner, 85, 90, 90, 85 per cent, all to be completed in 60 minutes.

(c) 400 metres kick at a steady pace.

(d) 16 × 50 metres with 5 seconds rest interval between each, at steadily increasing speed.

6 A.M.

(a) 400 metres swimming any style as a loosen up.

(b) 16 × 50 metres sprints, one every 60 seconds at 95 per cent.

(c) 400 metres steady secondary stroke.

Sprint swimmers

each sprint. One minute between each effort.

(d) 4 'broken' 200 metres main-stroke efforts, with 1 minute between each effort.

(e) 4 'broken' 200 metres secondary stroke efforts, 1 minute between each effort.

(f) 16 × 25 metres butterfly sprints from push.

Distance and medley swimmers

(d) 16 × 50 metres sprints, with 15 seconds rest intervals at 90 per cent effort.

(e) 400 metres of steady kicking.

(f) 16 × 50 metres sprints, with 10 seconds rest intervals at 88 per cent effort.

(g) 400 metres of non-stop pull (legs tied).

(h) 16 × 50 metres sprints with 7 seconds rest intervals at 85 per cent effort.

4 P.M.

(a) 200 metres butterfly at a steady speed.

(b) 200 metres backstroke at a steady speed.

(c) 200 metres breaststroke at a steady speed.

(d) 200 metres medley at a steady speed.

(e) 10 × 150 metres efforts, one effort every 5 minutes at 90 per cent from dive with emphasis on maximum effort on the final 50 metres.

(f) 10 × 50 metres kick sprints, one every 90 seconds at 90 per cent (all styles).

(g) 800 metres of swimming trying to maintain a low stroke rating. Steady speed.

(h) Relays to cover 400 metres (all strokes).

4 P.M.

(a) 200 metres butterfly at a steady speed.

(b) 200 metres backstroke at a steady speed.

(c) 200 metres breaststroke at a steady speed.

(d) 200 metres medley at a steady speed.

(e) 4 × 400 metres efforts, one every 10 minutes at 85, 87, 90 and 92 per cent.

(f) 400 metres of medley kick at a steady speed.

(g) 4 'broken' 400 metres efforts, i.e. 8 × 50 metres sprints with 10 seconds rest intervals, 5 minutes between each 'broken' 400 metres. Effort to be at 90–93 per cent.

(h) 400 metres of swimming trying to maintain low stroke rating. Steady speed.

3rd day 6 A.M.

(a) 8 × 100 metres medleys, one every 2 minutes.

6 A.M.

(a) 8 × 100 metres medleys, one every 2 minutes.

Sprint swimmers

(b) 1 × 400 metres 'broken' at 90 per cent.

(c) 1 × 400 metres kick 'broken' at 90 per cent.

(d) 2 × 200 metres 'broken' at 92 per cent with 2 minutes rest between each effort.

(e) 2 × 200 metres 'broken' pulls at 92 per cent with 2 minutes rest between each effort.

(f) 4 × 100 metres 'broken' mainstroke at 95 per cent with 2 minutes rest between each effort.

(g) 4 × 100 metres 'broken' kicks at 95 per cent with 2 minutes rest between each effort.

(h) 32 × 25 metres sprints from push at near maximum speed (all strokes).

4 P.M.

(a) A 'broken' 400 metres medley as a loosen up.

(b) 1500 metres at 85–90 per cent timed and recorded.

(c) 16 × 50 metres kick, or pull, or secondary stroke sprints, at 90 per cent, one every 90 seconds.

(d) 32 × 25 metres sprints from push, one sprint every 30 seconds.

(e) 8 × 50 metres 'polo' sprints, one every 90 seconds.

4th day A.M.

Rest morning.

4 P.M.

(a) 200 metres medley loosen up.

(b) 24 × 50 metres sprints 'going on the minute' at 85 per cent and gradually up to 95 per cent.

(c) 200 metres backstroke at 85 per cent.

(d) 200 metres breaststroke at 85 per cent.

Distances and medley swimmers

(b) 24 × 100 metres efforts with 20 seconds rest between each sprint, at 85 to 90 per cent.

(c) 4 × 100 metres kick sprints, one every 2¼ minutes at 85 per cent effort.

(d) 4 × 100 metres secondary stroke sprints at 90 per cent effort, one every 2 minutes.

(e) 4 × 100 metres pull (legs tied) sprints at 90 per cent, one every 2 minutes.

(f) 400 metres effort for even pace swimming at 90 per cent.

4 P.M.

(a) 400 metres of any stroke as a loosen up.

(b) 20 × 200 metres efforts, one every 4 minutes at 85–90 per cent.

(c) 32 × 25 metres sprints from push with 10 seconds rest intervals.

A.M.

Rest morning.

4 P.M.

(a) 6 × 50 metres kick sprints.

(b) 100 metres steady stroke.

(c) 1500 metres at 85 per cent.

(d) 10 minutes rest.

Sprint swimmers

(e) 200 metres butterfly at 85 per cent.

(f) 400 metres kick as a medley.
(g) 24 × 50 metres sprints, one every 75 seconds at near maximum speed.
(h) 16 × 25 metres kick or pull. Sprints to be from push.

5th day 6 A.M.
(a) A 'broken' 400 metres medley or a 'broken' 400 metres of secondary stroke as a loosen up.
(b) 800 metres at 90 per cent effort, timed and recorded.

(c) Sprinters to form 3-man relays and swim 50 metre dashes for 30 minutes (1,000 metres each man approximately.)
(d) 200 metres of steady kick.
(e) 200 metres of steady pull (legs tied).
(f) 32 × 50 metres with 10 seconds rest intervals at 90–92 per cent (forcing the distance swimmers along).

4 P.M.
(a) 4 × 100 metres medleys as a loosen up.
(b) Eight special dive 100 metres sprints one every 4 or 5 minutes. Timed and recorded.
(c) 400 metres steady kick.

(d) 16 × 50 metres kick sprints, one every 90 seconds at 95 per cent.
(e) 400 metres medley at a steady speed.

Distance and medley swimmers

(e) 2 × 800 metres efforts at 85 and 90 per cent with 5 minutes between each effort.
(f) 10 minutes rest.
(g) 4 × 400 metres efforts at 92 per cent with 5 minutes between each effort.

6 A.M.
(a) 4 × 200 metres medleys at 80, 85, 90 and 95 per cent efforts, one every 4 minutes.
(b) A timed and recorded circuit of
   (i) 200 metres of each of the 4 kicks.
   (ii) 200 metres of each of the 4 strokes.
   (iii) 200 metres of each of the 4 pulls (legs tied).
(c) 32 × 50 metres with 10 seconds rest intervals at 90–92 per cent.

4 P.M.
(a) 400 metres medley in reverse order.
(b) 3 × 100 metres efforts, at 90 per cent with 5 minutes rest between each effort.
(c) 4 × 200 metres kick or pull sprints, one every 4 minutes at 90 per cent.

Sprint swimmers   *Distance and medley swimmers*

(f) 16 × 50 metres pull (legs tied)
sprints at 95 per cent, one every 75
seconds.

(g) 2 × 200 metres medleys at a
steady speed.

6th day A.M.   A.M.
Rest morning.   Rest morning.

4 P.M.   4 P.M.

(a) 400 metres loosen-up on any   (a) 400 metres loosen-up on any
stroke or kick.   stroke or kick.

(b) Team leaders select and control (b) Team leaders select and control
a programme of relays to cover 1500 a programme of relays to cover 1500
metres (3 members to a team).   metres (3 members to a team).

(c) 32 × 25 metres sprints from   (c) 32 × 25 metres sprints from
push with 10 seconds rest intervals. push with 10 seconds rest intervals.

(d) 16 walk back 50 metre sprints   (d) 800 metres 'lungbuster' non-
(special), some can be kick or   stop.
secondary stroke at 95 per cent
effort.

(e) Up to 800 metres ironing out   (e) Up to 800 metres ironing out
weaknesses in the stroke.   weaknesses in the stroke.

Remarks

November sees the introduction of 'broken' work for the sprinters.
I find that swimmers will try to put more effort into 'broken'
training. The rest intervals, no matter how short, seem to give them
the desire to sprint harder. 'Broken' work also brings a new look to
the programme, just when it is needed. The total mileage is possibly
500 by the end of November for although the swimmers have been
programmed for 564 miles (distance swimmers) and 533 miles
(sprinters), I have found that the pupils drop about 10 per cent of
the allotted schedules, due to illness, school exams, swim meets
away from home, etc. From observation I have also found that at
least 500 miles must be covered before the mature swimmer reaches
top form for distances in excess of 100 metres. Of course younger
swimmers, especially the under 10 years age group, can come up to
top form much faster.

Of interest may be the figures for sprinting 50 metres at maximum
speed on a group of three boys and three girls all aged 10
years.

Month	Average training mileage for the season	Average 100 per cent 50 metres time
October	220 miles	37·8 seconds
November	381 miles	36·6 seconds
December	376 miles	36·0 seconds
January	450 miles	34·9 seconds
February	532 miles	34·1 seconds
March	578 miles	33·6 seconds
April	597 miles	34·0 seconds
		(4 swimmers only)

If training log books are kept the distance swimmers should compare the previous months' times with November's. Not only should time trials be improving but at least 50 per cent of all distance training times should be on up grade. When your distance performers find difficulty bettering training times, say for example the repeat 1,000 metre efforts, alter their programme for a while by working them with the sprint team. Often sprint swimmers can get a 'new life' by working with the distance team for a day or two. Incentive can be maintained at this time because school vacation is about to commence and the swimmers are looking forward to the break. Secondly the local (State) championships are only 6 or 7 weeks away and, as these are usually the basis for selection for the National titles, the individual starts to realize the purpose for all the hard work. November is a demanding month. Training is almost at maximum pressure and school examinations are conducted this month. However pupils seem to get through November, the first real danger in the Southern Hemisphere comes in December. Year after year I have noticed that a definite flat spot occurs some two weeks after the school examinations are over. It is unwise to press the team extremely hard as soon as school vacation commences. Conscientious students have depleted their nervous energy reserves by swotting and sweating it out over a week or more of examinations. A sure way to flatten the team is to disregard this fact and work them to exhaustion. At the end of November the leading team members are subjected to a blood analysis, the readings being carefully interpreted and adjustments made to the individuals overall training routine.

Seventh Month, December

Calisthenics: Only as warm-up exercises before Dynastatics, weight training, etc. As special exercises for the development of strength, flexibility or endurance in 'your' stroke.

Dynastatics, Rubbers, etc.: Two sessions of 15 or even 20 minutes per day. Since school vacation is on there should be no excuses for missing this important adjunct of training. Remember that American World Record Holders do this resistance machine exercises right up to the eve of this important event.

Weight training: I now advocate cutting the weight training session down from 90 minutes a week to three shorter work-outs of about 20 minutes. Strength is maintained when even 10 minute sessions are carried out daily. I have known top sprinters to maintain peak condition with one swim session and one 15 minute weight training session daily. This of course is at the top of the season, not at the beginning.

Water mileage: Distance and 400 metres medley swimmers, 30, 30, 28, 26. Grand total for season, 678 miles. Sprinters and 200 metres medley swimmers, 25, 25, 24, 20. Grand total for season, 627 miles.

Here is the schedule from the third week of December:

Sprint swimmers
1st day 8 A.M.
(a) 4 × 100 metres kick, all strokes as a loosen up, one every 2 minutes.

(b) 4 × 100 metres medleys, one every 2 minutes as a further warm up.

(c) 4 × 200 metres efforts, one every 5 minutes at 85, 85, 90 and 90 per cent effort on the mainstroke.
(d) 200 metres kick, steady.

(e) 8 × 25 metres kick sprints, one every 30 seconds at maximum speed.
(f) 200 metres medley, steady.

Distance and medley swimmers
7 A.M.
(a) 2 × 200 metres medley as a loosen up.

(b) Four sets of 5 × 100 metres 'repeats' aiming to swim at race pace for each 100 metres with correct turns.
(c) 200 metres kick, steady.

(d) 8 × 25 metres kick sprint, one every 30 seconds at maximum speed.
(e) 400 metres pull (legs tied) at 85 per cent.
(f) Four broken 400 metres efforts (10 seconds rest intervals) aiming to better or approach the world records for the swimmers' sex and age, etc. 8–10 minutes between each effort.

Sprint swimmers

(g) 16 × 25 metres butterfly sprints at near maximum speed.

(h) 8 × 25 metres 'walk back' sprints aiming for best time plus 2·2 seconds.

4 P.M.

(a) 8 × 100 metres medleys as a loosen up, one every 2 minutes.

(b) 8 × 50 metres kick sprints, one every 75 seconds, but aiming for near maximum speed, e.g. freestyle kickers to better 40 seconds, backstroke kickers 50 seconds, breaststroke kickers 45 seconds, and butterfly kickers 42 seconds.

(c) 200 metres loosening up swim on any style.

(d) Six very special dive 100 metres repeats on the mainstroke, one sprint every 5 minutes aiming for best time plus 4·5 seconds or less.

(e) 200 metres kick steady.

(f) 200 metres pull (legs tied) steady.

(g) 16 dive 50 metre sprints, with a turn at the end of the 50 metres, one every 3 minutes at near maximum speed.

(h) Starts, turns, finishes (10 minutes).

2nd day 8 A.M.

(a) 400 metres of your stroke as a loosen up.

(b) Four sets of 4 × 100 metres repeats, going 'on the minute', with 4 minutes rest between each set. Make each set harder than the previous set, e.g. 85, 90, 93 and 95 + per cent.

(c) 200 metres kick steady.

Distance and medley swimmers

4 P.M.

(a) 4 × 100 metres medley, one every 2 minutes as a loosen up.

(b) 3,000 metres as a weekly effort each 800 metres to become faster than the previous one.

(c) 200 metres kick steady.

(d) 200 metres pull steady.

(e) A 'broken' 800 metres (10 seconds rest between each 50 metres, gradually increasing the speed until near maximum at the end.

7 A.M.

(a) 400 metres of any strokes as a loosen up.

(b) Eight efforts of 300 metres, one effort every 9 or 10 minutes, all at 85–90 per cent, e.g. swimmer who swims 5 minutes for 400 metres would be expected to record about 4 minutes for the 300 metres.

(c) 200 metres kick steady.

Sprint swimmers

(d) 200 metres pull steady. (Note at this point pull (legs tied) is finished for the season.)

(e) 10 × 75 metres sprints with emphasis on the speed out of the 50 metres turn for the last 25 metres. These to be from dive and aiming for almost race pace.

(f) Turns, 10 minutes.

12 NOON

(a) 400 metres loosen up, any stroke or any kick.

(b) 1,000 metres of relays, in teams of 3, over various short distances from 20 metres to 50 metres, 75 per cent to be on the mainstroke. These to be at near maximum speed.

(c) Starts, 10 minutes.

6 P.M.

(a) 400 metres loosen up, any style.

(b) 1 × 400 metres at 90 per cent.

(c) 2 × 200 metres at 92 per cent, with 5 minutes rest between efforts.

(d) 200 metres kick steady.

(e) 200 metres medley steady.

(f) 4 × 100 metres from dive, one every 5 or 6 minutes at 95 per cent.
(g) 8 × 50 metres sprints at maximum speed, going 'on the minute', the added times for the eight 50 metres to better the world record for 400 metres.
(h) Finish, 'take over' practice.

3rd day 8 A.M.

(a) 4 × 100 metres medley (in reverse order) as a loosen up.

(b) 8 × 150 metres sprints, from push, one every 5 minutes aiming to 'push on hard' from the 100

Distance and medley swimmers

(d) 200 metres pull (legs tied) or a 200 metre medley.

(e) A 'broken mile', i.e. 32 × 50 metres with 10 seconds rest intervals throughout, non-stop. The effort should gradually increase throughout.

12 NOON

(a) 400 metres of any stroke as a loosen up.

(b) Three special 400 metres efforts, one every 10 minutes at 90–95 per cent, timed and recorded for future reference.

5 P.M.

(a) 400 metres of any stroke as a loosen up.

(b) 3 × 200 metres kick sprints, one every 6 minutes at 85 per cent.

(c) 3 × 200 metres pull (legs tied) sprint, one every 6 minutes at 85 per cent.

(d) 3 × 200 metres medley, one every 6 minutes at 85 per cent.

(e) 3 × 200 metres mainstroke, one every 5 minutes at 90 per cent.

(f) Finish, turns and 'take over' practice.

7 A.M.

(a) 800 metres 'lungbuster' as a warm up.

(b) 400 metres kick effort (timed).

Sprint swimmers

metre mark, emphasis being on even speed throughout, at 90–93 per cent effort, mostly on mainstroke.

(c) 200 metres kick, steady.

(d) 200 metres backstroke, steady.

(e) 4 × 100 metres very special kick sprints, one every 4 minutes aiming to beat set standards, these are 88 seconds (free), 90 seconds (breast), 90 seconds (fly), 95 seconds (back).

(f) 200 metres loosening up any style.

(g) Six dive 50 metre sprints, one every 5 minutes with a gun start. All at near maximum speed.

Rest

4 P.M.

(a) 800 metres of stroke mechanics on your race stroke. This does not have to be 800 metres non-stop but say, 8 × 100 metres trying to iron out a particular discrepancy in the stroke, etc. Note: It is advisable to do 'stroke correction' at near race speed, not at a slow pace. The two

Distance and medley swimmers

(c) 400 metres pull (legs tied). Timed.

(d) 16 × 100 metres push effort as a tough endurance grind, having only 10 seconds rest between each 100 metres. Constant speed is the aim.

(e) Turning practice. (10 minutes).

1 P.M.

(a) 400 metres warm up on any stroke.

(b) 800 metres as a race pace effort, timed and recorded.

(c) 200 metres kick, steady.

(d) 200 metres pull, steady.

(e) 400 metres at race pace timed and recorded.

(f) 5 minutes rest.

(g) 400 metres at race pace plus 5 seconds.

(h) 200 metres kick, steady.

(i) 200 metres medley, steady.

(j) A 'broken' 800 metres with 5 seconds rest intervals.

(k) 200 metres to 400 metres cool down for stroke 'brush up'.

Rest

Sprint swimmers

techniques can be entirely different, faults being emphasised at speed, that are not so apparent at a slow stroke rate.

(b) Three special 200 metres efforts, emphasising even speed throughout, and a definite 'push on hard' attitude after the 100 metres mark. These are from dive and one effort every 10 minutes. Swimmers would be expected to get to within 5 seconds of their personal best time on all these sprints.

(c) 200 metres kick, steady.

(d) 200 metres kick as an effort at 95 per cent.

(e) 200 metres medley, steady.

(f) Relays, 3 men to a team, to swim non-stop until each team has covered 72 laps of a 50 metres pool. The teams should be in their own age groups, or like stroke and should aim to better the existing Team records for the 2¼ miles.

(g) Turns (10 minutes).

4th day   8 A.M.

(a) 400 metres medley as a loosen up.

(b) Four sets of 'broken' 400 metres, i.e. 8 × 50 metres with 10 seconds rest intervals, at 85, 90 and 95 per cent and 95 per cent with 10 minutes rest between each set.

(c) 200 metres kick, steady.

(d) 4 × 50 metres kick sprints, aiming for personal records, one every 4 minutes.

(e) 200 metres medley, steady.

(f) Four dive 50 metres sprints aiming for your best time plus 1·5 seconds.

Distance and medley swimmers

7 A.M.

(a) 400 metres medley as a loosen up.

(b) 64 × 50 metres 'on the minute' non-stop throughout, aiming for constant times in sets of 8, e.g. 8 sprints at 39 seconds, 8 sprints at 38 seconds, 8 sprints at 37 seconds, etc.

(c) 400 metres legs tied as an effort. This is the last time legs tied is performed as such by the distance swimmers. Some legs trail (feet not tied) is performed from time to time.

(d) 16 × 25 metres sprints from dive.

Sprint swimmers
12 NOON
(a) 400 metres loosen up, any style.

(b) 16 special 'walk backs' 50 metres sprints, aiming for your best time plus 2 seconds.
(c) 16 × 25 metres sprints at maximum speed from dive or 3-man relays each to cover 16 × 25 metres. (Do all strokes.)

6 P.M.
(a) 600 metres loosen up and stroke mechanics.
(b) Eight 'broken' 200 metres efforts one every 6 minutes, aiming to better the world record for 200 metres for at least four of the efforts. (10 seconds rest intervals.)

5th day
Rest morning.

6 P.M.
(a) *Special time trial night.*
(a) 400 metres loosen up on any style.
(b) 8 × 25 metres sprints, as a pre-time trial warm up.
(c) Three special 100 metres time trials about 10 minutes apart. The first trial at 95 per cent, the second at 98 per cent and the third at 95 per cent.
(d) 200 metres kick, steady.
(e) 200 metres medley, steady.
(f) 16 × 25 metres kick sprints at maximum speed, one every 60 seconds.
(g) 200 metres cool down, any style.

Distance and medley swimmers
12 NOON
(a) 400 metres on any stroke or a 400 metres medley as a loosen up.
(b) 1,000 metres at race pace, timed and recorded, aiming to better personal record.
(c) 10 minutes rest.

(d) 1,000 metres at race pace plus 15 seconds.

6 P.M.
(a) 600 metres loosen up concentrating on stroke mechanics.
(b) Eight 'broken' 200 metres efforts, one every 6 minutes, aiming to better the world record for 200 metres for at least four of the efforts. (10 seconds rest intervals.) This means that girls would have to swim about 31·5 seconds for each lap and the men about 28·8 seconds.

8 A.M.
(a) 3,000 metres Fartlek.
(b) 32 × 25 metres sprints from push (usually across the pool), with 10 seconds rest intervals.

Rest afternoon.

Sprint swimmers
6th day   8 A.M.
(Long morning).
(a) 1500 metres on stroke work.
(b) 800 metres kick, one lap fast one lap slow throughout.
(c) 4 × 400 metres medleys.
(d) 16 × 50 metres 'on the minute' aiming for constant speed, e.g. your best time plus 5 seconds.

12 NOON
(a) 32 × 50 metres every 90 seconds aiming for best time plus 2·5 seconds.

6 P.M.
(a) 800 metres for style as a loosen up.
(b) 8 × 100 metres kick sprints every second one at near maximum speed.
(c) Form relays, 3 men to a team and using various strokes and various kicks until one mile has been covered by each swimmer.

Distance and medley swimmers

Rest morning.

12 NOON
(a) A warm up similar to their warm up used for competition.

(b) 1500 metres time trial.

Rest afternoon

Remarks

December is the month which will indicate to the coach if his work is going to pay handsome rewards or not. It is, as you can see from the programme, very demanding work. It is also the last extremely hard month. The work is more specialized but the rest periods are longer. Emphasis is placed on starting, turning and finishing, and all these items can be practised at race pace in the various training relays. During this month I start individual cards to record racing turns against the stop-watch. At the conclusion of training sessions I sit myself in line with the turning flags, 5 metres from the end of the pool. Individually the swimmers race past me, tumble and return to the flags. An assistant records the times. These are done in series of ten. The times are averaged and a slight improvement is expected each day.

The 75 metre sprints are timed and a large comparitor reads off the equivalent 100 metre time, e.g. 45 seconds for 75 metres equals 60 seconds for 100 metres. The swimmer uses this comparitor to condition his mind to various speeds. This system also applies for the 150 metre sprints. You will notice that starting times are brought back to 8 a.m. and that often a special midday session is included. The swimmers should be enthused into making their midday efforts the best work of the day.

The distance performers will find some segments of their training almost unbearable, e.g. the 16 × 100 metres push efforts with 10 seconds rest intervals. While the constant pressure is being applied throughout this month you must be sure that the swimmers have adequate food before the training sessions. High blood-sugar levels must be maintained if the quality of the work is to remain first-rate throughout the whole session.

Training records should be kept for the three man relay teams. I group the swimmers together into the age divisions and/or strokes. Our squad records will serve as a guide to other groups.

Senior Men – 30 minute relays: 61½ laps of 50 metres.

Senior Women – 30 minute relays: 58¼ laps of 50 metres.

Junior Men – 30 minute relays: 60 laps of 50 metres.

Junior Women – 30 minute relays: 57½ laps of 50 metres.

The swimmers' body weight will now be steady. Some coaches now supplement the team's normal diet with food additives. In Australia the most 'popular' vitamin addition is wheat-germ oil. For sprinters with a natural six beat leg action I feel it is a good idea to have them aim for personal kick records during December. Even poor kickers can, with concentration, considerably reduce their kick sprint times. The developing of a strong leg drive is of course, of paramount importance to breaststroke and butterfly swimmers.

Here are a few kicking times of interest:

In Australia, the late John Marshall, multiple world record holder, was the best of all our kickers. He was capable of breaking 6 minutes for the 440 yards on the kick board. John Konrads at 6 minutes 30 seconds, Ilsa Konrads at 6 minutes 27 seconds, Lorraine Crapp under 6 minutes 20 seconds, appear to be the outstanding kickers in recent years. Over 100 metres Jon Henricks 1 minute 17·4 seconds, David Dickson 1 minute 19·0 seconds were outstanding whilst Marlene Dayman 1 minute 22·6 seconds and Dawn Fraser 1 minute 24·4 seconds were the best girls. All won numerous National freestyle sprint titles.

In breaststroke multiple National title winner, Heather Saville was constantly under 1 minute 30·0 seconds for 100 metres breaststroke kick, her best being 1 minute 27·9 seconds. Her 200 metre kick time was 3 minutes 07·0 seconds. The best overseas time I have a record of is 1 minute 13 seconds for 100 metres dolphin kick by Indiana champion Fred Schmidt.

PART FOUR

Eighth Month, January

   Calisthenics and Dynastatics: Combined sessions, down to four sessions of 20 minutes weekly.

   Weight training: Nil.

   Water mileage: Distance and 400 metres medley swimmers, 28, 24, 11½, 20. Grand total for season 761½ miles. Sprinters and 200 metres medley swimmers, 24, 20, 10, 20. Grand total for season, 701 miles.

   Note: I have set out here the tapering off week. However, the week before this, the work load is lessened, the rest periods lengthened and the number of sessions decreased from ten to eight.

TAPER WEEK

Sprint swimmers

1st *day, Monday* 10 A.M.

(a) 600 metres loosen up, working on stroke.

(b) 8 × 25 metres from push, one every 30 seconds.

(c) 2 × 200 metres efforts, one at 90 per cent, one at 85 per cent, with 5 minutes between each effort.

(d) 200 metres kick, one lap fast, one lap slow throughout.

(e) 200 metres medley, steady.

(f) 8 × 50 metres sprints from dive ('walk backs') at near maximum speed, e.g. best time plus 1 second.

(g) 16 × 25 metres from drive at maximum speed.

(h) 200 metres to 400 metres cool down.

6 P.M.

(a) Start approximating the warm up procedure that you will use for your races, e.g. 600 metres loosen up, 1 lap steady, 1 lap fast, throughout.

Distance swimmers

1st *day, Monday* 10 A.M.

(a) 600 metres loosen up, working on stroke.

(b) 8 × 25 metres from push, one every 30 seconds.

(c) 4 × 200 metres efforts, two at 90 per cent, two at 85 per cent, with 5 minutes between each effort.

(d) 400 metres medley, steady.

(e) A 'broken' 400 metres effort (10 seconds rest intervals) at 90 per cent effort.

(f) 8 × 50 metres sprints (from push) at planned race pace.

(g) 200 metres cool down.

6 P.M.

(a) Start approximating the warm up procedure that you will use for your distances races, e.g. 400 metres loosen up at a steady speed.

A 'broken' 200 metres (10 seconds

Sprint swimmers
100 metres kick, 1 lap steady, 1 lap fast.
2 × 50 metres sprints at race pace from push.
4 × 25 metres from dive, timed and discussed.
100 metres to 200 metres cool down.
(b) Six special dive 100 metres, to be completed in 30 minutes, aiming for your best series. (Previous series have been recorded on personal cards.)
(c) 400 metres kick, 1 lap fast, 1 lap steady throughout.
(d) 16 × 25 metres from push OR relays across the pool, 3-man teams to the equivalent.
(e) Starts, turns, finishes, and take-over practices.

Distance and medley swimmers
rest intervals).
200 metres kick, 1 lap fast, 1 lap steady, throughout.
1 × 100 metres from push at race pace (timed and discussed).
4 × 25 metres sprints from push.
100 metres cool down.
(b) 400 metres effort at 90+ per cent (timed and recorded on your personal card).

(c) 200 metres medley, steady.

(d) A 'broken' 800 metres (10 seconds rest intervals at 90 per cent).

(e) 200 metres cool down for stroke or turning practice.

2nd day, Tuesday   10 A.M.
(a) 600 metres loosen up, working on stroke.
(b) A 'broken' 400 metres (with 10 seconds rest intervals) at 90 per cent.

(c) 400 metres kick, 1 lap fast, 1 lap steady throughout.
(d) A 'broken' 400 metres with 15 seconds rest intervals, at 90 per cent.
(e) 16 × 25 metres sprints at 90 per cent.
(f) 200 metres medley cool down.

2nd day, Tuesday   10 A.M.
(a) 600 metres loosen up, working on stroke.
(b) 4 × 200 metres efforts at 90 per cent one effort every 5 minutes, aiming for regular speed throughout, e.g. each 50 metres to be say, 32 seconds.
(c) 200 metres medley, steady.

(d) A 'broken' 800 metres with 15 seconds rest intervals, at 85 per cent.

6 P.M.
(a) The pre-race warm up as recommended for Monday evening.
(b) Four special 150 metres sprints to be completed in 20 minutes (aiming for your best series), recorded on your personal card.
(c) 4 × 50 metres kick sprints, one every 90 seconds at 95 per cent effort.
(d) 200 metres medley, steady.

6 P.M.
(a) The pre-race warm up as recommended for Monday evening.
(b) A 'broken' 800 metres with 10 seconds rest intervals at 90 per cent.

(c) 4 × 50 metres kick sprints, one every 90 seconds at 95 per cent effort.
(d) 200 metres medley, steady.

Sprint swimmers

(e) 8 × 50 metres from dive, at best time plus 1 second with a fast turn at the end of each 50 metres (one every 3 minutes).

(f) Starts, turns and finishes. (10 minutes).
(g) Up to 800 metres steady stroking as a cool down.

3rd day, Wednesday
Rest morning

6 P.M.
(a) The pre-race warm up procedure as for Monday evening.
(b) 200 metres effort as a pre-race time trial, at 95 per cent effort.

(c) 200 metres kick, 1 lap fast, 1 lap steady throughout.
(d) Three-man relay teams. Each team to cover 24 × 50 metres. The teams to be handicapped to aim for a close finish.
(e) 400 metres cool down.

4th day, Thursday
Rest morning.

7 P.M.
(a) The pre-race warm up procedure as for Monday evening.
(b) 100 metres effort at 95 per cent (final pre-race sprint)
(c) 200 metres medley, steady or 200 metres stroking, steady.
(d) 2 × 50 metres sprints from dive at race speed, 5 minutes between each sprint (final pre-race 50 metres sprints).
(e) 8 × 25 metres sprints, from dive in your racing lane.
(f) Turns, finishes in your lane.

Distance and medley swimmers

(e) 8 × 50 metres from push at race pace, e.g. if you aim to do 5 minutes for 400 metres your push 50 metres should be 37 seconds each (one sprint every 60 seconds).
(f) Turns, preferably in the lane you will race in.
(g) Up to 400 metres steady stroking as a cool down.

3rd day, Wednesday
Rest morning.

6 P.M.
(a) The pre-race warm up procedure as for Monday evening.
(b) 400 metres effort at 95 per cent timed and recorded. This is a pre-race time trial, and a good time should be recorded without too much stress.
(c) 200 metres kick, 1 lap fast, 1 lap steady throughout.
(d) Three-man relay teams, each team to cover 24 × 50 metres (work in with the sprinters for this exercise).
(e) 400 metres cool down.

4th day, Thursday
Rest morning.

7 P.M.
(a) The pre-race warm up procedure as for Monday evening.
(b) 200 metres effort at 95 per cent (final pre-race sprint).
(c) 200 metres medley, steady or 200 metres stroking, steady.
(d) A 'broken' 400 metres with 10 seconds rest intervals at 90 per cent.

(e) 800 metres cool down, 1 lap steady, 1 lap fast.
(f) Final pre-race team instructions.

Sprint swimmers

(g) Up to 400 metres cool down.

(h) Final pre-race team instructions.

5th day, Friday

Complete rest day, no unusual activities. Take in an afternoon movie, etc., if tension is mounting. OR, come to the pool for a steady 600 metres and up to 4 × 25 metres sprints.

Saturday, Race day

Heats 10 A.M.

(a) The pre-race warm up as previously practiced.

(b) Receive heat racing instructions.

(c) Heats.

(d) Post race cool down swim of up to 500 metres.

(e) Instructions for finals and discussion on the heats swim.

Distance swimmers

5th day, Friday

Rest morning.

P.M.

(a) The pre-race warm up procedure as for Monday evening.

(b) Final individual race instructions.

Saturday, Race day

Heats 10 A.M.

(a) The pre-race warm up as previously practised.

(b) Heats.

(c) Post race cool down recovery swim of up to 500 metres.

(d) Instructions for finals and discussion on the heats swim.

Remarks

January in Australia is the month of the State titles. Your performances in these titles usually determines if you are to start in the National titles in February. Top performers usually train on hard during January and have only a taper down for the Nationals, this way they only have to reach one 'peak' in the summer season.

You will notice that I have moved the daily training times back to the times that we anticipate the heat and finals times will be held. This procedure also allows the swimmer to sleep in each morning, a feature I feel is full of merit. I have noticed that when State or National heats are held at 8.30 or 9 a.m., many swimmers are still 'half asleep' or sluggish. Many top performers missed getting into the finals simply because they (1) have not been physiologically awake long enough, (2) they have underestimated the speed required to make the finals and therefore swimmers with less ability, but who have swum a 100 per cent effort, have replaced them in the finals, or (3) they just have not been accustomed to swimming a 100 per cent effort at 9 a.m. Because of these features I have seen National champions in lanes 1 or 8, or not at all.

The coach must make sure that this month he is fully aware of all his pupils' thoughts, fears, apprehensions and desires. This is the one month the coach can make or break the individual or the team. Pupils will now become extra sensitive to the approaching events. Some will 'go into their shells' and will need that friendly word of encouragement, that little extra attention that makes him know that you care, even if he isn't the number one star of the team. Some pupils will tend to develop certain idiosyncrasies to counteract a lack of confidence. The coach must now be his strongest, a real tower of strength for the pupil to rely upon. Personal record cards should be kept at this time of the season, especially for the senior swimmer so that the coach and the pupil may compare final pre-race trials from the previous season. This is one way to assess prospects and discuss tactics. The idea of giving the pre-race warm up, all the week prior to the titles, is to (1) eliminate unusual instructions to the pupil on the race day, (2) allow the coach more time on race day to concentrate upon other important matters, (3) allow the pupil to do a warm up procedure that has given him excellent training times during the week.

Friday, or the day before the competitions begin, is a day that training may or may not be carried out. Some pupils, especially the nervous types, prefer to swim in order to break the length of the long day of tension and pre-race nerves. Other pupils will prefer to stay out of the water completely. Care should be taken by pupils not to:

(1) Overeat, because of nerves and tension.
(2) Do any silly or unusual activities.
(3) Sleep or rest too much and become sluggish.
(4) Become constipated.

Ninth Month, February

Calisthenics and Dynastatics: Combined session of four times weekly, each session to be 20 minutes.

Weight training: Nil.

Water mileage: Let us presume that you have to reach a second 'peak' this month, if so you are advised to completely repeat last month's programme.

Distance and 400 metre medley swimmers, 28, 24, 11½, 20. Grand total for season, 845 miles. Sprinters and 200 metre medley swimmers, 24, 20, 10, 20. Grand total for season, 775 miles.

Remarks

The swimmer and the coach are now under the heaviest mental pressure for the season. More than ever the pupil should become an individual as far as coaching instructions are concerned. You are strongly advised to incorporate Chapter 7, *Team Tit-Bits,* and include these items in the February programme. *Practical Psychology in Coaching* (Chapter 4) will also give invaluable information to coach and pupil alike.

The good points gained from last month's taper off and competition can be repeated, the mistakes you made can be rectified. Swimmers who have qualified for the Nationals should have a complete medical check up at the end of January, and if necessary vitamin B_{12} and/or iron shots could be administered by the team doctor. Refer to Chapter 10, *Notes from my Olympic Notebook,* the section concerning haemoglobin levels.

From past records these improvements should be expected between your State titles and the Nationals, even though both efforts are 100 per cent.

100 metres from 0·8 seconds to 1·1 seconds.
200 metres from 1·8 seconds to 4·2 seconds.
400 metres from 3·9 seconds to 5·5 seconds.
800 metres from 7·0 seconds to 12·5 seconds.
1500 metres from 10·0 seconds to 17·8 seconds.

Bear in mind that part of this improvement will be the direct result of the pupil presumably having harder competition in the Nationals, also that in the distance events the pupil may have been needing a hard 'warm-up' swim in his State titles. However, the greater overall improvement will come from the benefit of an intelligent tapering down programme. Unfortunately many coaches do not seem to be able to control this all-important feature.

Tenth Month, March

Calisthenics and Dynastatics: Nil.

Weight training: Weight training can now be re-commenced. Thirty-minute sessions using medium weights, e.g. 12-year-olds to handle 24 lb., 15-year-olds to handle 30 lb. In other words twice your own number of years in pounds. The first week two sessions, the second week three sessions, the third and fourth week four sessions.

Water mileage: This is not a set figure for March, but each session should cover 2 miles. March therefore should total 80 miles, bringing the grand total for the season to 925 for the distance swimmers and 855 for the sprinters. Here are two sample programmes:

Sample programme No. 1
(a) 16 × 25 metres kick sprints for warm up and assembly.
(b) 20 minute eliminations in relays, across 50 metre pool.
(c) 1500 metre time trial either legs tied or kick with flippers.
(d) Water polo game.

Sample programme No. 2
(a) 16 × 50 metres medleys (this means about 12 metres on each of the four strokes). One medley every 60 seconds.
(b) Form three-man relays and time them over 1,500 metres kicking or pulling (each man will kick or pull 10 × 50 metres).
(c) 800 metres medley non-stop.
(d) Water polo game.

Remarks
During March sprinters and distance swimmers can reassemble into one unit. The coach can now form water polo teams, basketball teams, marathon swim teams, week-end touring parties, swim Bar-B-Ques and make this month a really great one with which to finish the season.

The weary, disinterested flattened swimmers will take on a renewed zest for the sport and finish the season wanting to come back again. The end will be sweet and not sour as is often the case.

Throughout the whole season of 10 months now present in Australia, the coach should regularly plan stroke instruction sessions, film sessions and swim meets against top squads. The team should swim once a week during April and May. These sessions need not be supervised. The success of next season depends on a fresh, revitalized coach, so these are the obvious months for the coach to rest up.

The weight training programme should be done four times a week. Secondary sports especially basketball, tennis or golf are recommended during this period. Dental work should also be attended to now. Since the Easter vacation usually falls in this period, I strongly advise the swimming families to make this their major annual holiday.

E

9 A Work Programme for a Junior Squad

This chapter is designed to meet most of the needs of a Junior Squad, a 'Y' team, a country squad, etc., who do not, because of the lack of professional coaches or adequate facilities, train as hard or as long as the leading city groups. Within this work-out is incorporated all the essential features of an international schedule. You may apply this work-out to your squad with full confidence that you are on the right track. Only the quantity and the speed of the work-out has been reduced. The schedule is suitable for all age groups and all strokes. Obviously a nine-year-old girl will not work with the same intensity as a 15-year-old boy. The actual pressure applied to each swimmer within the squad, must be determined by the club coach. Common sense is the keynote.

The basic aim is for 20 miles a week. I wish to emphasize that continuity of the work-out is the most important feature. The squad that works at a good rate over a long period will have sound results. This schedule covers 24 weeks and is designed mainly for the summer term.

This work-out will deal only with water conditioning, but for best results, conditioning and stroke technique are necessary.

I have set the schedule out in three weekly segments. It will take you a week to have the squad working efficiently, then for the next two weeks you should consolidate the work-out. It is important, that during the first weeks you should devote all the water time to swimming all strokes and kicking all kicks, irrespective of the stroke the individual is specializing in, you must do a general programme. During the first weeks, not too much pressure is applied as far as effort is concerned as long as the squad is moving along at a reasonable speed. It is important that after the first week, once your swimmers have become accustomed to the water and the schedule, they should aim to do the work-out practically non-stop. By this I mean that perhaps 30 seconds or so between each section would be adequate. There should be no need for the swimmers to leave the water at all. You could reasonably expect to do the work-out in about 80 minutes. Keep in mind also that the first month should include stroke correction. A good plan is to take four boys for style check on Monday morning, and then four girls on Monday afternoon and keep this programme going for six training days. In this way you will have given individual style checks to 24 boys and 24 girls once a week. Perhaps you could spend five minutes on each swimmer, ironing out his or her worst fault first. Only try to eliminate or rectify one fault at a time. This is the system I use.

If you are so inclined, it is advisable to:

(a) Take some basic measurements of your pupils.

(b) Have the local Sports Medicine doctor check the swimmers over before the season starts, with emphasis placed on ears, nose and chest.

(c) Have a haemoglobin test taken.

Weeks 1, 2 and 3 (getting wet)

Work out eight to ten sessions a week, rest two full days, say Wednesday and Sunday.

Do ten minutes stretching exercises a day.

Start log. Record body weight.

MORNINGS – all strokes (20 minutes)

500 metres freestyle.

200 metres backstroke.

200 metres breaststroke.

100 metres butterfly.

Pulls (15 minutes)

400 metres of mainstroke with legs trailing (not tied).

200 metres of secondary stroke with legs trailing (not tied).

Kicks (15 minutes)

400 metres of mainstroke kicking.

200 metres of secondary stroke kicking.

Basic conditioning (15 minutes)

400 metres of mainstroke at 80 per cent non-stop.

200 metres of secondary stroke at 80 per cent non-stop.

EVENINGS – Warm up (10 minutes)

500 metres of steady stroke swimming.

Kicks (20 minutes)

4 × 200 metres kicks, one 200 metres of each of the four styles.

Pulls (20 minutes)

4 × 200 metres pulls, one 200 metres of each of the four styles.

Basic conditioning

1,200 metres of mainstroke non-stop with the 'up' laps fast and the 'down' laps stroking it out.

Weeks 4, 5 and 6 (basic conditioning)

Work out twelve sessions a week, rest one full day.

Do 15 minutes strengthening exercises daily (dynastatics, dialex, rubbers, isometrics, etc.) six times a week.

MORNINGS – all strokes (not to take more than 18 minutes)

1. 200 metres freestyle at 75 per cent effort non-stop.
2. 200 metres breaststroke at 75 per cent effort non-stop.
3. 200 metres backstroke at 75 per cent effort non-stop.
4. 200 metres medley at 75 per cent effort non-stop.

Kicks (not to take more than 20 minutes)

1. 200 metres freestyle kick aiming to better 4 minutes.
2. 200 metres backstroke kick aiming to better 5 minutes.
3. 200 metres breaststroke kick aiming to better $4\frac{1}{2}$ minutes.
4. 200 metres dolphin kick aiming to better $4\frac{1}{2}$ minutes.

Pulls (not to take more than 15 minutes)

1. 300 metres freestyle pull with legs tied aiming to better 6 minutes.
2. 200 metres backstroke pull with legs tied aiming to better $4\frac{1}{2}$ minutes.
3. 100 metres breaststroke pull with legs tied aiming to better 3 minutes.

Conditioning

1. 800 metres of bilateral breathing freestyle at 80 per cent effort.
2. 20 × 25 metres dive sprints of butterfly or freestyle.

EVENINGS – Warm up (10 minutes)

1. 200 metres medley of kick at a steady rate.
2. 200 metres medley non-stop at a steady rate.

Kicks (15 minutes)

1. 200 metres freestyle kick aiming to better $4\frac{1}{2}$ minutes.

2. 4 × 100 metres mainstroke kick sprints departing every $2\frac{1}{4}$ minutes and aiming to better 2 minutes.

Pulls (15 minutes)

1. 200 metres freestyle pulling (with legs tied) aiming to better 4 minutes.

2. 4 × 100 metres mainstroke pulling departing every $2\frac{1}{4}$ minutes and aiming to better 1 minute 50 seconds.

Conditioning

1. 24 × 50 metres at 75 per cent effort with emphasis on stroke departing every minute.

Weeks 7, 8 and 9 (more conditioning)

Work out twelve sessions weekly, rest one full day and do a weekly time trial.

Strengthening exercises, increase to 20 minutes a day, six times a week.

MORNINGS – Warm up (25 minutes)

10 × 100 metres medleys departing every $2\frac{1}{4}$ minutes.

Kicks (not to take more than 25 minutes)

1. 6 × 100 metres kicks, departing every $2\frac{1}{4}$ minutes.

2. 1 × 100 metres backstroke kicks.

3. 1 × 100 metres breaststroke kicks.

4. 2 × 100 metres dolphin kicks.

Pulls (10 minutes)

1. 500 metres non-stop pulling at a steady rate with some fast sections interspersed.

Conditioning (15 minutes)

3 × 200 metres efforts on the mainstroke at 80 per cent effort departing every 5 minutes.

EVENINGS – Warm up (12 minutes)

5 × 100 metres medleys, but in reverse order of strokes, departing every $2\frac{1}{4}$ minutes.

Conditioning (this section to take not more than 40 minutes)

15 × 100 metres at 75–80 per cent effort, mixing all strokes and departing every $2\frac{1}{2}$ minutes

Kicks (13 minutes)

500 metres non-stop kicking at a steady rate with some fast sections interspersed.

Conditioning (20 minutes maximum)

20 × 25 metres sprints breathing every four strokes on crawl, or every three strokes on 'fly

Weeks 10, 11 *and* 12 (*endurance*)

Work out twelve sessions weekly, have one full rest day and do a weekly time trial

Exercises remain at 20 minutes, six times a week

Once a week substitute 1 × 3,000 metres or 2 × 1,500 metres for the evening work-out.

MORNINGS – Warm up (20 minutes)

400 metres kick medley.

400 metres medley or 2 × 200 metres medley.

Kicks (not to take more than 13 minutes)

10 × 50 metres kick sprints departing every 1¼ minutes.

Pulls (10 minutes)

10 × 50 metres pull sprints (with legs tied) departing every minute.

Conditioning (30 minutes)

30 × 50 metres sprints departing every minute, the 'up' sprints to be 90 per cent, the 'down' sprints to be 85 per cent for stroke perfection.

EVENINGS – Warm up (10 minutes)

500 metres steady non-stop swimming changing stroke and speed often.

Conditioning (40 minutes)

5 × 300 metres at 80–85 per cent effort departing every 8 minutes.

Speed

20 'walk back' sprints of 50 metres at 95 per cent effort with correct start.

or

a three-man team relay swimming non-stop until each member swum 20 × 50 metres.

Weeks 13, 14 *and* 15 (*endurance and speed*)

Work out eleven sessions weekly, having one rest morning each week plus one full rest day.

One time trial over your race distance.

Alter exercise sessions to two 10-minute periods daily preferably before swim work-outs.

Once a week substitute 3 × 800 metres at 90, 92 and 90 per cent efforts for the morning work-out. Do the warm up section first.

MORNINGS – Warm up (10 minutes)

5 × 100 metres medleys departing every 2 minutes.

Speed kick (12 minutes)

1. 8 × 50 metres kick sprints starting off at 85 per cent and gradually increasing to 95 per cent, departing every $1\frac{1}{4}$ minutes.

2. 100 metres slow kick cool down.

Speed pull (12 minutes)

1. 8 × 50 metres pull sprints starting at 95 per cent and easing back to 85 per cent, departing every $1\frac{1}{4}$ minutes.

2. 100 metres slow legs trail cool down.

Speed (44 minutes)

10 dive 75 metres sprints with correct turns at 88–92 per cent effort, departing every 4 minutes.

EVENINGS – Warm up (15 minutes)

4 × 50 metres kicks.

4 × 50 metres pulls.

4 × 50 metres stroke.

Speed (30 minutes)

20 push off 50 metres at 95 per cent effort departing every 90 seconds.

More speed (20 minutes)

20 × 25 metres very hard sprints from dive, every other one to be butterfly.

Cool down

Up to 400 metres for relaxing.

Weeks 16, 17 *and* 18 (*more speed*)

Work out eleven times weekly having one rest morning each week plus one full rest day.

One time trial at 97 per cent as well as one time trial at 90 per cent over your race distance.

Exercise periods to be two 10-minute sessions daily preferably before swim work-outs.

Twice a week substitute 4 × 400 metres at 90, 92, 94 and 92 per cent for the morning work-out. Do the warm up section first.

MORNINGS – Warm up (10 minutes)

500 metres at a medium pace.

Speed kick (16 minutes)

200 metres kick in under 3 minutes 40 seconds.

2 × 100 metres kick sprints each under 1 minute 45 seconds.

4 × 50 metres kick sprints each under 50 seconds.
Speed pulls (16 minutes)
200 metres pull in under 3 minutes 30 seconds.

2 × 100 metres pull sprints each under 1 minute 40 seconds.
4 × 50 metres pull sprints each under 45 seconds.
Speed (40 minutes)
1 × 200 metres sprint at 92 per cent.
2 × 100 metres sprints at 94 per cent.
4 × 50 metres sprints at 96 per cent.
8 × 25 metres sprints at 98 per cent.
Cool down with a steady 400 metres.
EVENINGS – Warm up (12 minutes)
400 metres of stroking
8 × 25 metres push offs (not timed)
Speed (30 minutes)
10 × 50 metres 'walk back' sprints at best time plus 3 seconds.
Super speed (20 minutes)
1 × 25 metres dive sprints at maximum speed.
Relays – form three-man teams and sprint over 50 metres for 10,
15 or 20 minutes non-stop.
Cool down with a steady 200 metres.

Weeks 19, 20 *and* 21 (*racing period*)
Work out ten times weekly having two half rest days and one full
rest day each week.
Exercise periods to be reduced to one 10-minute session daily.
Substitute the taper section at appropriate place if needed.
MORNINGS – Warm up (20 minutes)
300 metres of steady paced swimming.
200 metres kick in 3 minutes 50 seconds.
200 metres legs trail in 3 minutes 30 seconds.
Speed sprints (30 minutes)
4 × 100 metres at 92, 94, 96 and 92 per cent – one sprint every
5 minutes.
4 × 50 metres kick sprints at 96, 94, 92 and 90 per cent – one
sprint every 2 minutes.
Super speed sprints (40 minutes)
Twenty sprints across the pool and back (usually about 40 metres)

departing every 2 minutes and concentrating on correct starts and turns.

Cool down with 200 to 400 metres steady stroking.

EVENINGS – Warm up (20 minutes)

400 metres of stroke swimming.

100 metres kick in 1 minute 50 seconds.

100 metres pull in 1 minute 40 seconds.

Speed sprints (18 minutes)

3 × 200 metres at 92, 94 and 90 per cent departing every 6 minutes.

Super speed sprints

3 × 75 metres sprints at 90–95 per cent departing every 3 minutes.

6 × 25 metres sprints at maximum speed.

Cool down with up to 400 metres of steady stroking.

Weeks 22, 23 and 24 (top of the peak)

Work out eight times weekly, sleeping in on at least four mornings and having a full rest day as well.

Exercise periods to be reduced to one 10-minute session on every second day, preferably the rest morning.

Substitute the taper section at the appropriate place if needed.

MORNINGS and/or EVENINGS

Warm up (20 minutes)

400 metres warm up of stroke.

100 metres kick at a steady speed.

100 metres pull at a steady speed.

4 × 25 metres from push.

Speed (20 minutes)

1 × 150 metres sprint at 90 per cent.

1 × 100 metres sprint at 92 per cent.

4 × 50 metres sprints at 94 per cent.

Relax (10 minutes)

400 metres of any of the strokes.

Super speed sprints (20 minutes)

2 × 50 metres at maximum speed.

10 starts (15 metres sprints)

10 turns (at full race pace).

Cool down with up to 600 metres for stroke, starts and turns.

10 Notes from my Olympic Notebook

Collecting important and true data can be of assistance in planning future work-outs and seasons. Extracts from my notebook may be of assistance to others. Only factual information has been recorded. As an observer I logged about 130 significant facts at Mexico City and these varied from:

'(39) U.S.A. girl breaststroke swimmers swim a series of 25 metres freestyle sprints in their pre-race warm up.'

and

'(70) The Russian team performed 20 minutes hard and fast calisthenic movements on the pool side before each training session.'

to

'(96) Due to the efforts of the Australian Sports Medicine doctors in organizing and supervising the eating, drinking and washing habits of the swim team, the Australians had far less infections of the stomach than any other team.'

Whilst my observations at Mexico were of interest to me the following details on the Australian team may be of benefit to others. The ideal time to test and record data on teams is obviously whilst they are in a training camp; however, so far in Australia only one worthwhile attempt has been made in this regard, namely by Forbes and Ursula Carlile on the 1960 team to Rome. More of this type of valuable information is greatly needed by coaches and sports medicine personnel. Prior to leaving their home cities to train at Scarborough, the Australian swimmers were given an exhaustive physical test. The result of this test is given at the end of this chapter (Fig. 4).

The training undertaken at Scarborough, Queensland, for the

1968 Olympic Games preparation was the most intensive six weeks group work-out ever done in Australia. Not only was the mileage high (218 miles) but the intensity of the training was first-class. The squad averaged 36⅓ miles a week, having only three rest days in the six-week period. Sprinters carried out a different schedule to the distance swimmers. It is significant to note that during this stressing period the squad officially bettered 28 National Records and equalled two others. Minor stress signs were evident in most pupils, but we usually swam through these, easing back on the effort when skin rashes, early morning colds, muscle weariness, etc. appeared. We had two severe fatigue cases, one suspected appendicitis and one chronic sinusitis.

Overleaf is an analysis of the work-outs for the 100 metre and 200 metre swimmers.

In addition it included warm ups, cool downs and stroke work as basic training.

Remarks

Special sections were included where the squad swam as far as 800 metres controlling their breath, e.g. 16 × 50 metres with only ten breaths each 50 metres.

For some sessions I worked the whole team on a common programme but as a rule the distance swimmers worked out on a different schedule.

Analysis of distance swimmers (page 120)

Remarks

The programmes were 'padded' with basic work, stroke correction, starts, turns, finishes, take overs, etc.

One typical training session from each week at Scarborough

1st week: 4 × 100 metres medleys as a warm up, every 2 minutes.

40 × 50 metres every 50 seconds at 90–93 per cent (sets of 10).

200 metres kick, relax.

200 metres pull, relax.

8 × 200 metres every 3 or 3½ minutes, at 88–90 per cent going out steady for the first 100 metres and coming home hard.

12 × 25 metres from push on all strokes.

200 metres cool down. (3 miles)

Sprinters

Details Stroke	1st week	2nd week	3rd week	4th week	5th week	6th week
25 metres	60	30	36	128	120	88
50 metres	196	192	288	192	200	196
100 metres	49	76	68	68	70	144
200 metres	59	39	43	5	20	24
400 metres	13	10	7	9	4	4
800 metres	1	1	1	3	1	–
1,500 metres	1	1	4	–	1	–
Kick 50 metres	48	8	–	16	32	40
100 metres	16	21	–	–	8	16
200 metres	9	10	14	4	4	–
400 metres	2	8	8	8	–	–
Pull 50 metres	–	–	–	16	24	32
100 metres	–	19	–	–	8	16
200 metres	6	5	11	5	4	–
400 metres	2	–	1	2	–	–

Distance Swimmers

Details *Stroke* 50 metres	1st week 168	2nd week 216	3rd week 224	4th week 176	5th week 160	6th week 148
100 metres	56	80	60	32	40	48
200 metres	5	17	25	31	36	32
400 metres	17	19	23	26	32	20
800 metres	2	3	7	7	6	8
1,500 metres	1	4	–	3	3	3
3,000 metres	1	1	1	1	1	–
Kick 100 metres	4	–	25	8	8	16
200 metres	4	14	10	10	4	4
400 metres	8	8	8	–	–	–
Pull 100 metres	4	–	17	–	8	16
200 metres	5	13	6	6	4	–
400 metres	2	–	1	1	–	–

2nd week: 8 × 100 metres medleys every 2 minutes.

8 × 100 metres kick every 2¼ minutes.

8 × 100 metres pull every 2 minutes.

8 × 100 metres mixed strokes, every 2 minutes.

40 × 50 metres with 10 seconds rest.   (3¼ miles)

3rd week: 800 metres controlling breathing.

200 metres kick, relax.

200 metres pull, relax.

8 × 100 metres hard, in breathing pattern.

200 metres kick, relax.

200 metres pull, relax.

16 × 100 metres hard.

200 metres secondary strokes.

200 metres polo.

16 dive 50 metres.

Starts, turns, take-overs.   (3¼ miles)

4th week: 4 × 100 metres medleys as a warm up.

400 metres stroke (style work).

8 × 100 metres every 4 minutes, going out at 85 per cent, back at 95 per cent.

16 × 50 metres every 90 seconds from push. (HARD)

8 × 50 metres kick sprints. (HARD)

8 × 50 metres pull sprints. (HARD)

16 × 25 metres at faster than race speed, dive.

16 dive 50 metres at race pace for STYLE.

800 metres relax, lengthening out stroke.

or, 20 fast across and backs with tumble.   (3¼ miles)

5th week: 400 metres for stroke.

4 × 100 metres kick sprints.

4 × 100 metres pull sprints.

400 metres for stroke.

32 × 50 metres sprints from dive.

1,500 metres of speed play.

Starts, turns, take-overs.

6th week: 400 metres medley as a warm up.

6 × 100 metres mainstroke, every 2 minutes.

6 × 100 metres kick as sprints.

6 × 100 metres pulls as sprints.

6 × 100 metres mainstroke from dive as hard sprints.

32 × 50 metres sprints, going on the minute.

Bodyweight of Olympic Finalists

Name	Age	National Titles Feb. 68		6/8/68		18/8/68		27/8/68		10/9/68		11/10/68	
Girls		st.	lb.	st.	lb.	st.	lb.	st.	lb.	st.	lb.	st.	lb.
Bell	21	9	0	9	6½	9	8¾	9	7	9	6½	9	5
Deakes	14	8	12	9	6½	9	13½	9	9¼	9	10½	9	5¼
Eddy	15	7	10	8	4½	8	6½	8	4¾	8	4¾	—	
Langford	14	7	10	8	3½	8	6½	8	6	8	5¼	8	3½
McClements	17	10	4	10	7	10	10¾	10	11½	10	12½	11	5½
Moras	14	8	0	8	2½	8	4½	8	5¼	8	4½	8	1
Playfair	14	9	0	9	2	9	2½	9	3	9	4¾	9	0½
Steinbeck	17	10	0	10	10½	10	10½	10	9¾	10	10¼	10	8½
Watson	15	9	5	10	9	10	8	10	5¼	10	6½	10	6¾
Boys													
Byrom	17	11	8	12	5½	11	13½	11	11½	11	10	11	11
Cusack	17	11	0	11	3	11	0¾	11	0½	11	0¼	11	1
Brough	17	12	6	12	11	12	9¾	12	13	12	10¼	12	6
O'Brien	21	16	2	15	5	15	0½	14	8	14	2½	13	13¾
Rogers	20	12	3	12	2	12	6½	12	3½	12	2½	11	13
Wenden	18	12	0	12	2	12	1¼	11	12½	11	13¼	11	13
White	17	12	10	12	11	12	9½	12	8	12	5½	11	11
Windle	23	12	2	11	10	11	10¾	11	6¼	11	8¾	11	3

It is interesting to note that matured Mike Wenden kept close to his racing weight during the whole preparation, as did Moras, while Playfair steadily increased despite the heavy training load. Note also the weight pattern of gold medallist Lyn McClements.

Haemoglobin Levels

Haemoglobin levels were taken at regular intervals to help assess the stress load. Vitamin B_{12} injections were given as a precautionary measure throughout the training period and especially at Mexico, where it was anticipated that the levels would drop after the first few weeks of acclimatization.

Note the sharp increase in the levels upon arriving at Mexico. I altered the individual training loads according to the haemoglobin levels, especially in the last month. Girls whose levels dropped below the 13 gm level rarely performed well.

Haemoglobin levels of Olympic Finalists (in gm.)

Name	Age	Scarborough 8/8/68	7/9/68	Mexico 24/9/68	3/10/68	Remarks
Girls						*Mexico*
Bell	21	13.7	13.6	12.8	13.8	7th in final 200 metres freestyle.
Eddy	15	13.9	14.4	13.9	14.2	Relay.
Langford	14	15.1	14.5	15.0	—	7th in 800 metres final freestyle.
McClements	17	15.4	—	14.7	15.5	1st in 100 metres final butterfly, 65·5 seconds.
Moras	14	14.2	14.2	13.1	15.2	3rd in 400 metres final and 4th in 800 metres final freestyle.
Playfair	14	14.5	—	13.9	15.8	100 metres breastroke, 1·15·9, relay.
Steinbeck	17	13.7	14.4	—	14.5	100 metres freestyle, 60·6 relay.

Name	Age	Scarborough		Mexico		Remarks
		8/8/68	7/9/68	24/9/68	3/10/68	
Girls						*Mexico*
Watson	15	14.5	13.7	15.0	14.4	4th in 200 metres final backstroke.
Boys Brough	17	15.1	14.9	14.3	16.0	3rd in 1500 metres final and 4th in 400 metres final freestyle.
Byrom	17	14.5	15.1	15.0	16.2	100 metres backstroke in 61·9, relay.
Cusack	17	15.1	14.6	14.7	15.8	Relay.
O'Brien	21	16.5	16.2	16.0	17.0	100 metres breaststroke in 68·6.
Rogers	20	14.7	15.1	15.5	15.5	200 metres freestyle relay.
Wenden	18	14.8	14.7	15.6	16.8	1st in 100 metres freestyle, 52·2 seconds. 1st in 200 metres freestyle, 1·55·2 seconds.
White	17	14.5	15.0	15.0	15.5	4th in 1500 metres freestyle, and 5th in 400 metres freestyle.
Windle	23	13.8	14.6	14.7	15.5	6th in 200 metres freestyle.

Early Morning Heart Rates

Swimmers were instructed to keep a log of early morning heart rates. Unfortunately there was no control on these as the swimmers took the counts before arising, therefore the records are not complete.

The graph (Fig. 2) shows the heart rates of the Australian 4 × 200 metres relay which placed second to U.S.A. in the Olympic final. The time of the team was 7 minutes 53·7 seconds, the first time all members of an Australian team have bettered 2 minutes for 200 metres. It is worth noting that Michael Wenden's heart rate was consistently high, whereas the heart rates of Graham White and Greg Rogers were in line with swimmers who have trained for long periods over long distances.

A low resting heart rate is an indication of the efficiency of the heart muscle. A heart that has grown large and strong through continued work over a long period will have a greater contractile force. This in turn, will force through more blood each beat than the untrained heart, and as a consequence, the trained heart will not have to do so many beats per minute to perform the same amount of work.

It appears that the heart increases in size and strength at least for the first ten years of training, judging from the following research extracts:

'Mitchell found that pulse averaged 69 for the first year of training, 64·5 for the second, 56·8 for the third. Cotton reports that unusually low pulse rates have been found among athletes. The averages of Olympic runners measured by Bramwell and Ellis are: sprinters, 66, middle distance runners, 63, long distance runners, 61, and marathon runners, 59.

'Cotton measured eight champion swimmers who were assembled for a national meet at Sydney, Australia. Five of these were Olympic men. The mean basal pulses, measured in a hotel the evening before the meet were 52, 50, 42, 40, 53, 47, 49, 47, with a mean of 47·5. This report shows that normal young men with almost no athletic history average in basal pulse rate 66; those with average athletic history average 63; those with relatively greater athletic history average 57. Superior athletes average 53; Olympic athletes average 50, and Olympic swimmers with ten years' training average 47.

'White collected a number of electro-cardiograms of athletes with extremely low pulses. Mac Mitchell had a basal pulse of 37 and it had been as low as 31. Glen Cunningham had a pulse rate of 38 to 40. Nurmi's was 42. Dr. George Deaver has predicted that these men with low pulses will live a long time.'

Incidentally the lowest heart rates I have personally recorded on top flight swimmers are, Dawn Fraser 42, Jan Turner 48, Julie McDonald 45, Graham White 40, and Murray Garretty 45. All had had at least five years of hard training when these rates were counted.

Simple incentive tables were kept by some swimmers. I have

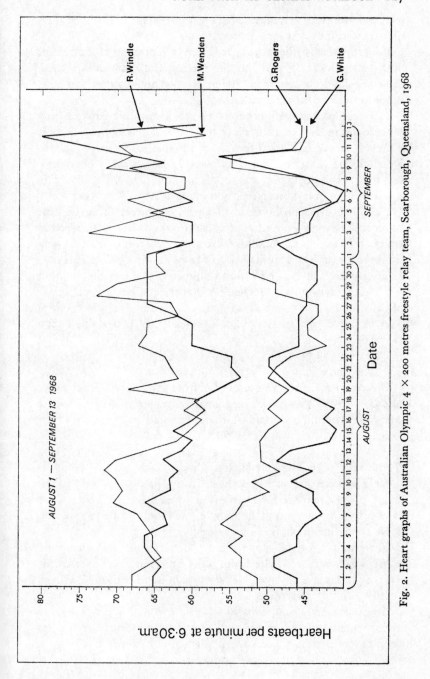

Fig. 2. Heart graphs of Australian Olympic 4 × 200 metres freestyle relay team, Scarborough, Queensland, 1968

included distance swimmer Graham White's sheet (Fig. 3). The sheet is of value for several reasons.

1. It graphically illustrates that White is improving at a nice rate over distances of 100, 200 and 400 metres, and that perhaps these distances should be his main targets. His 800 and 1500 metres have not improved at the same rate.

2. By comparing two distances one can assess the relative merits of these distances. Let us compare the 100 and 400 metres. White is 6 metres behind the world record for 100 metres. Over 400 metres he is only 11·1 metres behind the world's fastest even though the 400 metres is four times further than the 100 metres. Relatively he is a much better swimmer over 400 metres than 100 metres.

I also suggested to the team that personal target sheets be kept to record the number of times that certain distances are bettered in training. I have found that this motivating card can be of great help in propping up jaded spirits, whilst heavy training is in progress.

The coach can use the card to point out to the swimmer that although he has not yet reached his best time of last season, he has already bettered last season's 'targets' many times. It is a methodical way to prove that the swimmer is consistently better this season than last.

The Long Range View

If you care to chart up a graph sheet from your Target Sheet it can. also be very enlightening. I suggest you draw up a Target Sheet to suit your style, distance and ultimate time and paste it in your log book.

Target Sheet of Julie McDonald (see p. 130)

Here is how you mark your sheet. Every time you pass a 'Target Time' place a mark in the appropriate square. In Julie's case, if she does a 67 for 100 metres she puts one tick only in the 67 seconds square, not one in 68, 69 or 70 as well.

For example, in 1965 Julie swam 100 metres in 70 seconds eight times, whereas in 1966 she swam 70 seconds ten times, etc. As the years of training go by, you will see that you are becoming a much more consistent performer.

Swimmers were individually interviewed and their replies to twenty questions were recorded. The questions included such items as, years of training, years of supplementary exercise, pattern of

GRAHAM WHITE 100metres FREESTYLE

1 second = 1·8 metres

					metres short
World record		52·2		100 m	
Australian record		53·7		97·3m	2·7
Graham White	1966	58·5	≈89·0m		11·0
" "	1967	57·1	≈91·1m		8·9
" "	1968	56·4	≈92·5m		7·5
" "	1969	55·5 *till 29·2·69*	≈94·0m		6·0

GRAHAM WHITE 200metres FREESTYLE

1 second = 1·7 metres

					metres short
World record		1 ·54·5		200 m	
Australian record		1 ·57·9	≈194·6m		5·4
Graham White	1966	2·08·7	≈175·8m		24·2
" "	1967	2·05·5	≈181·3m		18·7
" "	1968	2·02·3	≈186·9m		13·1
" "	1969	2·00·8 *till 29·2·69*	≈189·4m		10·6

GRAHAM WHITE 400metres FREESTYLE

1 second = 1·6 metres

					metres short
World record		4·06·5		400 m	
Australian record		4·12·4	≈389·6m		10·4
Graham White	1966	4·29·8	≈362·9m		37·1
" "	1967	4·23·2	≈373·3m		26·7
" "	1968	4·14·7	≈386·8m		13·2
" "	1969	4·13·6 *till 29·2·69*	≈388·9m		11·1

GRAHAM WHITE 800metres FREESTYLE

1 second = 1·5 metres

					metres short
World record		8·34·3		800 m	
Australian record		8·47·3	≈780·5m		19·5
Graham White	1966	9·19·3	≈732·5m		67·5
" "	1967	9·13·3	≈741·5m		58·5
" "	1968	8·48·0	≈779·4m		20·6
" "	1969	8·54·2 *till 29·2·69*	≈770·1m		29·9

GRAHAM WHITE 1500metres FREESTYLE

1 second = 1·4 metres

					metres short
World record		16·08·5		1500 m	
Australian record		16·41·5	1455·8m		44·2
Graham White	1966	17·45·5	1371·2m		128·8
" "	1967	17·25·5	1403·2m		96·8
" "	1968	16·41·5	1455·8m		44·2
" "	1969	16·56·4 *till 29·2·69*	1439·9m		60·1

Fig. 3. Graham White's incentive sheet

Target Time for 100 m.	70 secs.	69 secs.	68 secs.	67 secs.	66 secs.	65 secs.	64 secs.
1965–66	//// ////	////	//	/	/		
1966–67	////// //////	///// /	////	///	//	/	
1967–68	/////// ///////	///// /////	///// ///	/////	///	///	/
1968–69	/////// ///////	/////// ///////	/////// /////	/////// ////	///// //	//// //	//

menstruation, ultimate swimming ambitions, etc. No attempt will be made here to fully analyse the answers. These points, however, seem important.

1. Over half of the female swimmers have irregularities in their menstruation cycle at some time during the training year.

2. The swimmers who performed best at Mexico had had over six years of hard training behind them.

3. Only two members of the team did not take supplementary vitamins or minerals.

4. All swimmers did land exercises. However it is worth noting that the hardest land worker, Michael Wenden, won two gold medals and set one world record whereas the swimmer with the least land exercise training behind her, Lyn McClements, also won a gold medal.

5. From an hereditary point of view only one swimmer had a parent of outstanding athletic ability whereas four pupils had at least one parent with moderate athletic ability. The majority had parents with little or no athletic ability.

6. Five members of the team came from families in the higher income bracket, four pupils came from families in the low income bracket. Fifteen pupils could be considered coming from middle earning families.

7. The swimmers were asked a particular question, 'What is your ultimate aim in swimming?' Some replies indicated the swimmer's tremendous desire to push aside present barriers, others showed an

Figure 4.
RESULTS OF PHYSICAL TESTS GIVEN TO AUSTRALIANS PRIOR TO 1960 OLYMPICS.

Name	Sport	Sex	Event	E.C.G.	Heart score	Blood group	Cardio-thoracic ratio c.m.s.	Clinical	Blood Pressure	Pulse rate	Orthopaedic	Chest expansion	Urine	Weight	Right grip	Push	Pull	Standing broad jump	Hb Gms.	H-crit	Erythrocyte sedimentation rate	Red blood corpuscles	Hyman's Test Index		Max. expiratory pressure	Maximum oxygen intake		
																							Vital capacity	Max. breath holding		Max. pulse rate	Aerobic cap age corrected	Fitness index
R. Boyle (17 yrs)	Aths	F+	Sprint	N.A.D.	90	O+	10·1:26·2	Heart Grade I Systolic	120/60	72	Back slightly reduced range	3″	Clear	9 st. 2 lb.	52	91	28	6′ 7½″	15·4	42%	10	5·6	34	30 ·529	75			
R. Doubell (23 yrs)	Aths	M	Endurance	Satis.	100	AB+	11·6:30·6	Acute pharyngitis	115/68	52	Satis.	3½″	Trace albumin	10 st. 1 lb.	78	84	43	7′ 7″	16·4	46%	6	5·8	52	40 ·729	60	111	4·1	64
S. Eddy (15 yrs)	Swim	F+	Endurance	T flattened and diphosic	90	O−	12·0:26·6	N.A.D.	120/65	60	Satis.	3″	Clear	8 st. 2¼ lb.	28	54	25	5′ 9½″	15·1	45%	4	5·7	38	48	40	150	2·9	55
P. Gray (17 yrs)	Swim	F+	Endurance	Flat T in III	80	A+	10·8:26·7	N.A.D.	140/80	60	Satis.	3½″	Nil	8 st. 7 lb.	42	61	30	6′ 10″	15·4	47%	8	5·6	33	47 ·539	70	148	2·9	54
J. McDonald (16 yrs)	Swim	F+	Endurance	T III a little flat	96	A+	11·6:29·4	Satis.	130/70	60	Satis.	2½″	Clear	10 st. 6 lb.	52	74	24	6′ 0″	15·4	45%	7	5·3	35	47 ·562	65	143	3·2	48
S. McKenzie (17 yrs)	Swim	F+	Endurance	T III−ve	96	A+	13·6:31·0	Satis.	117/68	60	Lumbar lordosis	3″	Clear	—	57	68	34	5′ 10″	16·1	45%	14	5·0	44	52 ·590	60	140	3·1	40
P. G. Norman (26 yrs)	Aths	M	Sprint	T III flat	106	A−	13·5:31·4	Satis.	135/80	66	Satis.	4½″	Trace albumin	12 st.	102	132	75	8′ 2½″	15·9	45%	2	7·7	47	50 ·927	130			
G. White (17 yrs)	Swim	M	Endurance	S−T elevated and depressed	110	O+	13·8:31·4	Satis.	125/80	72	Satis.	2″	Trace albumin	12 st. 12 lb.	82	96	62	6′ 6″	16·3	46%	1	5·9	48	53 ·770	90	124	3·6	44

uncanny ability to predict future times, whilst others again were indicative of a 'soft' attitude. Here are some replies:

'I want to record 65·5 in the Olympic final. I want to swim in the British Commonwealth Games in Edinburgh.' *Lyn McClements* who won the Olympic title in 65·5 seconds.

'I want to be the first man to break 16 minutes for 1500 metres.' – *Greg Brough.*

'More than anything I want to break a world record.' – *Karen Moras.* (She did, in March 1970, 800 metres.)

'I want to do what no other Australian swimmer has done – that is represent Australia at three Olympic Games and three British Commonwealth Games.' – *Graham White.*

11 Girls

Pre-puberty girls are almost on a par physically with boys their own age. Up to twelve years most coaches with mixed squads have found that the girls can often do the work-outs, the repeats, better than the opposite sex. Their endurance and recovery is sometimes superior.

However, after puberty the boys experience a greater growth spurt and quickly increase in muscle mass. Girls are weaker generally speaking because of the relative size of the muscle mass and because of the inherent muscle strength comparison. Boys have a greater thoracic area and consequently a larger aerobic capacity. Girls have approximately 10 per cent less haemoglobin than boys and as a general rule this is what the girls trail the boys by; 10 per cent in growth, strength, endurance and speed.

The table below is of interest showing the closeness of both sexes to twelve years.

Victorian State Winning Times 1969

	Boys	Girls	Difference (50 metres)
7 years	40·5	41·5	1·0
8 years	35·5	38·2	2·7
9 years	35·3	35·5	·2
10 years	34·1	32·6	—1·5
			(100 metres)
11 years	1·10·4	1· 8·2	—2·2
12 years	1· 6·1	1· 8·2	1·9
13 years	1· 2·2	1· 7·7	5·5
14 years	59·8	1· 4·4	4·6

Mentally, however, the girls fare better. As a general rule up to

Fourth Form (15 years) girls apply themselves better to schooling and swimming. On the average they are ahead of the boys scholastically to this point.

Menstruation in Relation to Swimming

The onset of puberty, or the developing of a child into adulthood, is heralded by many visible and invisible physiological changes in the body. The pituitary, situated at the base of the brain in close proximity to the optic mechanism is the controlling factor in this change.

In girls puberty usually occurs between the ages of eleven and fifteen years when the secondary sex characters begin to appear. (I have actually had one swimmer who was sixteen before the cycle commenced.) These include the widening of the hips, the enlargement of the breasts, the growth of the pubic hair and the general maturity of the body. The commencement of the menstrual cycle, or menstruation is allied with these physical developments. In swimmers menstruation usually occurs a little earlier than normal. The cause of this is believed to be due to the advance development of the swimmer brought about through training.

Menstruation is the term applied to the haemorrhaging of the blood from the membraneous lining of the uterus into the vagina and appearing externally. This menstrual flow, once instituted, occurs approximately every four weeks, and has a duration of three to seven days. Variations to this cycle can be caused, however, by (a) emotional stress, (b) anaemia, (c) illness, (d) strenuous exercise, (e) pregnancy.

Emotional disturbances such as worry over school examinations, the approach of the championship race, loss of form, etc., can upset the cycle. One Australian swimmer who was a world record holder, failed to have her period on the predicted date. This was three weeks before the Olympic Games. Because of worry over the situation the swimmer completely lost form. Nine weeks eventually separated the two periods. This disturbance is known as amenorrhoea, and the physician should be consulted should it occur. A complete rest from training and the cycle is usually reinstituted.

Sometimes associated with menstruation are physical disturbances which, although not serious, are amplified by anxiety. They include, swelling and tenderness of the breasts (mastalgia), enlargement of the thyroid gland, throbbing pain in the lower back or abdomen, sweating, flushing of the skin, headaches, elevation of the temperature and fainting. These ailments in mild form are natural occurrences, but vary greatly in intensity with individuals. Medical advice must be sought for serious or prolonged disturbances.

Swimming can be continued throughout the menstrual period without repercussions. Championships or important events need not be missed because of this inconvenience. During menstruation girls often produce their best efforts, others fail and this is probably due to anxiety, or more probably because of the weariness of body that menstruation brings. No risk to health is likely to be incurred during or after a hard swim.

It should be mentioned that cases of uterine cramp may occur during or after a severe swim. This distress can be relieved by (a) the application of heat to the abdomen, usually in the form of a hot water bottle, (b) warm blankets to the rest of the body, (c) keep the swimmer off her feet, (d) administer a hot drink and aspirin, (e) a drink of brandy and water.

There is usually a drop in body temperature just prior to the commencement of the monthly period. This drop of temperature can sometimes be used as a guide in easing off the load of training. Often you will hear one girl comment on 'how cold the water is today' when actually conditions are normal. From observation I have found her period is close at hand.

Complete abstinence from training during menstruation is not recommended. The disinclination for physical exertion at this time is great and the training schedule can be planned that one or two rest days correspond with this period. The first and second days of menstruation are usually the most severe in pain, the tendency being for the discomfort to gradually diminish after the third day. The intensity of the work-out should depend on the individual and the severity of the period.

At the commencement of the swimming season, when easy conditioning work is being undertaken, a rest from training for the first two days of the period is a good idea, especially if training is outdoors in cold water. Upon my advice my older girls (over sixteen years) often train through on one or two 'rest days' during the month, thereby having a credit of two days when the period commences. They can then have one or two days out of the water if they wish.

If a girl has severe pain during her periods the following aspects must be considered if considering racing: (a) the importance of the event, (b) the water temperature, (c) the general health of the swimmer, (d) the distance of the event, (e) the possible severity of the swim, (f) the swimmer's past experience of racing during menstrual cycle.

Through the loss of blood during menstruation, there is a loss of iron from the system. This can sometimes be rectified by the inclusion of an iron tonic or iron tablets in the diet.

The intake of iron is a tricky business. Iron taken orally is often assimilated by the lining of the stomach. The best system I know and one approved by the Sports Medicine Doctors is to take one of the slow diffusing time capsule types, three or four times a week. This will prove adequate and will prevent any side effects such as constipation. Incidentally there is some evidence that long term iron medication can give rise to liver damage. Since the 'multi vitamin' type capsules usually contain iron I think it is wise completely to stop taking all vitamin capsules when not in hard training.

Water Retention. During the days prior to menstruation there is an accumulation of sodium chloride within the intercellular tissues causing a retention of water. Often there is a visible swelling in the lower abdomen. There is an increase in body weight usually from two to four pounds as well as a feeling of 'being swollen'. These two symptoms can affect performance.

Treatment is helpful for those who complain of these symptoms. The aim is to prevent retention of water and to stimulate the excretion of salt and water by a suitable diuretic. Proprietary preparations are readily available.

Depending upon the importance of the event, and the age of the pupil and the parents' consent, it is often advisable to place the girl on an oral preparation to delay the onset of menstruation. Before this treatment is commenced I send my pupils to a gynaecologist for advice. These oral preparations contain two female hormones and they suppress the normal mechanism of the cycle, and whichever preparation is being taken the period will not occur. A wise policy is to start the preparation some two months before the event to ensure that the pupil is compatible with the treatment. Some oral preparations can cause temporary side effects but since there are more than twenty of these preparations on the market a suitable one can be found.

Immediately the important races are over the treatment can

cease and the menstruation cycle will commence. Many of my pupils have had outstanding results whilst taking the oral preparation.

Effect of Menstruation on Sports Performance. At the Sport-Medical Congress during the Olympic Games in Finland in 1952, Ingram reported on the results of a group of 107 female champions, consisting of 9 swimmers, 13 gymnasts, 28 basketball and baseball players, 14 skiers and skaters and 43 track and field athletes, aged 15–25 years. With the exception of four, all had taken part in competition events during menstruation, without experiencing disturbances of any kind; twenty reported that their performances during menstruation were better than usual and five had attained their record scores at this time. No effect of menstruation on athletic efficiency was noted by 45, and poorer than normal results by 39.

Since the 1956 Olympic Games, it has been ascertained that at least 21 gold medals in track and swimming events have been won during menstruation.

Not a single female competitor abstained from a contest because of menstruation. Incidentally, many women athletes have been pregnant, some being 2, 3 and 4 months.

Childbirth in Athletes and Swimmers. In respect of the duration of labour, a group of 94 athletes and swimmers was compared with a group who had not participated in competitive sports: the mean total time for the former was 17 hours 27 minutes as against 21 hours 26 minutes for the latter. For the swimmers the second stage of labour lasted 40·2 minutes and for the baseball players 55·4 minutes; as against 1 hour 1 minute for the controls.

12 The World's Greatest Woman Swimmer

A Brief History

Few coaches have the opportunity to observe a really great swimmer in private life, training and racing over an extended period as I had during the experience of training Dawn Fraser, undoubtedly the world's greatest woman freestyle swimmer.

A book of this size does not allow space to tell the full story, but I will put down important training and allied matters that occurred over the twelve years of our swimming association.

It is a fact that Dawn spent her early childhood in the industrial suburb of Balmain. Because of the home economic situation, Dawn had often to battle for herself, make decisions, take responsibility and look after others. As a consequence her formal education was neglected. The environment of the neighbourhood it appears, gave Dawn a toughened exterior whereas inwardly she was quite a sensitive person. Running up the steep Balmain hills barefooted and climbing over back fences developed in her the physical toughness that would be called on in later years to win three successive Olympic gold medals.

A legacy from her father of bronchial asthma aggravated by the smoggy dockside atmosphere was an encumberance Dawn carried throughout her swimming life.

I still recall the first day I met her. Lithe and lean in her black 'Speedo', running along the side of the pool and hurtling into the water like a black panther, she was just 14 years of age. She had absolutely no womanly development; actually she looked for all the world like a wiry young boy with her short-cropped hair. Being the only one in the pool on a schoolday I soon discovered that she was 'playing truant'. Over a cup of coffee at the pool kiosk I learnt that Dawn had an aimless existence, she had no idea of her own potential. To me in those brief few moments I had seen her in the pool it was obvious that she had a natural greatness in the water. I persuaded her to join my coaching team – headquartered at the Drummoyne Swimming Pool – which at this time was particularly strong having seven National champions. However, I didn't see Dawn for months after this original meeting. She had gone 'bush'.

Towards the end of the 1952 season she poked her nose inside the pool and I made sure this time that she didn't get away. She managed to handle stroke instruction very well, but she was not too keen on squad training. I was lucky to see her three times a week, she seemed to always have an excuse for not being at training, 'in bed with the flu', 'fell off my bike', 'had to look after the next door neighbour's kids', etc.

At the end of the first season it was evident that if I could harness this great talent I would have a National champion. Dawn's improvement on limited work was so rapid that we decided to attempt the New South Wales 100 yards record which stood at 61 seconds. It was a solo swim and I can still remember the timekeepers from the N.S.W. Women's Swimming Association shaking their heads as Dawn failed three times that Saturday afternoon. This was the turning point in Dawn's career. It was as if her wheels had been put on the right track. She now knew what she wanted to do most of all.

On reflecting upon that first year I now realize that champions, even in the initial stages, single themselves out from the crowd by their water compatibility and aggressiveness. I have also realized since then that there exist people who just have to succeed. Some fall into the category of Dawn who had many shortcomings in her home life, and was determined somehow to compensate for them. I also learnt that it is possible for dedicated athletes to overcome respiratory illnesses and reach the upper strata of sport.

During the first year it is doubtful if Dawn covered 50 miles in training. I kept a log from the second season until 1964 and during that period she covered 4,161 miles. Her best mileage year was 1960 when she trained over 469 miles.

The commencement of the second season saw Dawn exercising once a week and swimming eight times weekly. This season she was placed third in the Nationals in 69 seconds. She had grown to 5 feet 7 inches and weighed 9 stone 10 lb.

That year my tutor, physiology Professor Frank Cotton put Dawn through an exhaustive battery of physical tests. Important things which came from this examination were: Dawn had a weakness of the lower back, she was also anaemic (blood count below 80 per cent) and the chest X-ray revealed suspect shadows. I think this was the final scare that induced Dawn to give up smoking.

You may think that a lot of this material I have written is of no consequence, but I feel it is important. It may inspire some other child, somewhere to change their mode of living and dedicate their energy output to sport.

In her third season I concentrated upon increasing Dawn's weekly swimming mileage as well as building her physically. You must remember she often missed meals, preferring to subsist on milk shakes. By February 1956 she had reached 5 feet 8¼ inches and weighed 10 stone 5 lb. Her blood count had been increased by vitamin supplementation and her mileage was now nearing 800 miles which, of course, was far below that of her contemporaries.

That month she smashed the world record for 100 metres and 110 yards, a record that had stood for twenty years.

Now Dawn's sights were on the Melbourne Olympic Games of 1956. With such a goal I had no difficulty inducing her to undertake a more intense course of land conditioning.

It is worth mentioning that at this stage I had several male swimmers swimming 100 metres well under the minute. Dawn trailed these swimmers in squad work-outs and I have no doubt this is one reason she became so aggressive in her sprinting. It is history now that Dawn went on to win the 100 metre Olympic title in World Record time of 62 seconds.

The following facts are, in the main, dry statistics but some could be of material assistance to coaches and aspiring champions.

Dawn Fraser's annual swimming

	Miles	Hours of weight training	Season's best time for 100 metres
1952		No Record kept	
1953	220		69·3
1954	283	30	67·0
1955	260	33	66·1
1956	398	53	62·0
1957	261	16	61·6
1958	428	49	61·6
1959	464	28	60·2
1960	469	63	60·4
1961	348	38	60·3
1962	444	41	59·9
1963	303	40	60·2
1964	283	38	58·9
TOTAL	4,161	429	
AVERAGE	346¾	39	

Note: This record is reasonably accurate as I have kept Dawn Fraser's bound log books.

The following are details of haemoglobin levels kept during the 1962 season. During this time Dawn's diet was being supplemented with iron and vitamin B_{12} tablets.

Plate 1. (*Above, left*) Land Conditioning – Dynastatic Exercise 1 (*see* p. 154). Virginia Rickard demonstrates the correct wrist and elbow position for fast repetitions. Plate 2. (*Above, right*) Dynastatic Exercise 2 (*see* p. 154) Vicki Williams shows how to regulate the resistance by holding the loose cord

Plate 3. (*Left*) Dynastatic Exercise 3 (*see* p. 154). Jane Comerford has her arm in a strong pull position. Plate 4 (*Right*) Dynastatic Exercise 4 (*see* p. 154). Six seconds at maximum pressure is adequate for the isometric position in butterfly and breaststroke

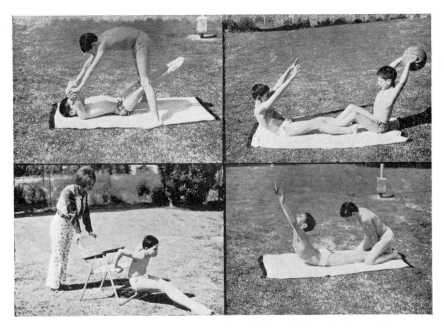

Plates 5–8. Land Conditioning – Standard exercises without weights. (*Top, left*) Exercise 1 (*see* p. 157). Raising partners. (*Top, right*) 2. Ball passing in pairs (*see* p. 157). (*Below, left*) 3. Back press from chair (*see* p. 157). (*Below, right*) 4. Back arching (*see* p. 157).

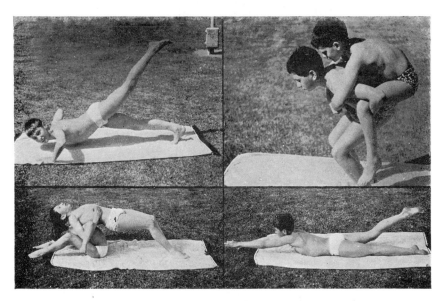

Plates 9–12. (*Top, left*) 5. Body presses with alternate leg raising (*see* p. 157). (*Top, right*) 6. Half squats with partner on back (*see* p. 157). (*Below, left*) 7. Back to back pullovers (*see* p. 157). (*Below, right*) 8. Swimming (arms and legs (*see* p. 158)

Plates 13–16. Land Conditioning – Weight training. (*Top, left*) 1. Lift and Press (*see* p. 159). (*Top, right*) 2. Horizontal pullovers (*see* p. 159). (*Below, left*) 3. Half squats (*see* p. 159). (*Below, right*) 4. French curl (*see* p. 159)

Plates 17–20. (*Top*, *left*) 5. Counsilman's arm rotators (*see* p. 159). (*Top*, *right*) 6. Back lift (*see* p. 159). (*Below*, *left*) 7. Wrist curls (*see* p. 159). (*Below*, *right*) 8. Alternate front and back press (*see* p. 160)

	%	Gms.
5th August 1962	88	12·6
19th August 1962	90	13·0
2nd September 1962	88	12·6
16th September 1962	86	12·2
30th September 1962	88	12·6
13th October 1962	92	13·1
27th October 1962 (World Record 59·5 sec.)	98	14·0

A complete record of early morning heart rates was not kept but these random counts show the increasing efficiency of her developing athletic heart. During December 1958 I had a wonderful opportunity to observe the champion's resting heart rate. She was in bed for almost a week with a severe bout of influenza.

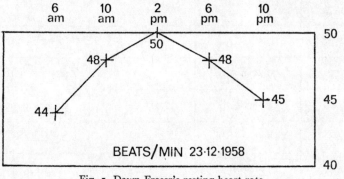

Fig. 5. Dawn Fraser's resting heart rate

Once Dawn's physique had 'set' her yearly body weight fluctuation only varied 5 or 6 lb. This was due to Dawn keeping close to her physical peak throughout the whole year. Just how fit I kept her can be gauged by these times in 1962:

F

November 1961	63·1 seconds	January 1962	60·8 seconds
December 1961	62·4 seconds	February 1962	60·4 seconds
March 1962	60·4 seconds	August 1962	62·4 seconds
April 1962	—	September 1962	62·2 seconds
May 1962	—	October 1962	62·0 seconds
June 1962	64·0 seconds	November 1962	59·9 seconds
July 1962	63·2 seconds		

Here is a table of her annual racing weights:

	Peak racing weight	Peak racing height	Peak haemoglobin level
1952	—	—	—
1953	9 st. 10 lb.	5′ 7″	—
1954	10 st.	—	83 per cent
1955	10 st. 3 lb.	—	88 per cent
1956	10 st. 5 lb.	5′ 7½″	93 per cent
1957	—	—	—
1958	10 st.	—	88 per cent
1959	10 st. 6½ lb.	5′ 8″	92 per cent
1960	10 st. 8¼ lb.	5′ 8¼″	94 per cent
1961	10 st. 4½ lb.	5′ 8¼″	14 gm.
1962	10 st. 8 lb.	5′ 8¼″	14 gm.
1963	10 st. 8 lb.	5′ 8¼″	13·8 gm.
1964	10 st. 8 lb.	5′ 8¼″	13·6 gm.

Dawn seemed to be beset with an extremely high number of viruses and infections, etc. They included repeated asthmatic attacks (in her early career), numerous bouts of influenza, bronchitis and several instances of proven pneumonia, and swollen glands. She had allergies and the one we feared most of all was fresh paint. Freshly painted swimming pool surrounds were disastrous to our plans. Dawn had many muscle 'breakdowns', which included several recurring bouts of tendonitis. She had a chipped vertebrae from a car accident. Hardly a season went by when Dawn was not out of the training pool with at least a couple of serious illnesses. Perhaps the most frightening was a prolonged bout of hepatitis. It took Dawn many months to finally throw off this serious disease, which unfortunately is usually taken far too lightly by swimmers.

Dawn usually insisted on training during her menstruation cycle and she would never put off a race, no matter how minor, because of this inconvenience. Cold water temperatures often caused her to have severe pains in the region of the kidneys. That there was no permanent detrimental effect from all these disorders is underlined by the fact that Dawn gave birth to a lovely daughter with a minimum of discomfort and she herself is enjoying fine health.

In a previous chapter I have stated that Dawn swam 100 metres in 67 seconds in the Mexican Olympic pool after being out of training for four years. This last sentence tends to prove an original thought I had regarding Dawn Fraser: that as a swimmer she was ten years ahead of her time. That there is no doubt in my mind that she would have won her fourth sprint gold medal at Mexico, had she been eligible to swim.

In conclusion these points may be of interest.

1. Observation and films have proven that no one has had a freestyle technique comparable with Dawn's.

2. She had tremendous aggression in her races and even from the earliest days never entered a race thinking she might be beaten.

3. Because of training her physique changed from scrawny and under-nourished to a lean and powerful one.

4. Her ability to converse well and mix with any company was due to her association with the swimming fraternity and her numerous swimming trips.

5. Her swimming strength was almost equally divided below the

waist and above the waist, e.g. best 50 metre kick 38·0 seconds, best 50 metre legs tied time 31·8 seconds.

6. Dawn was competent at all strokes. World record in freestyle and butterfly, National record in medley.

7. Her training consisted of perhaps 50 per cent mainstroke in various forms, 15 per cent kicking practice, 10 per cent legs tied training, 25 per cent on the other strokes.

13 Land Conditioning

Basic Physiology

Think of conditioning and you instinctively think of fitness. But what is fitness? Is it good health? Or the ability to perform life's functions without undue stress? For the purpose of this chapter fitness can be broken into two sections – muscular fitness and organic fitness. Muscular fitness encompasses all the important items needed to execute the strokes, e.g. strength, speed, endurance, recuperative ability, flexibility, etc. Organic fitness is the respiratory and circulatory fitness that, to put it simply, allows the long distance swimmer or runner to grind out over the distances. Both are indispensable to today's swimmer.

Some activities, such as weight lifting and hammer throwing, need mainly only muscular fitness. In endurance work we need organic fitness but since it is becoming increasingly evident that swimmers are now starting to turn distance races virtually to sprints a fine balance of both types of fitness is required.

First of all it is essential to remember that we are born into either the first or the second category. Most people have both qualities but one type of fitness will always be dominant. For example the coach may feel that a certain swimmer will make a great 'sprinter' but the balance of the two fitnesses may be leaning towards endurance. These border line cases of sprinter-distance men are numerous. I always wanted Dawn Fraser to be a great 400 metre swimmer because the ease of her stroke indicated to me that she could 'swim all day'. She did reach world class over that distance but her muscular fitness was superior to her organic fitness and she predominated as a sprinter. Two examples at the other end of the scale were Murray Rose and John Konrads.

Anatomically the body can be subdivided into three categories.

145

This is called Somato typing. The groups are endomorphs, meso-morphs and ectomorphs. The coach must be familiar with the characteristics of each type so that he can channel the swimmer along the correct lines, each type having properties that the other two do not possess.

Endomorphs usually have little or no athletic ability. Endomorphs are usually short of height and carry a lot of body fat. They are chunky and have very little muscle. The inexperienced coach or swim teacher can be misled by the endomorph who comes to the pool for a swim lesson. Because they have surplus adipose tissue the endomorph floats well, and because of this they learn to swim faster and do it with apparent ease compared with the other body types. Parents and some coaches tend to think that they have a born cham-pion on their hands and they start to push the swimmer into swimming as a competitive sport. How wrong they are. I cannot recall ever having seen an endomorph in top-class still water swimming.

The ectomorph is thin and tall, the bones are usually light. Arms and legs are long and lean. Ectomorphs are usually prone to cold, chest complaints, asthmatic and allied nervous disorders. They cannot stand cold water. They usually perform well in endurance athletic events but they do not, as a general rule, adapt well to heavy physical work.

Ectomorphs show up relatively well in backstroke events. Australia's greatest backstrokers, David Thiele, John Monckton and Peter Reynolds have all had some ectomorphic qualities but they have been fortified with the better attributes of the mesomorphic body type. I believe that the very best swimmers contain a com-bination of the ecto-mesomorphic body types.

Mesomorphs can be described as having a 'square' and hard body with a long trunk. Ribs are usually strong and prominent. The waist is low and slender. The arms are evenly proportioned. Feet and hands are broad and strong.

Look for the ecto-mesomorphs and you have a good foundation with which to start. Wenden, Devitt, Rose, Fraser (Australia), Schollander, Clark, Stouder, Hickcox, McKenzie (U.S.A.), Matthes, McGregor, Mosconi (Europe) are all examples of the ecto-meso-morphic body. Other intangibles that show through in these two body types are courage and the desire to compete.

Flexibility is a component of muscular fitness. It is becoming increasingly difficult to reach world class without super flexibility. Roland Matthes, perhaps the greatest stylist at the Mexico Olympics, has super flexibility in all joints. His backstroke wins and world records depend upon this flexibility. If his shoulders were not flexible he would not be able to place his straight arms directly behind his shoulders; if his forearm and wrist joints were not flexible he would not be able to place his hands into the water without distortion. His leg drive has great fluidity and flexibility in the ankle and knee joints. Flexibility can be improved by training. The ability of the extension of a joint to move over a greater range with apparent ease depends upon the 'looseness' of the joint and the physical characteristics of the muscles acting as prime movers. This is why some characteristics of the ectomorph are desirable (super flexible types). Super flexibility is necessary in the legs of top breaststrokers. True, Jastremski was not a super-flexible type but I am sure that his coach James Counsilman would be the first to admit that he would have been even greater had 'Chet' had more flexibility. The ability to twist the lower leg, and turn the toes out-ankles in, is a decided asset to the breaststroker. The ability to 'flick' the ankle at the end of the leg drive can only be maximum when flexibility is maximum. If you have long lean legs you must maintain or increase their flexibility should you commence exercises to develop or strengthen them. Do not sacrifice flexibility for strength. Develop the two simultaneously.

Muscles are, I suppose, machines that can be used for converting chemical energy into mechanical movement. Muscles move us, they propel us through the water. Muscles are made up of numerous fibres that vary from 1/25th of an inch to $1\frac{1}{2}$ inches in length and are extremely thin. These fibres are grouped together, all wrapped in bundles and connected to one another. Each fibre has one or perhaps two nerves acting upon it as well as a fine network of minute blood vessels – capillaries.

When a muscle is exercised regularly we actually increase the thickness of each fibre up to a point, the more we exercise, the thicker each fibre becomes. However, we cannot increase the length of the fibres or their numbers. Muscular exercise and therefore muscular fitness increases the thickness of the muscle fibre whereas organic training is thought to increase the number of capillaries around each muscle fibre. Within and around the working muscle there takes place 32 chemical reactions to 'convert' energy and to discharge waste products. It is known that mesomorphic body types, because of the 'bulk' of their muscle fibres 'tie up' very early in an event, possibly due to their inability to discharge their muscular waste products and the congestion of blood that quickly builds up. Therefore it is important not to over-develop the swimming muscles by the incorrect or indiscriminate use of exercises or equipment. All muscles play a part in swimming even though it may not be apparent immediately.

Briefly the main muscle groups are:

Arm depressors: Pectoralis major, latissimus dorsi, teres major and the triceps.

Arm rotators: Subscapularis, teres major, pectoralis major.

Arm extensors: Triceps.

Arm recovery: Brachialis and deltoid.

Hip flexors: Psoas.

Leg extensors: Quadriceps, gastrocemius, gluteus.

Types of Exercises

There are three movements:

Isotonic. All swimming movements are isotonic, that is, the muscles and levers are in constant motion.

Intermediary. If I were to lift a bar up to a certain point and hold it static for say 3 seconds then lift it 6 inches higher and again hold it for 3 seconds, etc., this is known as intermediary exercise.

Isometric. Is where a muscle works but there is no movement. For example if I were to press my palms against each other and hold the press for a few seconds this is termed isometric. Six seconds is the accepted time phase for each isometric contraction.

Isotonic movements build endurance especially if used with a light weight. Developing children should do mostly isotonic movements through the full range of the movement.

Intermediary exercises add variety to a conditioning programme. Their real value is a mystery.

Isometric exercises add great strength to the muscles exercised but should be confined to physically mature swimmers, in moderation to the young.

When a muscle is worked regularly it increases in size, in strength, but it becomes heavier. Specific swimming muscles exercised regularly against resistance will, if all other things be equal, make you swim faster. The type of exercise you do, the amount you do, the resistance used, etc., depend upon your age, sex, physical development and the swimming events you are training for. From the above you can see that there are many variables and consequently just as many weight training systems. Today's schedules usually concentrate upon the muscles used for 'your' stroke.

Here are some fundamentals I have discovered and use:

(a) Movements with light weights or little resistance repeated many times will develop endurance, e.g. 500 repetitions × 15 lb. resistance.

(b) Movements with heavy weights or much resistance repeated only a few times will develop strength (sprinters).

(c) Movements with heavy weights or much resistance repeated many times will develop bulk, and must be avoided.

(d) Movements with medium weights or medium resistance repeated a medium amount of times will develop an equal amount of strength and endurance.

(e) All movements must be taken through their full range ('short' movements destroy flexibility).

(f) Exercises that imitate the actual swimming movements obviously are most beneficial.

(g) The best programmes are those that combine, in this order, warm-up exercises, stretching exercises, isometric exercises, isotonic movements.

(h) Avoid movements that develop muscles not required for power in swimming (biceps, deltoids, gastrocnemius).

(i) What weight to use may be estimated from a formula I devised:

Sprinter swimmers

	Weight to use		Repetitions
Age (years	+ Body weight (stones)	+ 20	× body weight (stones)
e.g. 12	+ 8	+ 20 ×	8
	40 pounds	×	8 repetitions

Distance swimmers

Age (years)	+ body weight (stones)	× age (years)	+ body weight
e.g. 12	+ 8	× 12	+ 8
	20 pounds	× 20 repetitions	

(j) Most benefit can be derived from the weight training and resistance sections by incorporating isometric, intermediary and isotonic exercises.

(k) Stretching and flexibility movements are of little benefit for the very young, but are essentials for the matured swimmers.

(l) Do not hold isometrics for 10 or 12 seconds as some authorities advocate – 5 or 6 seconds will be adequate.

The Australian scene, especially in the country areas, is such that a fairly heavy dosage of conditioning exercises must be carried out as a complementary to swimming. Indoor heated pools and allied facilities are few and far between. Secondly, the school system of physical conditioning leaves a lot to be desired, chiefly because of the lack of adequate sports areas and equipment. American school children (ages 6–11 years) are bigger, taller, and I suppose stronger than their Australian contemporaries (I have anatomical measurements for these two nations).

In the capital cities where water conditioning can be carried out for 10 or 11 months of each year there is still the need for land strengthening and flexibility exercises.

This simple, but well controlled test of 1961 gives a clue as to why we should maintain strength movements throughout the whole season.

Name   1 × *Max. press with bar bell (in pounds)*

	JULY	AUG.	SEPT.	OCT.	NOV.	DEC.
Fraser, Dawn	85	92½	100	95	—	82½
Dickson, David	97½	110	127½	—	120	110
Ryan, John	90	105	120	—	112½	—
Krieg, Dale	77½	85	90	88	78	72½
Aunger, Kym	85	97½	115	107½	105	105
	NO SWIMMING 3 hours weight training weekly			NO WEIGHT TRAINING Swimming about 15–22 miles weekly		

We realize that supreme strength is not needed for swimming, and it has been known for a long time that strength does not increase by just swimming only.

Whereas strength decreases in the water, flexibility increases. However the range of flexibility can be increased even more so by suitable exercises. Super-flexibility is of paramount importance for breaststroke and butterfly swimmers.

I had a very satisfying experience whilst coaching a partially spastic 14-year-old boy, Tony Cram. His deformed left foot had a restricted flexibility of 44 degrees. I designed a special shoe, which when worn forced his ankle joint to work over a gradually increasing range. After 20 weeks his ankle flexibility had increased to 67 degrees. Not only could Tony walk with less limp but he went on to win the National Junior butterfly title.

The following principles must be borne in mind when organizing a land conditioning programme:

(a) Age of pupil – if overall development is needed first, then specific exercises later.

(b) Time available. Eliminate unnecessary warm-ups and 'doubtful' and harmful exercises.

(c) Is strength required – or endurance – or both?

(d) Flexibility is just as important.

(e) Can some exercises be done at home to save travel time?

(f) Testing, measuring and motivation are helpful.

(g) All pupils do not need the same amount of work.

There is no doubt that Australia ruled the swimming world during the 1950s simply because we heard that 'the Americans were doing exercises with weights and that John Marshall was doing flexibility exercises and pulling movements'. We did not know for certain what exercises were being done, but in typical Australian 'have-a-go' style, coaches such as Carlile, Guthrie, Herford, Talbot, Cusack and myself 'designed' our own weight training programmes Being isolated from the world scene at times can be advantageous. This was one occasion. We over-compensated, we designed better weight training and flexibility work-outs than the rest of the world. The same scene was duplicated in our pool training, although we did not know it, we were working harder in the pool and out of it.

Every few years a new 'trend' will flash upon the conditioning scene. Some of these are purely commercial in concept, designed to sell books or equipment. Others are worth including in your programme. There can be no doubt that Michael Wenden owes his success to strength developed through conscientious adherence to isometric exercises, or that Karen Moras and Diana Rickard are helped by the daily use of their Dynastatic machines.

The Dynastatic (Australia) or Exogenie (U.S.A.) machine has

indeed proved beneficial in developing stroke strength in young pupils. Its main attributes being that it is light and portable and therefore the work-outs can be done at school. Also stroke principles such as elbow lift and firm wrist can be ingrained into the pupil.

Forbes Carlile introduced this important piece of training equipment into Australia four years ago after watching Sharon Stouder do her daily 10-minute work-out under the watchful eye of coach Don Gambrill. Sharon and quite a few more of Gambrill's pupils went on to win gold medals at Tokyo. The dynastatic exercises are now well established in Australia and I have set out Carlile's system below.

These exercises should be carried out for 20 *to* 30 *minutes daily* during the winter season, and for 10 to 20 minutes daily during the summer.

WARMING UP AND FLEXIBILITY

1. DOWNWARD AND SIDEWAYS STRETCHES
   Bending at waist with legs straight.
   > 8 full stretches. Stretch down, stretch up.
   >> Stretch down and to left, stretch up.
   >> Stretch down and to right, stretch up.

2. BACK 'SCRATCHES'
   With elbow high, arm bent and reaching behind the head across the back. Stretch the shoulder-joint by pulling on the elbow with the other hand.
   > 6 × 6 repetitions on alternate arms.

3. TOWEL DISLOCATIONS
   Hold ends of towel with wide hand grip. Limber the straight arms over the head. Each day start *gently* and gradually narrow the grip. Keep at this shoulder flexibility exercise but do not try for too much too soon. 15 repetitions.

4. ANKLE STRETCHERS – KNEELING
   Point feet and sit on heels. Heels must be kept together. Limber down '1–2–3'. 12 repetitions.

5. PULL BACKS
   Lie face down, arch back and grasp pointed feet. Pull with arms and throw head back, then relax. 12 repetitions.

ABDOMINAL AND STRENGTHENING EXERCISES

6. BACKSTROKE KICKING

Lie on back with arms extended above the head. Point feet, keeping legs straight and heels off the ground. Lift legs alternately in fast tempo. 100 times.

7. SQUAT-THRUST JUMPS

Squat, hands outside knees on ground. Thrust legs out behind, keeping back straight. Return to squat position – then jump high and return to squatting position. 24 times. Rest for 10 seconds every six repetitions when necessary.

8. FRONT CRAWL KICKING

Lie face down with arms stretched beyond the head. Point feet, keeping legs straight and feet off ground, lift legs alternately in fast tempo. 100 times.

DYNASTATIC EXERCISES

Swimmers of all ages will benefit greatly by carrying out these special exercises regularly, from 5 to 20 minutes daily. There are no 'gimmicks' and the schedules are designed so that there are no time-wasting changes in positioning and adjustments to the apparatus. Every swimmer works individually. Make the most of the fact that with the Dynastatic you have a *controlled resistance* which you should increase as you grow stronger. The resistance is constant from the beginning until the end of the pull which is a great advantage over cheaper spring and expanding devices.

General aim

To strengthen the particular muscles and muscle-fibre groups. used in the various styles. You copy closely the technically correct action. In this way good technique is learned whilst muscular strength and endurance is increased. Pay particular attention to the instruction to KEEP THE ELBOWS UP.

Instructions

Set up the Dynastatic with the door attachment placed either on the top or at the side of the door which is closed (and preferably locked to prevent an unexpected opening from the other side). Adjust the resistance by depressing the ball bearing near the top of the Dynastatic and turn the cylinder.

Exercise 1. For all strokes (See plate 1)

Fast repetitions. (Isotonics)

Set the resistance on the Dynastatic so that you can carry out the exercise illustrated with a fairly fast, rhythmical action for 5 minutes. Hold the hands flat in the grips and keep the elbows high as the arms press down and back, beyond the thighs. Work in one or two minute bursts with a 10-second rest interval between each burst.

The harder you work the hotter the metal cylinder of the Dynastatic will become. This is a good test of how much effort you are putting into it. Increase the resistance week by week.

Exercise 2. For all strokes (See plate 2)

Slow pull-throughs and 6-second holds. (Isometrics)

Dial back the resistance on the Dynastatic so that the cords are slack with the resistance nearly zero. Taking about 20 seconds for the pull-through movement, regulate the resistance by holding the loose cord with the other hand so that you can barely move the pulling arm. Repeat alternately five times with each arm.

Keep the elbows high and push back beyond the thigh.

SIX-SECOND HOLDS. Select four positions from the start of the pull to the final push back. Hold the slack cord with the other hand and make the strongest possible static (isometric) contraction at each of the four positions for 6 seconds. Carry out this exercise with each arm.

Exercise 3. For Backstroke (See plate 3)

Sit or stand with your back to the Dynastatic and carry out the backstroke exercise regulating the resistance by holding the loose cord in the other hand. Carry out slow pull-throughs and 6-second holds as described for Exercise 2. Note that the first part of the arm stroke should be made with the arm nearly straight, but early in the pull the elbow should bend, keeping the hand in front of the elbow.

Exercise 4. Butterfly and Breaststroke (See plate 4)

Hold four positions of the butterfly and breaststroke pull each for 6 seconds in the static (isometric) position. Keep the elbows high and the hands in the flat 'swimming' position. To obtain the four positions through the pull, stand at various distances from the Dynastatic. In addition to this exercise, butterfly and breaststroke specialists should carry out exercises 1 and 2 to help gain strength and endurance. Repeat twice.

Over the years I have discovered that some pupils respond better to a programme of swimming 50 per cent, exercising 50 per cent. I will explain this. Two of my greatest girl swimmers, both Olympians, had only limited success when working solely in the pool. They were National champions Alva Colquhoun and Jan Turner. Alva was a bad asthmatic, so bad in fact that in water work-outs we would often have to pull her from the pool gasping and distressed. Treatment would follow with a subsequent lightening of the swim load. In order to keep up a measure of strength we decided to do light weight training and allied exercises. At one exercise, walking on her hands, Alva became so proficient that she could circumnavigate a 50 metre pool. From this point she became a world class swimmer dropping into the 62+ seconds for 100 metres. This was 1960. Her programme briefly was:

Swimming: basic miles per week, 10
Swimming: effort work per week, 2
Exercises: calisthenics, etc. per week, 2 hours
Exercises: light weight training per week, 2 hours

On swimming only, Alva never raced well, was always fatigued. Jan Turner was a similar case, but a stronger girl. On 'just swimming' Jan managed to get to 64 for the 100 metres. On a programme of mixed weights and swimming she bettered 63 seconds. There is no doubt in my mind that some swimmers would be better conditioned if some of their water was transferred to land conditioning. I have often observed how many swimmers will, after only a month or 6 weeks of water work reach their best time for the season for 50 metres. This period has been preceded by a weight training season during the off months. Often the sprint time is not repeated until almost at the end of the swim season. I feel that sprinters derive more benefit from land exercises than do the distance students.

Two short stories are worth telling here because they involve great Australian swimmers, David Dickson and John Ryan. John Ryan, known fondly as 'Foot' is the best kick board sprinter I have coached. John's best time of 34·6 seconds for 50 metres kick on the flutter board was successfully reduced to 32·4 seconds after just one month of ankle flexibility exercises. Even as dramatic was the 'discovery' by David Dickson. During a 'walk back' session of 50 metre sprints David discovered that if he did five body presses (or push-ups) before a sprint his time was up to ·6 of a second faster. After seeing the pink flushing of the blood in the pectorals, the trapezius and the triceps and up into the throat after each 'set of five push-ups', I had no doubt as to why David's times were faster. David applied his secret weapon successfully in winning many National sprint titles.

At the time of writing there is controversy about the benefits of warm-ups on athletic performances generally. The experiment Professor Frank Cotton and myself carried out on Jon Henricks may be worthy of further investigation. We decided to give Jon a 'warm-up using exercises and equipment' but no swimming. Jon warmed-up on pulleys, stationary bicycle, weights and callisthenics. His rectal temperature rose to 100·4°. That night he set a new world 100 metres record.

The following day he was stiff from the unaccustomed exercises.

Over the years I have shaken my exercise class down into what I consider a very workable system getting the most benefit to each pupil in a minimum of time.

Here is my system at the gymnasium:

(a) We do very little, if any, warm-up exercises.

(b) We do eight hard standard exercises without weights.

(c) We do 10 minutes exercises on rubber cords or pulleys.

(d) We do eight standard exercises with weights.

(e) We do 15 minutes of dynastatics.

(f) We vary the duration, load and sequence often.

(g) We swim where possible after each work-out.

Away from the gym class

(h) We do 12 minutes dynastatics daily.

(i) We do ankle flexibility movements for breaststrokers.

(j) A bush walk of 9–12 miles every three weeks at an altitude of 2,000–4,000 feet.

Section (a): Five minutes at the most should be used for warm-up movements and these should be restricted to stretching and flexibility exercises such as:

1. Half squats. 1 minute.

2. Crossing of arms and legs, 1 minute.

3. Head to knees, 1 minute.

4. Rowing, 1 minute.

Some pupils eliminate the warm-up section. They replace it by getting out of the car a mile away and jogging to the gymnasium.

Section (b) (eight hard standard exercises)

1. *Raising partners* (See plate 5)

A lies on back with hands grasping opposite elbows behind head. B leans on A's elbows. A forces the weight of B's body up, at the same time raising his legs.

Repetitions: five sets of ten movements each partner.

2. *Ball passing in pairs* (See plate 6)

A and B interlock feet or place feet in special leather rungs. A with arms extended overhead sits up and throws medicine ball to B. B catches ball and lies back with ball extended behind head. Repetitions: The ball to pass 100 times or 2 × 50.

3. *Back press from chair* (See plate 7)

Subject keeps elbows tucked in close to sides and from a floor-sitting position pushes body up and down. Keep legs as straight as possible and toes pointed. Repetitions: five sets of ten movements.

4. *Back arching (feet held)* (See plate 8)

A's feet are anchored by B (or under some immoveable object, A now arches up and back as far as possible with arms extended in front.

Repetitions: two sets of twenty movements each partner.

5. *Body presses with alternate leg raising* (See plate 9)

As the chest and head dip down in the body press the face is turned to the left and at the same time the right leg is lifted. The arms then press up straight and the leg returns to the floor. Next time the face turns right and the left leg is lifted.

Repetitions: five sets of ten movements, done at a steady rate.

6. *Half squats with partner on back* (See plate 10)

With a partner of equal weight straddled on the back, A goes steadily down into a half squat position, then returns to the straight body position. Keep heels on floor.

Repetitions: 2 × 10 movements each partner.

7. *Back to back pullovers* (See plate 11)

A and B sit back to back with arms interlocked at elbows. A leans back with force as B leans his head down to his knees.

Then B forces up and back on to A who now has his head on his knees.

Repetitions: thirty movements.

8. *Swimming* (*arms and legs*) (See plate 12)

With straight arms and legs whip the legs and arms up and down fast, the upward movement of the left arm to coincide with the upward movement of the right leg, and vice versa. Arch back and hold head high.

Repetitions: three sets of 60 seconds each set.

Section (*c*) (*i*) Tension work with rubber cords or pulleys. (Do either section)

1. *Freestyle arm action.* (With emphasis on high elbow recovery do the complete freestyle arm action taking care to co-ordinate correctly.)

Repetitions: six sets of 30 seconds.

2. *Butterfly or Breaststroke or Freestyle intermediaries*

In three positions of the pull hold the stretched cords for 5 seconds. Raise elbows and wrists.

Repetitions: 5 seconds in each of three positions (three run throughs).

3. *Double arm backstroke pull and push*

In three positions of the pull hold the stretched cords for 5 seconds. Keep wrists firm and elbows forward.

Repetitions: 5 seconds in each of three positions (three run throughs).

OR

Section (*c*) (*ii*) *Pulleys.*

1. *Kiphuth's arm action on bench*

Lying on a bench with back arched and head high pull the handles down and through the freestyle movement alternately.

Repetitions: At least 100 movements with weights that will just allow you to do twenty at a time.

2. *Breaststroke arms*

Standing in a bent forward position do a complete arm action including recovery of the breaststroke. Pupils may also learn their 'breathing timing' during this exercise.

Repetitions: At least 100 movements with weights that will allow you to do only twenty at a time.

3. *Backstroke arms*

Lying on a bench do the double backstroke pull and push or alternate arm actions.

Repetitions: At least 100 movements with weights that will allow you to do twenty at a time.

Section (d) Weight training

1. *Lift and Press* (used as a warm-up) (See plate 13)

Lift the barbell from a comfortable position in front of the feet. Keep wrists curled out. Lift weight and straighten legs at same time.

Repetitions: three sets of ten movements.

2. *Horizontal pullovers* (See plate 14)

Lying on the floor (for safety) with the arms extended behind the head slowly lift the bar up to the vertical. Keep knees bent up. Then return the bar to the floor. Keep hands only shoulder width apart.

3. *Half squats* (See plate 15)

Standing with feet apart and the bar on the shoulders, bend the knees forward until the straight upper trunk squats half-way down. Keep heels on floor. Return to upright position.

4. *French curl with double bounce* (See plate 16)

In a standing or kneeling position and with the bar held overhead and the hands fairly close together slowly bend the elbows until the bar is as low as possible. Keep the upper trunk straight, then do two little 'bounces' with the bar and return it to the straight position. Keep the elbows tucked in tightly throughout.

5. *Counsilman's arm rotators* (See plate 17)

Lying on back with bar held in behind the head slowly raise and lower the bar to the vertical. Keep the elbows on floor throughout.

6. *Back lifts* (See plate 18)

With the bar held behind the buttocks and the trunk slightly bent forward the arms press back and upwards in an arc. Return to starting position.

7. *Wrist curls* (See plate 19)

Sitting upon a chair with the forearms resting on the thighs, by extending and flexing the wrists and fingers the bar rolls forward and backward. Either a bar or heavy dumb bell can be used.

8. *Alternate front and back press* (See plate 20)

Standing position press the bar up above the head then return the bar down on to the shoulders. Then do a back press and return the bar to the chest.

Section (e) 15 minutes Dynastatics from the section previously outlined.

SPECIAL EXERCISES

Section (i) Ankle flexibility

1. Sitting on a chair with one leg upon the knee the hands press down on the toes then pull back hard on the toes forcing the ankle joint through its greatest range (Fig. 6a). Repetitions: two sets of ten ups and ten down each foot.

2. The same sitting position; however, this time with one hand on the heel, press down and at the same time with the other hand pull the toes up; then reverse (Fig. 6b).

Repetitions: two sets of ten ups and down each foot.

3. In a sitting position point one leg straight out and have the toe describe the largest possible circle without moving the knee (Fig. 6c).

Repetitions: ten revolutions each way with each foot.

Shoulder flexibility exercises

1. Shoulder flexibility can be maintained and increased by exercise. Grip a towel at the ends and without dropping one shoulder blade (keep shoulders level) take the towel from in front of the thighs over the head and down to the buttocks (Fig. 7). After a few days take a shorter grip on the towel and repeat.

Repetitions: 25 complete movements.

Backstroke 'press and pull'

1. Backstroke arm strength as well as technique can be developed by this exercise. Lying on a bench with the arm overhead at the entry position A presses down against B's hand as an isometric exercise for 6 seconds. A's arm then executes the

Fig. 6a. Ankle flexibility – 1

Fig. 6b. Ankle flexibility – 2

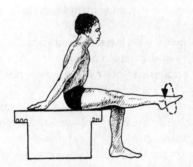

Fig. 6c. Ankle flexibility – 3

Fig. 7. Shoulder flexibility

Fig. 8. Backstroke 'press and pull'

complete arm movement slowly against the resistance of B's hand.

Repetitions: twenty movements each arm.

In the cold winter season we aim to bush walk 100 miles, usually in rugged country and at altitudes of over 2,000 feet. The pace is never less than 3 miles per hour and in mountainous country this can be quite tough. Our longest overnight bush walk has been 37 miles and our fastest forced march has been 13 miles in 2 hours 30 minutes. The value of such exercise is (a) cardio-respiratory, (b) builds up good team spirit, (c) a diversion from general routine, (d) general leg exercise (which is completely ignored in our weight training programme. Ages range from 9 to 20 years.

This set of calisthenic type exercises are standard movements and would ideally suit a group where equipment was not available. There is no doubt, that if done correctly, they will improve (a) flexibility, (b) cardio-respiratory, fitness and in some cases (c) strength. This schedule done three times weekly would be adequate for most. It is compiled to be used in conjunction with Chapter 9, *A Work Programme for a Junior Squad*.

FLEXIBILITY AND STRENGTHENING EXERCISES
(Based upon Kiphuth)

1. Lying on side with bottom arm stretched out on floor beyond head and top of hand on floor opposite shoulder for support. Keep

back arched and ankles pointed, whip single leg up and down in short beats (fifty each side).

2. Sitting position on floor, neck firm, legs apart. Bend trunk forward and downward and raise sitting position (25–50 times).

3. Lie on back with arms stretched overhead. Swing up and over through the sitting position to a forward bend putting hands on each ankle alternately (15–40 times).

4. Sitting position, neck firm, raise the knees alternatively in a follow motion, similar to riding a bicycle (50–100 times).

5. Lying on side with legs together and top hand on floor for support keeping the back arched throughout the exercise, whip the legs backward and forwards alternatively. (Freestyle kick on the side – 100 each side).

6. Sitting position, legs flat on floor and hands on floor at back of hips. Push up to back leaning position and then return to sitting position (30–50 times).

7. Sitting in the hurdle position grasping each ankle, bend trunk sideways and downwards on to extended leg and return to starting position (20–30 times).

8. Lying on back with hips and knees flexed (knees bent) and arms at side. Slowly draw knees to chin and return to starting position. Keep feet off floor (20 times).

9. Lie face downwards, resting on elbows, thighs, legs and top of insteps. Pulling in hard with abdomen and squeezing down hard with buttocks, lift the hips off the floor whilst resting on elbows and forearms (30 times).

10. Sitting, hips firm, or neck firm, or fully extended overhead and clasped and legs stretched out together. Double knee raising and double knee extension to the starting position. Legs are kept off the floor throughout the exercise and the trunk at right angle if possible (20–50 times).

11. Lying, face down with hands clasped and stretched overhead. Raise the head and chest keeping feet on floor and return to starting position (20–40 times).

12. Lying on the back, arms stretched to the sides horizontally, hips and knees flexed with knees above to abdomen. Slowly roll the legs from side to side keeping the thighs and legs close to the body and the arms and shoulders on the floor throughout. Turn the head away from the twist to aid in keeping the shoulders flat (50 times).

13. Sitting position, legs apart and arms spread sideways horizon-

tally. Swing the arms and legs across the midline of the body and then back to the starting position, i.e. crossing of arms and legs (50 times).

14. Lying face down, neck firm, toes pointed. Rotate the pelvis by drawing down with the buttocks and up with the abdomen, then relax. This exercise should first be practised in a standing position with the clasped arms extended overhead (30 times).

15. Sitting position, legs flat on floor and arms in free position hanging at sides of trunk. Raise both legs off the ground as high as possible and touch toes returning to starting position. Keep knees straight, toes pointed, legs off floor throughout movement (50 times).

16. Lying on back with hands on back of neck, raise trunk to half sitting position with trunk in a half twist to the left. At the same time raise the left knee so that the right elbow and left knee touch each other or the elbow passes the knee, then slowly lower the trunk to the floor and extend leg to starting position (15 times each side or 30 times alternately).

17. Sitting position, neck firm, legs flat on floor. Twist the trunk to the left crossing the left leg to the right. Then twist to the opposite side and change the leg movement executing in rhythm with heels on floor throughout the exercise (50 times).

18. Sitting position on floor, legs flat on floor, arms hip firm, neck firm or clasped and extended overhead. Whip legs up and down alternatively in a follow motion from the hips. Legs are off floor throughout movement and arms are kept upright, i.e. backstroke kick (100 times).

19. Lying face downward with arms at sides and palms pressed down on the floor, raise both legs and return to starting position, toes pointed, legs straight (20–40 times).

20. Lying on back, hands at back of neck or free position. Swing the trunk up through the sitting position, then forward and downwards as far as possible, flexing the hips and the knees until the heels are touching the buttocks. Return to the starting position on the floor. When the arms are held on a free position then reach forward as far as possible (30–50 times).

21. Lying face down, arms and legs extended. Whip the arms and legs up and down in rhythm alternatively. Called freestyle arms and legs (200 times).

22. Lying on back with legs together, knees bend and feet on the floor, heels in close to the buttocks and neck firm. Slowly lift the

hips off the floor as high as possible and return to starting position (30–40 times).

23. The body resting on the straightened arms and insteps (not the toes). Single leg raising (20–40 times).

24. Sitting on heels with knees flexed. Bend backwards in extension of the spine and hips until head touches floor. Return to standing position. Arms should assist in support. Knees to stay on floor throughout (20–40 times).

25. Lying on side with the lower arm extended out overhead and the top arm used for support. Keep ankles and knees together and raise both legs sideways and upwards and then return to starting position. Back well arched throughout (25 times each side in rhythm).

26. Lying face down with arms extended out beyond head, with hands, arms and chest and legs as high off the ground as possible, spread arms and legs and return to starting position. Back to be arched throughout (45 times in rhythm).

27. 'Double Movements'. Lying face down with arms fully extended overhead and partner's pressure support on the ankles. Slowly raise arms, head and trunk and return to starting position, keeping arms fully extended (25 times).

28. Lying face downwards with arms folded and forehead resting on hands with support applied to upper back. Slowly raise both legs off floor and return to starting position. Toes pointed, legs straight throughout (25 times slowly and in rhythm).

29. Lying on side with neck firm and legs spread with pressure support at the ankles raise trunk sideways and upwards returning to the starting position (15–30 times each side).

30. Lying on stomach with neck firm and pressure applied to ankles, slowly raise chest and head and swing slowly from side to side (20–40 times).

31. Lying on back with both legs perpendicular and hands on back of neck, firm pressure is applied by partner on the elbows. Slowly swing the legs from side to side through the perpendicular (30–50 times).

32. Lying on the back with arms stretched out overhead and back of hands together. The partner squeezes the back of the hands together with his knees and puts pressure on the elbows to keep them close and straight. Slowly raise knees into chin (40–60 times).

14 A Few Thoughts on Freestyle Sprinting

Sprint records are at last becoming 'respectable' although they are still a long way from the ultimate. At the time of writing they present an exciting challenge to the enthusiastic. We have not yet reached that standard where four or five people are tied on the world mark awaiting freak circumstances in order for one of them to shave a tenth of a second off the record.

The door is still open. Let us analyse the present world record holders for 100 metres freestyle. Dawn Fraser was ahead of her time. Having trained her for twelve years, I realize that, although she was an almost perfect racing machine, she had shortcomings in her training schedules and in her health that must have prevented her from swimming even faster. For example Dawn did not have the use of static exercise machines (exogenies, etc.), she had a low blood count, her turns were not the ultimate and anyway most of her fine swims were recorded with hand touch turns. Training sessions were often missed because of colds, pneumonia, backaches, social obligations (as much as 50 per cent of a week's sessions would be missed at times). So you see there is plenty of scope for improvement. There must be a dozen Dawn Fraser's about who will have the health and the opportunity to fill in the gaps in Dawn's training regime.

Michael Wenden's world title for the 100 metres was made with electronic timing (records a slower time than hand held watches), his turn was perhaps the slowest of all the finalists, his record was created after days of hard racing at altitude (Michael had eleven races in ten days), so you see circumstances could have been more conducive to breaking a world record. Therefore it is a simple matter for us to predict that another 'Wenden' with a faster turn and a fresh body will drop that world mark again, and again. Nevertheless these two great performers have most of the qualities that a coach dreams of in the ultimate pupil.

Logically sprint swimmers should perform their best at an age when their physical and mental development reach a peak, and the sum total of sprinting experience can be called upon. For sundry reasons perhaps social, domestic or the lack of opportunity, a sprinter may never reach a 'peak'.

Male Olympic 100 metres winners are becoming younger, e.g. Walter Riz 1948 (23), Clark Scholes 1952 (22), Jon Henricks 1956 (21), John Devitt 1960 (23), Don Schollander 1964 (17), Michael Wenden 1968 (18), and each four years the Olympic record drops lower. The fact that Olympic sprint heats, semi-finals and finals usually occur within 36 or 48 hours gives an advantage to the younger swimmer who has a greater resilience and recovery capacity. World records are often created by persons older than the reigning Olympic champion under conditions that require only one maximum effort.

Irrespective of the age or the circumstances, one overriding essential cannot be ignored – this is the experience of sprinting. In other words sprinting begets sprinters. Speed is improved by experience in the ability to sprint. To give a faultless all-out effort over 100 or 200 metres with a whip-like start, a faultless turn, perfect stroke mechanics, can only be expected after hundreds of races over the distance. David Dickson's performances at Tokyo in 1964 are an example. Each effort over 100 metres he assures me was 'absolute maximum', but his times for successive swims were 55·1, 54·9, 54·6, 54·1 seconds. Australian sprint stars would be extremely lucky to have a dozen maximum 100 metres races in a year's racing. This is far from adequate. In sprint swimming the movements must be almost instinctive and this is where repetition and experience count. Special skills involving 'natural' movements can be speeded up by practice, whereas it is hard to develop speed in 'unnatural' movements.

Physical Attributes

A pre-requisite for freestyle sprinting is a body type of mesomedial characteristics. It is not essential to be extra tall but the body should have a certain compactness. Strength without over-bulk should be evident even at a casual glance, especially in the upper body. Henricks, Devitt and Schollander all had well developed thighs. The ideal body type in my opinion can be likened to a racing dog. Length and strength in hands and feet are important, but since Wenden has swum as fast as 51·4 seconds for 100 metres with a definite cross kicking action, there is room for investigation in the sprinting leg drive. The upper body muscle groups should present a smooth contour and incidentally some of my fastest sprinters have had smooth skin surfaces. Since about 19 square feet of body surface is involved, this can be an advantage.

A body weight of 168 to 186 pounds has been the range of the last four Olympic 100 metres winners, heights varied between 71 and 73 inches. The sprinter should be endowed with natural speed in his everyday actions. His reflexes must be sharp. He must have a fast reaction time. He should have an innate rapidity of muscular movement, a feature that is only improved minimally by training. Often however, at first glance these features may not be discernible, for instance, Schollander, Spitz and Wenden have an explosive sprint output in the water but in everyday life they would appear to be rather 'quiet'. Wenden even speaks slowly.

Greater Endurance for Sprinters is what we are seeking

Most reasonable swimmers have the speed to cover 30, 40 or 50 metres at a pace that if they could keep going at this same rate would approach or better the National mark for 100 or 200 metres. A failing endurance factor causing diminishing speed over the balance of the distance is the reason we fail. Sprint swimmers need a special kinds of endurance. They need:

(1) Nervous endurance.
(2) Pain endurance.
(3) Fatigue endurance.
(4) Rhythmic, dynamic endurance.
(5) Power endurance.

Nervous endurance is the ability of the competitor to maintain emotional stability under mental strain. The days and hours prior to the important event can be nerve-racking and often disastrous to the swimmer who cannot control his nerves. He will be 'washed out' before he steps on the block.

Pain endurance is the ability of the competitor to maintain or even increase his work output against the build-up of physical and mental pain as the gruelling race proceeds. Some people have a greater tolerance to pain than others. It is this intangible that separates the 'quitter' from the record breaker. The pain endurance factor must also be present in the training work-outs, as Doctor James Counsilman points out in his *Hurt, Pain and Agony Concept* – call it 'grit', call it 'guts' or willpower, without pain endurance you will not succeed. An adage of mine that I continually toss to the team is apt here, 'no pain – no gain'.

Fatigue endurance is mostly physiological and chemical. The body's capacity to dissipate waste gases and work by-products, its ability to buffer spiralling acid levels, to tolerate a rising oxygen debt or to maintain an above-average blood-sugar curve are as a rule, out of our control. Fatigue endurance, or the body's ability to endure prolonged work stress and still maintain a balancing chemical turnover is mostly innate. Diet and training can improve these situations but only minimally.

Rhythmic dynamic endurance is the ability to hold 'form' in the stroke mechanics, below and above the water without any appreciable falling away of technique, throughout the whole race. A percentage of swimmers, especially the young, 'go to pieces' in the final 25 metres of a race when the pressure is at maximum. The finest example I have seen of rhythmic endurance was Dawn Fraser who held perfect form of stroke against all challengers. The only lapse Dawn had was in the concluding stages of the Tokyo Olympics 100 metres final when her stroke rhythm deteriorated under pressure. It was the closest she ever went to being defeated in a sprint.

Power endurance. The ability to control your nerves, hold your stroke, endure pain and fatigue are valuable assets only if you have power endurance. To be able to exert the optimum maximal pressure on each stroke, each leg drive, throughout the whole sprint is the only way to put up a 100 per cent performance. It is no use going through the actions if the power is not applied and maintained. Michael Wenden's sprint performances at the Mexico Olympics were classic examples of power endurance. Every stroke appeared to be full of applied power. It appeared to me that this power endurance manifested itself forcibly in the closing stages of his events when he gradually pulled away from world record holders Ken Walsh (100 metres) and Don Schollander (200 metres).

A 'distance' background. Is it just coincidental or good planning that a greater percentage of Aussie sprint stars have been distance champions in their formative years? In my case it is planned; all our young swimmers train and compete over the longer distances. Australia's greatest sprinters Dawn Fraser, Lorraine Crapp, Ilsa Konrads, Jon Henricks, John Devitt and Michael Wenden have all held titles and/or records for distances of 400 metres or greater. As they reached swimming maturity they have concentrated on the sprint events with outstanding success. In the years prior to 1950 there were a remarkable number of 'speedy squibs' in Australia. Coaches and pupils alike believed that by repeating 25 metre or 33 metre sprints they would achieve sprint success. The pupils had no background of 'over distance speed swims'. Consequently they were extremely fast for the first 50 metres but faded dismally after the turn. Since swimming movements are not 'natural' in the strictest sense, maximum 100 or 200 metre output can only be given by performers who have trained and raced long and hard over the greater distances in the stroke formative years.

A sprinter's aggression – the killer instinct. Do not confuse this with the 'grim determination' of a long distance swimmer – a sprinter's killer instinct is an explosive intangible. His whole being throbs with a controlled fierceness. He will win. Losing never enters his head. He is extremely confident. I feel the attitude can be best summed up by 'famous last words' – Jon Henricks (1956 Melbourne): 'These b—— have a cheek lining up against me. I'll kill them.' Dawn Fraser (1960 Rome): 'Swim in your own lane (so and so). If you get into mine I'll swim right over the b—— top of you'. Mike Wenden (1968 Mexico): 'Stop worrying coach – I'll win'. This 'force' rarely asserts itself in training work-outs but manifests itself in important events. Great sprinters are born with this 'fire' and without it can never be really great. The coaches, by talk and motivation, can induce a pseudo-killer instinct, but if the genuine article is not there in the inherent make-up of the sprinter, then that 1 per cent we look for is missing.

Education – Intelligence. Most male Olympic sprint winners since the end of the war have been University students. In my own group one pupil in three is either a state or commonwealth scholarship winner. From this we may assume that intelligence is a pre-requisite for swimming. My top sprinters are also near the top of their form at school. They are significantly more advanced at school than the distance performers.

Average school marks (all subjects) – 10 sprinters   73·6

Average school marks (all subjects) – 10 distance swimmers 70·7

Boredom. The sprinter has a poor tolerance to long distance training. He can manage say 4,000 metres a session without complaining but his mentality is such that a long or dull programme bores him. The fun or excitement of a sprint series, the challenge of a training relay will enthuse him but suggest a 3,000 metre grind or a series of 400 metre 'repeats' to the older sprinter and he is bored stiff, even rebellious.

Sprinters have a greater amount of innate swimming ability. They are half born, half made. Their output of nervous energy, their resting metabolism is at a higher level than the mile men. Sprinters, because of this fast and high output of energy need to replace it quickly. They must recharge their 'batteries'. They are great sleepers.

Jon Henricks could 'sleep on a barbed wire fence', Wenden and Fraser could sleep heavily through noise and hubbub of an Olympic village even in the middle of the day.

The Stroke for Sprinting. The stroke is covered fully in Chapter 15.

Stroke rates for 50 metres. Of necessity, sprinters have higher turnover of the arms than the distance men. This needs no explanation. Care should be taken to see that the push through is not shortened. Emphasis should be made, that during training, sprinters are to push back to a point 4 inches beyond the leg of their costumes, making sure, however, that they do this by an extension of the arm and hand and not by distorting a straight spine. In training we know this push through as 'flick back'.

At present I am experimenting with a new hand entry for sprinters. The hand is being placed into the water 'little finger first'. The arm does not over reach. The hand is 'cocked' firm at the wrist. The hand 'spades' into the water and there is practically no glide. By placing the hand in 'little finger first' the forearm and hand present a flat surface area to pull with, right from the commencement of the stroke.

The following are the stroke rates for 50 metres from push of Olympic sprint winners during speed – Henricks 52, Devitt 59, Schollander 50, Wenden 56.

Note: Henricks and Schollander are extremely good on a flutter board whereas Devitt and Wenden are not very efficient.

Breathing Patterns. During 'walk backs' I have my sprinters imitate the breathing sequence that they will actually use in the race.

Repeatedly sprinting with your personal breathing sequence eliminates confusion in this department on the day of the big event. I do not believe that the swimmer should go out the first 50 metres with as few breaths as possible, as some coaches advocate. I feel that a premature building of the oxygen debt can have disastrous effects in the final stages, especially in a 200 metres sprint. A pattern I like to use is – dive, 4 strokes, breathe, 4 strokes, breathe, 4 strokes, then normal breathing until the last 7 or 8 metres of the event, where if possible the swimmer goes to the wall without a breath. Wenden in his classic 200 metres Olympic win breathed on every stroke, whereas in the 100 metres breathed as I have outlined.

Distribution of effort in a sprint. Sprint swimmers have not, as yet, reached that stage in overall development where they can maintain a 100 per cent effort all the way. This was demonstrated dramatically at Mexico. World record holder Zorn expended too much energy in the first 50 metres of the Olympic final, leading the field at the turn in 24·4 seconds. He finished last. Wenden, conserving just that little extra reserve energy over the first 25 to 30 metres, was a body length behind at the 50 metre mark, but he finished first with a new world record. Walsh who also controlled his first 50 metres finished a close second.

15 *The Freestyle Strokes*

Note, I said strokes, for there are two freestyle strokes, or at least two distinct sets of features that separate the sprint stroke from that of the distance men. If you saw Wenden win the 100 metres at Mexico and Burton win the 1,500 metres, both in Olympic record time, you will know what I mean. You could never imagine Wenden winning the 1,500 metres with his stroke or conversely Burton winning the 100 metres with his (Burton's) stroke.

The sprint stroke, strangely, has not changed much over the last few decades, except for the period when the Japanese dominated world swimming in the 1930s. Most Olympic sprint champions have been influenced by Weissmuller, and his other principles, consciously or sub-consciously. The main changes have been made in the stroke rate, the leg drive, and the breathing action.

My most successful area of coaching has been in the production of 100 metres freestyle Sprint Champions and I have had Olympic Sprint Champions since 1956. Here are the salient differences between the sprint and the distance stroke.

Body Position

Sprinters, the body rides high, back clear of water, head high with the water breaking about the eyebrows. The legs as a consequence are a little deep, but by arching the back they do not go too deep.

Distance, the body assumes a flat line, with the head much lower, and the feet much higher. There is no back arching.

Recovery

Sprinters. The hand pushes well back to the end of the bathers, but 3 inches shorter than this when sprinting hard. The elbow emerges first and is lifted fairly high but the hand never leaves the water by more than an inch or so. The arm does not swing wide because this would tend to twist the body by giving the hips a side wobble. The arm travels close to the side of the body and enters the water with the thumb in line with the nose. There is no extension of the shoulder. The hand enters the water just before the elbow. At this point the arm is not absolutely straight, a slight bend is maintained at the elbow and wrist. Too much nonsense has been written and spoken about relaxation during the recovery. Certainly there is less tension in the muscles as the arm recovers but you cannot flash over 100 metres in less than 60 seconds with the arms recovering like broken limbs. There is a firmness in the recovery which immediately fuses with power when the arm enters the water.

Distance. The hand has pushed back further than the sprinter; the elbow still emerges first but the elbow is not carried quite so high. The hand is still kept low. The actual entry is made in just a little wide of centre with the arm much longer out in front than that of the sprinter. However, the hand does enter the water before the elbow. There is much less tension in the recovery muscles.

The Stroke
Sprinters. The hand moves down into the first pressure area fairly quickly with emphasis being placed on a cocked elbow and wrist. There is a bending of the elbow but not as much as the distance men, the tendency being to take the arm through straighter and consequently with less shoulder roll, such as Steve Clark, former world record holder used. The hands do cross the centre line. Swimmers such as Wenden, Fraser, Clark and Schollander all pull their hands well across the centre. The hands are pulled through deeper than the distance men. Keep in mind that sprinters as a general rule are stronger physically than distance men and can apply more force to the straight lever. After the hand has passed under the umbilicus it continues its backward push but starts to move out to the side passing under the hip bone and leaving the water about 2 inches wide of the leg.

Distance. The hand enters the water slightly 'longer' than the sprinters. Moras, Windle (Australia) do drop rather 'short' but Meyer, Burton, Kinsella (U.S.A.), Brough and White (Australia) have a slight stretch and the hand does not sink to the first pressure point as quickly or as sharply as the sprinters. In other words there

Fig. 9. THE FREESTYLE STROKE

(a) The working arm should be more than half way through the push as the other hand enters the water

(b) Maintain a high and flat position in the water

(c) As the leading hand presses down, slightly lift the elbow

(d) The arms are now windmilling; that is, the elbows are directly opposite each other

(e) The power of the pull is emphasized by the boomerang shape of the working arm

(f) As the leading hand enters the water the face starts turning smoothly in the bow wave

(g) At the end of the forceful exhalation, the face is in a good position to take in more air

(h) As the recovering arm moves forward the face is returned to the centre, either in time with the hand or slightly in advance of the hand for sprinters. Distance swimmers recover the hand well before the face reaches the centre. This is known as late breathing

is a definite glide. The one thing that impressed me immensely at Mexico was the extremely smooth stroking of Meyer and Burton. Prior to Mexico the fastest 1,500 metres I had seen was a 16 minutes 41 seconds by my distance star Graham White. His stroke is rather hurried. I imagined that to swim under 16 minutes 20 seconds, there would be practically no time for a glide but the smoothness of the hand entry and lack of 'froth and bubble' of the U.S. stars was impressive.

As the glide or 'feel phase' is completed the hand pulls deeper but along the central axis until it is almost under the diaphragm. The elbow is well bent, actually at an angle of about 95 degrees between the upper arm and the forearm (sprinters have an angle of about 110 degrees). At this point the hand moves across the centre line, as the working shoulder drops lower. It is this dropping of the shoulder over the working arm that gives strength and length to the stroke. Konrads, Windle and Windeatt actually pass the hand under the opposite hip. The arm gradually straightens and with a final flick or push the hand leaves the water about 2 or 3 inches below the end of the bathers and some 3 inches wide of the thigh.

The Timing of the Two Arms

Sprinters. This important aspect is determined by the cadence of the leg drive in both sprinters and distance students. As long ago as 1924 Weissmuller had one arm almost completely through the stroke as the other arm entered in front. Weissmuller had a regular six beat kick. Forty-four years later at Mexico City, Wenden had an almost identical timing, the difference being that Wenden has an irregular leg action – a definite cross kick. I advocate that as the leading hand sinks to a point 6 inches below the surface the pushing hand should be nearing the ¾ way mark.

Distance. Murray Rose, Jan Konrads, John Nelson all have the working hand directly under the solar plexus as the recovering hand enters the water. Robert Windle in his distance swims has one arm almost right through the push as the other arm takes the catch; which 'timing' to use depends on the kick action. Those with a leg trail style or a trail and cross leg action usually do best with the arm timing similar to Windle. Those with a regular kick swim best with a timing like Konrads.

The Head action and Breathing Timing

Sprints. Just as the recovery hand enters the water the face turns to take the breath. The head is held high. A considerable bow wave is created by the side of the face and this facilitates the inhalation. Then the face recovers back to the centre, now in time with the other arm which is, of course, recovering. A simple rule is that once the recovering hand reaches a point opposite the side-turned face, the thumb and nose move forward together. Wenden's face is a trifle later than his fast recovering arm, whereas Schollander turns his face into the water a fraction before his hand.

Distance. The head is carried a little lower than the sprinters but surprisingly not that much, the face being just down in the water. If the swimmer is breathing on one side only there is a slightly later timing than the sprinters. That is, the recovering hand enters the water then the face rolls up and out to take the breath. The head recovers a fraction after the new recovering hand passes the face. The cadence of distance swimmers movements allow ample time for very smooth breathing and head techniques. This controlled action gives the swimmer a sense of rhythm and timing for the whole stroke. The distance pupil commences exhaling when the mouth is facing the bottom of the pool. There is a gentle and continuous exhalation, all the air being cleared before the face emerges again. Sprinters use the explosive technique of forcibly exhaling the last of the air just before the mouth emerges, but this is not necessary for the distance swimmer.

THE FREESTYLE START

Prior to getting upon the block the swimmer's thoughts should be firmly fixed upon the action he is about to make. He should take no heed of other competitors. The starter blows his whistle and upon this signal the swimmer steps up on to the back of the block. The starter then commands 'Take your marks'; the swimmer steps up on to the front edge of the block, standing upright, arms dangling by the sides, eyes looking straight ahead. The feet are some 6 to 9 inches apart. The swimmer should have a very firm grip of the block by curling his big and second toes over the edge. He now bends forward from the waist until his hands are hanging loosely at a point some 12 inches above his feet. His knees are slightly bent, his eyes are looking at a point in the water some 3 or 4 metres up the pool. The gun fires and the swimmer first of all swings his arms in an upward movement describing a wide circle with his outstretched arms. The head has dropped down and the knees have assumed a bent attitude.

The tremendous momentum initiated by the circling arms working in conjunction with the pushing power of the legs and feet causes the now leaning forward body to hurtle out over the water. In the circling of the arms take care to keep the elbows almost straight and the fingers fully extended. Keep in mind that as the arms circle, the body leans forward, the centre of gravity alters. Therefore tremendous power must be exerted by the legs to force the heavy upper body into horizontal movement. Just before the arms complete their circle to an outstretched front position, the head is lifted sharply. The swimmer arches his back, his eyes are looking down the pool. He should 'float' through the air in this graceful back arched position for a fraction of a second before he suddenly lowers his head and his hands pierce the water at an acute angle. If the swimmer attempts to get out too far on his flight he will automatically 'jack-knife'. This entry creates great resistance. If the swimmer's trajectory is too low or the upper part of the body too high a feet first entry will result. This too is a faulty entry. I have observed that even amongst the National freestyle champions very little effort is made to have the hands enter the water thumbs touching, and the head well tucked down between the outstretched arms. The disadvantage of entering the water with the hands apart (even 12 inches) and the head slightly raised is considerable. You only have to observe the splash or impact wave created when this is done purposely to know what I mean. Care should also be taken to have the toes pointed back and not hooked during the flight and entry. The body, once it leaves the block until the first stroke, should be firm but not stiff except for that instant when the head is suddenly lifted and the back arched during the flight.

Once the body has entered the water care must be taken not to submerge too deeply, 18 to 20 inches of water over the back would be as deep as I would expect the adult diver to descend. By experience the swimmer should be able to judge the exact instance to commence a narrow flutter kick and the first arm pull and push to propel him to the surface. Tradition has set the pattern that from 3 to 6 narrow flutter kicks are performed rapidly before the first arm stroke is commenced. However, swimmers who are poor at kicking are ill-advised to do this. The present world record holder over 100 metres, Michael Wenden, has a long and slightly piked flight and entry, but derives practically no benefit from his legs in surfacing.

Finally far too many swimmers lift their heads prematurely in the underwater glide and their faces and foreheads cause front resistance and back of the head drag.

To be a great starter is dependent upon the swimmer having superb reflexes and almost automatic response to the starter's gun. United States sprinter Zac Zorn is easily the fastest starter I have ever seen. By the time the finalists in the Men's 100 metres event at Mexico had travelled 15 metres Zorn was 4 feet in front due to his superb reflex condition and starting technique. It was no fluke; I saw this happen three times.

Towards championship time, special gun start sessions should be conducted by the coach. The swimmer is timed from the gun to the 10 metre mark many times, varying his stance, his wind up, his flight and his entry until the stop-watch repeatedly shows which particular combination suits him best. I keep cards on the individual swimmers and by averaging out the timed starts daily it becomes apparent that the swimmer is becoming faster as he repeatedly practises this segment.

Breathing patterns should be individual. Timed trials over 50 metres using various breathing sequences will soon determine the one that suits the swimmer best. The majority of swimmers prefer to restrict the number of breaths they take in the first 25 or 30 metres of a sprint event. The number varies between 3 and 6. Certainly no breaths should be taken on the first stroke after the dive. I prefer the swimmer to become balanced in stroke before the first breath which could be 3, 4 or 5 strokes after he has surfaced. Distance performers go into a regular breathing pattern almost from the beginning of an event. Sometimes 4 strokes are taken without a breath at the commencement of their race.

THE FREESTYLE TURN

Even the very young swimmers are taught the following tumble turn. The fall back turn is not taught but a few do pick it up by imitating. There is no doubt as to the advantage of the tumble because as much as 8/10ths of a second can be gained by its correct execution. It is ironic that Dawn Fraser, world record holder over 100 metres at the time of writing, performed her best times with a fall back turn, but do not be misled, Dawn was always a little 'short of breath'. Pre-race nerves often aggravated an asthmatic complaint and she felt that she did not have sufficient energy coming back the second 50 metres of her event if she tumbled.

Some coaches say that the physical demand in carrying out a tumble robs the performer of energy in the succeeding laps. The answer to this is simply practice, practice, practice until the body adapts to the new stress. Simply, in other words, if you do tumble turns all the time during training it is not stressful to do it during a race.

One adjustment that could be made to swimmers who find it unduly hard to do the tumble during a race is to shorten the length of the glide away from the wall after the turn. Prolonged push offs are more fatiguing than the actual tumble when the oxygen debt is rapidly mounting. To be able to turn efficiently on either side is a distinct advantage for the advanced swimmer. However, there would not be one swimmer in ten at top championship level that can do this. Most swimmers having a 'favourite turning side'. There is no excuse for swimmers nowadays not to be competent in tumble turning because the winter short course season in Australia demands that the pupil perform over 1,500 turns a week in normal training sessions. Under my present training system it is a pre-requisite to tumble all the time in order to be a member of the top training 'chain'.

The Forward Roll Turn

As the swimmer approaches the wall he sights a pre-selected spot either on the wall or on the pool floor which will indicate to him that this is the time to tumble. Most swimmers prefer to be looking forward underwater to the wall. As each arm finishes its push it remains pressed in neatly by the side of the thigh, the head is quickly tucked down on to the chest and the momentum of the body is transferred into a forward roll. This movement is similar to the movement of a diver executing the forward roll in a one-and-a-half dive.

When the body is half-way through the roll, the body is momentarily balanced on the arms and hands which are pressed down. The feet are thrown over towards the wall in a straight, but not stiff, attitude.

As the legs move closer to the wall they bend at the knees so that the feet will touch the wall with bent knees and therefore be able to execute a strong push. As the feet are coming over, the swimmer drops one shoulder; this in turn causes the body to do a half twist, which allows the feet to land on the wall sideways.

The half twist continues as the body is vigorously pushed away from the wall and the body quickly gains a flat position.

Care should be taken to ensure that the turn is done close to the top of the water. A 'deep' turn can be most exhausting as well as time consuming.

16 Backstroke

I believe that backstrokers throughout the world can be separated into two groups: those who ride high over the water like Roland Matthes and those who swim with their head and shoulders well back, as does the Australian champion Karl Byrom. I also believe that in the last 20 years there have only been two classical backstroke champions, David Thiele (Australia) 1956–1960 Olympic Champion, and Roland Matthes (East Germany) Olympic Champion 1968.

These two back crawlers have similar styles and are in a class all on their own. I am sure that men's backstroke records will only be broken by swimmers with a physique and technique similar to these two giants of backstroke.

Briefly, they differ from all other backstrokers because of their natural body position in the water, and I say natural because they do not appear to be struggling to hold their bodies high.

Their heads are held at such an angle that the lobes of their ears are just clear of the water, but what makes the stroke look so polished is the fact that their shoulders and chest ride high out of the water. I have seen Thiele sprint with his body clear of water down to his navel. Their legs are fairly deep into the water and they have powerful kicks. An improvement on their times will come when someone can execute their stroke without too much effort and he can speed up their rather slow stroke rate. Here then is the style I advocate to aspiring backstrokers.

Head Position. The head is fairly high with the eyes looking up The head does not move from side to side. It acts as a pivot point for the shoulders; nevertheless it is not held stiffly. The lobes of the ears can touch the surface of the water when doing basic training, but at any speed at all the chin should be tilted forward into the neck thereby elevating the back of the head.

Body Position. The head being high, it naturally follows that if you keep the body straight the legs will be a little deep. The body lies in the water at an angle. If the top of the head is 8 inches out of the water the toes will be about 12 inches below the surface. There is a minimum of 'piking', but it is hard to stop the tail going down a little. The tops of the shoulders and the chest are clear of the water.

Arm recovery. The hand leaves the water with the little finger slightly leading and the arm straight at the commencement of the recovery. Whereas Thiele used to swing his arms at an angle of 45 degrees to the water, Matthes recovers his very high and straight. This is correct because the vertical recovery does not introduce a lateral hip sway, secondly it allows for a more rapid recovery. During the recovery there is a noticeable slackness of the wrist but otherwise the arms are recovered absolutely straight with the biceps passing close to the ears. As the hand reaches the highest point in the recovery phase the shoulder is rotated slightly and there is a noticeable lifting of the deltoid. This lift and stretch of the arm is then carried on until the hand enters the water, preferably with the little finger first. The hands enter the water at 'five minutes to one'; that is, just a fraction wide of the head. The anatomical structure of the shoulder joint makes it extremely hard to place the hands directly behind the head, so flexibility in the shoulder joint is a desirable asset.

The Entry, Pull and Push

The importance of the first part of the stroke is often underestimated. As the hand is virtually thrown into the water it presents, as soon as possible, a flat position. The arm is then pressed down and almost immediately starts its sideways pull. It should be mentioned here that the working shoulder pivots on the neck and drops lower to give greater strength and support to the pull. The opposite shoulder is lifted at this point to give balance. At this stage the arm is still straight and it is a mistake to bend the arm prematurely. From observation of the world's best, the arm actually drops to a point lower than the back, in other words, about 12 inches deep. The hand is held very firm, the fingers together and the arm pulls straight back until it is at a point just before the shoulder. At this point the arm bends, the elbow drops lower, the hand moves closer to the side of the body and also closer to the surface, some 6 inches deep. The hand and arm now present a boomerang shape and the forearm and hand start pushing back as parallel to the side of the body as possible. The hand continues the push until the arm is straight but just before it straightens fully the elbow rotates and the hand pushes down towards the bottom of the pool. This final push down is a strong flick. This flick was originated by James Counsilman and his pupil Tom Stock, and is a significant advancement on the stroke.

The Arm Co-ordination

One thing is common with all the world's best male backstrokers and this is the co-ordination of the arms. The pushing arm is nine-tenths through its cycle when the recovering arm enters the water. This co-ordination is a little difficult to teach the young because one arm (pushing) is assuming a bent attitude and therefore travels through the water a trifle faster than the older style straight arm pull and push. Observations on Christine Caron and Cathy Ferguson have shown that they have the pushing arm at a point three-quarter's way through, whereas Kaye Hall's pushing arm is closer to that of the males, namely practically right through the push as the opposite arm enters the water.

The Hand Withdrawal

At the end of the flick down, the hand is 2 or 3 inches wide of the thigh. The hand now turns outwards and the little finger emerges from the water first to commence the recovery.

Leg Drive – timing

The world's great backstrokers, Kiefer, Thiele, Monckton, Matthes, Tanaka, Caron, Muir, Hall, have all had strong regular six-beat kicks. The one exception was Tom Stock who had a six-beat kick for 100 metres and an irregular four-beat kick and trail for his 200 metre events.

Roland Matthes has a deeper kick than normal, his legs appear to be well down. This is of course due to his high head and shoulder position. Thiele also had this deep leg drive with super ankle flexibility and the toes being slightly turned in. It is important to remember that the knees should never be lifted high, never break the surface for instance. The secret of a good kick is to be able to initiate the leg drive from the thigh but also to be able to bend the knee so that the lower leg is deep in the water doing most of the work on the upward drive. Not enough importance is paid to leg drive in training sessions. There is only one way to develop a good leg drive – regular kick practice with arms extended behind the head with the fingers interlocked. Be sure to keep the rib cage high during these work-outs and the body stretched out.

The perfectly co-ordinated backstroker will dovetail the leg drive in with the arm action. As the left hand enters the water the right leg has just completed its upward kick and conversely as the right hand enters the left leg is finishing its upward thrust. Four other leg beats function between these two points. Finally remember the leg drive is a narrow one, it has to be to co-ordinate with the arms.

Breathing

It is now a universal practice to breathe in a regular pattern whereas a few years ago there was no planned breathing technique. Most top back crawlers breathe in on the left arm recovery and out on the right arm recovery, or vice versa. The system is good because it ties the co-ordination of the whole stroke together. The swimmer 'feels' co-ordinated. George Haines points out that the jaw should be relaxed to promote ease of breathing and lessen tension in the neck muscles. The amount of air inhaled should not be excessive. It should be a sharp inhalation.

Some important facts

(a) Ankle and shoulder flexibility is an asset.

(b) The world's greatest male backstroke swimmers have been tall, lean men, well over 6 feet.

(c) The backstroke race, because of the start, lends itself to equal lap swimming.

(d) Backstroke is the best stroke for pupils with asthmatic, bronchial or breathing complications.

(e) Backstroke is the easiest of all strokes to teach to the young, once the fear of being on the back is overcome.

CHRISTINE CARON

(An evaluation written in 1966 but still of practical interest.)

Former world record holder, Christine Caron (France) has an almost faultless style for a girl. Her racing start is the finest I have seen.

Here are details of Christine and her training:

BEST TIMES: 25 metres – 14·4
             50 metres – 30·5
           100 metres – 1·07·9
           200 metres – 2·28·6

Brief History

Christine has been training for seven years since the age of 10. She started as a freestyle swimmer but only had medium success. She is a member of the Racing Club of France. She does most of her training in a 25 metre indoor pool in Paris. She is coached by Madame Berlioux, who also coached her daughter, Monique, to the French backstroke titles for 12 successive years from 1941 to 1953.

Physique

Mlle Caron is very firmly built and in the last 12 months (1965–66) has put on to my reckoning, about 10 pounds (4·5 kg.). At present she weighs 63 kg. (140 lb.) and raced at Tokyo at 61 kg. (135 lb.) where she finished a fingernail second to Cathy Ferguson (U.S.A.).

Christine is 1 metre 70 cm. high (5 feet 7 inches). She has broad, solid shoulders similar to Dawn Fraser and she is small busted. She would be a 38–24–36 girl. She has short hair about 1 inch below her ears and she wears a cap. Her legs are firm and solid.

Body Position

If anything is wrong with Christine's style it is her body position. In my opinion, her rear end, especially her feet, are far too deep, obviously because of her head position. Her body lies at an angle of about 10 degrees below the water, taking her ears as the pivot point. (This is an observation from the side of the pool and therefore hard to judge.) Her lower legs and feet are deep and in a swim of 100 metres in 1·15·0 she will not create any above-water disturbance with her feet.

In the Tokyo Olympic final (1·07·9) her feet came level with the surface and her 'froth and bubble' was about 12 inches high. The rest of her body position remained the same.

Head position

Christine's head is carried a fraction higher than normal. It is held very firmly in place, not stiffly. It moves slightly from the central position on each stroke. The lobes of her ears are just clear of the water. Water never breaks across her face.

Arm Recovery

The arms are carried very high, similar to Duenkel and Ferguson (U.S.A.). The biceps pass within an inch or so to the side of the face. They recover very fast. At the top of the recovery they speed up and actually smash into the water in a 100 metres effort. The arms stretch well back and the hands are loose at the wrists. The hands enter the water right behind the head, that is, in line with her ears. At the moment of hand entry the shoulder is well into the water. Her little finger breaks water first, cutting in to make a hole for her hand that comes down like a blade.

Shoulder Reaching

Christine's shoulders are not as active as the two American champions, Ferguson and especially Duenkel throw their shoulders right back. Christine's arms more or less smash into the water in a natural position. She does not over reach.

Entry and Pull

Christine's arm work is really effective. The hand on entry, pushes straight down into a spot some 4 to 6 inches below the surface. Her 'working shoulder' drops down with it. She immediately starts to pull. Her hand has entered right behind her ear and for about 12 inches of hand-pull her arm is straight. However, well before her hand is level with her shoulder, she has 'cocked' her elbow (bent it) down deeper. Her arm position now resembles a 'boomerang'. Her hand (at shoulder level) passes her body at a point 16 inches wide of her body and about 5 inches deep. Her hand presents a really wonderful flat pulling and pushing surface. Her arm action is very similar to Graef or Mann (U.S.A.).

The Push

Christine has adopted a modified version of the *'push down'* originated by Tom Stock and now carried on by Mann and Graef (all Americans). When her hand is at lower-rib level it still maintains its very flat pushing surface but it moves in closer to the body. The elbow is still bent. At the waist level her hand is 8 inches away from her side. As it pushes further back her hand moves in closer to her thigh. When it has almost reached the end of its push the thumb turns in towards the thigh and the palm of the hand pushes *down* towards the bottom of the pool. At this point, of course, the arm is practically straight.

Arm Withdrawal

Her hands leave the water in two positions; (200 metres 2·28·6) the hands were being withdrawn exactly midway between the bottom of her bathers and her knee joint, that is, about 8 inches above her knee; in her shorter sprint (100 metres in 1·08·7) the stroke rate is higher and consequently the hands do not push back so far. They withdraw from the water about 10 inches from the knee joint. Her hands appear, when sprinting, to leave the water almost back of the hand first. They flick out very fast, the same as Cathy Ferguson's.

The Co-ordination of the Two Arms

Thompson Mann and Jed Graef (U.S.A.) have the 'working' arm 9/10ths of the way through the stroke when the recovery arm enters the water. Christine's 'working' arm is about three-quarters of the way through the stroke, that is, well into the final push stage, when her other arm smashes into the water behind her head. Both arm cycles are identical. Her stroke is well balanced.

Breathing

She carries her mouth partly open frequently during the race and she appears to inhale when the left arm is right at the top of the recovery. She exhales on the recovery of the right arm.

Leg Drive

Very powerful, very low, very rapid, describes Christine's kick. It is a conventional one with the knees always down. The lower leg is carried very low and of course her feet never break the surface. She 'toes in' a little but not excessively. Her knees never 'roll over' the centre line. Her lower leg drive is very rapid. That is, below the knee joint, her shins and feet angle down rather sharply and do kick very rapidly.

Warm-up

She does: (a) 400 metres of basic work on her back.

(b) 100 metres of back kick, arms extended overhead.

(c) 2 sprints of 15 metres out of the blocks.

(d) 1 sprint of 25 metres (timed).

(e) 3 or 4 turns.

(f) 50 metres slow backstroke then out.

This warm-up was done one hour before the race.

Splits and Stroke Rate in Races

Splits	35·3	1·13·9	1·53·6	2·33·0
Strokes	51	52	53	52
Splits	15·5	32·9	50·5	1·08·7
Strokes		52		54

Proportion of Strength

100 metres arms only (legs tied)   1·20·0 best time

100 metres kick (arms extended overhead)   1·24·0 best time

Annual Progression

Age	100 *metres*	200 *metres*
12	1·22·2	
13	1·19·0	
14	1·12·4	2·36·6
15	1·09·6	2·32·1
16	1·07·9	2·29·6
17	1·08·6	2·28·8

CATHY FERGUSON

The 1964 Olympic Champion and former world record holder, Cathy Ferguson, is a rather tall girl with short-cropped hair. Below the waist she is a little heavier than normal especially the upper thigh and around the knees. The upper legs are slightly similar to a cyclist's musculature. The calves are thick like Tanaka's but not so much so. Her body weight is about 10 stones 10 pounds. She is 5 feet 8 inches tall.

Characteristics

Coach Daland told me that 'she deserves any success that comes her way because of the way she attacks her training, and her consistency. Rather weak above the waist, he explained, *she is one of the few kids in the team who will rattle off 2,000 pulleys each night. She swims crawl in every 1,500 metre event she can get in except the National final 'just to keep up her endurance'.* She swims all strokes well and I put this down to the fact that we make our squad do plenty of medley work.'

Here are her annual best times.

Age	100 metres long course	200 metres long course
14	1·10·8	2·34·9
15	1·09·1	2·30·9
16	1·07·7	2·27·4
	(W.R.)	(W.R.)
17	1·08·1	2·28·0

Body Position

Cathy 'sits' slightly in the water but in a fairly normal line. Her knees never break the surface and from side observation they appear to be slightly higher than the hips. Her upper body is not too high out of the water and I suppose her chest and shoulders would be 2 inches above water level. Even when sprinting hard her body does not lift noticeably.

Head Position

Her head sits in a natural position with the waterline breaking across the lobes of her ears. The head is not held too high or back too far on each arm stroke. The head *sometimes* moves a little from left to right.

Arm Recovery

At the end of her stroke Cathy's recovering arm 'flicks' out fairly fast. This appears to be done intentionally and the arm recovers rapidly when sprinting. Her arm carries straight and high describing a perfect semi-circle. The arms are never wide of the body line and if anything tend to recover slightly over the body. As her arms near the water the fingers are slightly fanned. Her little finger leads first into the water. As with a lot of backstroke swimmers, Cathy's hand, when about 6 inches from the water, because of poor flexibility, angles slightly outwards. Her hands enter the water wider than normal.

Shoulder Reaching

Just before entry Cathy's upper arm and shoulder slightly over-reach backwards. In other words, the arms do not drop into the water in a natural way but appear to be stretching back.

Entry and Pull

Cathy's hand on entry slips slightly sideways missing just a little of the catch. After the hand has travelled about 6 inches it then presents a very flat area to the water. At this point the hand is about 6 inches below the surface. There is a bending of the forearm as the working shoulder drops into a strong position. Virtually all of the pull is with a straight arm and of course rather wide. Cathy's working arm is rather deep and when her hand is directly opposite the line of her shoulders it appears to be about 12 inches deep.

The Push

Cathy continues the arm action with an almost straight push to the side but fairly deep. The hand pushes well through and squeezes against the thigh midway between the knee and the hip. She does not use the push-down of Thompson Mann. Cathy's stroke is one that requires great strength and endurance if maximum speed is to be obtained over 100 metres or 200 metres. No doubt the fact that she does 2,000 pulley movements each night after training has a great bearing on her strength. Personally I consider her arm action outdated. If I am correct the harnessing of the power of Cathy Ferguson to an ideal arm stroke would further reduce the world records.

The Co-ordination of the Two Arms

The world record holders in men's backstroke are 9/10ths through their working arm stroke when the opposite arm enters the water. This of course is due to the fact that the bent arm push is very quick through the water. In Cathy's position, however, when one arm is entering the water the working arm is at a point past half-way and near to the three-quarters mark. The same situation is true when the arms are reversed.

The Withdrawal of the Hands

At the finish of the push against her thigh, Cathy's thumb leads out of the water but the hand is quickly turned over so that the little finger leads into the 'flick' recovery.

Leg Drive

If you have seen Japan's Tanaka kicking you will have a good idea of the action used by Cathy. She bends the lower leg very noticeably down into deep water while the upper leg only has a range of about 6 inches. Her foot would move through an area of at least 2 feet. She has a regular six-beat drive and when sprinting hard her feet come reasonably close to the surface leaving a trail of foam. She does not roll her knees across her body to any marked degree.

Breathing Pattern

Cathy very noticeably breathes in on her left arm stroke and out on the right every time.

Warm-up

Cathy's warm-up for competition is typical of the Daland school. The following is her preparation for racing:

Warm-up at 2.45 p.m.

1st race, 3.20 p.m.

300 metres freestyle in 4·30·0 at a fair speed but resting sometimes.

200 metres freestyle kick on a board at 53–54 seconds per lap.

200 metres freestyle at 45 seconds per lap with some stops.

5 minutes of fooling around with turns, backstroke starts and 10 metre bursts in all styles.

4 sprints each of 50 metres with 30 seconds rest between each sprint.

Times were:
50 metres butterfly	34·7
50 metres backstroke	34·7
50 metres breaststroke	44·0
50 metres freestyle	31·6

After 200 metres slow freestyle then 50 metres backstroke in 33·6.

Splits and stroke counts (over 200 metres at 100 per cent)

Splits	34·7	1·12·8	1·51·0	2·29·2
Strokes	51	51	53	56

Splits and stroke count (over 100 metres at 100 per cent)

Splits	15·7	33·6	51·3	1·09·0
Strokes		54		55

THE START

The rule on backstroke starting states, 'Competitors shall line up in the water facing the starting end with the hands resting on the end or the rail of the bath, or starting grips. The feet, including the toes shall be under the surface of the water. Standing in the gutters is prohibited. At the signal for starting they shall push off and swim upon their backs throughout the race. The hands resting on rails or end of bath must not be lifted before the signal of starting.'

The swimmer 'sits' comfortably in the water, the toes level on the wall just below the surface. The hands grip the starting rail at shoulder width, the arms are straight, the head is tilted slightly forward. Pushing pressure supplied along the toes but the bulk of it being in the vicinity of the big toe. The majority of the Olympic finalists had their feet level but some seem to think that there is less chance of slipping if one foot is placed on the wall lower than the other. The head moves forward and then the arms are thrown back in a vigorous up and sideways movement. At the same time the head is thrown back. Since a head weighs about 10 lb., considerable advantage can be gained by the correct execution of the head movement.

The hips are lifted as the arms pass to the side of the body, there is a slight arching of the back but it is imperative not to arch too great or the swimmer will dive too deep.

A good backstroke start is a combination of four points:

(a) The vigorous throwing back of the arms and head.

(b) The arching of the back correctly.

(c) Great pushing power applied by the feet.

(d) Straightening of the legs that will hurl the body away from the wall.

Only practice will dovetail these essentials into a smooth movement. As the body is thrown out over the water, the hands enter the water first, immediately followed by the back of the head and shoulders. A clean entry is essential and if you are fortunate enough to have a long lean body like Roland Matthes, you can gain a lot

Fig. 10. THE BACKSTROKE START. (a) A firm but comfortable grip should be made with the hands and the feet. The toes should be in a slip proof position ready for the tremendous push. (b) The hands and head are thrown back simultaneously

(c) By throwing the arms around instead of over, the body does not submerge too deep. (d) Do not arch the back excessively. Do not throw the head back too far

(e) A fairly flat entry is desirable. The position of the head usually determines this

from your streamlined plunge. The body submerges to a point where there is 12 inches of water above the chest. Deeper than this is too deep. The body glides through the water in a straight firm position, but care should now be taken not to arch the back. The head should be tilted back so that the ears are covered by the bicep muscles. When the body has reached a point in the glide when the swimmer feels that his momentum is about to decrease, vigorous kicking movements commence. There are usually 4 to 6 kicks depending on personal preference, and as the third kick is executed one arm is pulled through the complete pull-push cycle while the other arm is extended beyond the head. When the leading hand has reached the end of the push the second hand starts to pull through the water. Care should be taken to see that the body enters the water at an acute angle, not flat. A flat entry or a heels first entry causes tremendous resistance. A smooth trajectory can be governed by the position of the head as the body glides. If the head is held up the body will pop to the surface prematurely. If the head is held back too far the body will sink too deep. I advocate that the swimmer should pull back with the strongest arm first, and no inhalations be made for the first four strokes.

THE BACKSTROKE TURN

'Any competitor leaving his normal position on the back before his foremost hand has touched the end of the course for the purpose of turning or finishing shall be disqualified.' – Extract from *Australian Swimming Union Handbook*.

To be efficient in the backstroke turn the swimmer must,

(a) Approach the wall with confidence.

(b) Quickly place his feet on the wall where his hand has been.

(c) Push off from the wall with a minimum of resistance.

(d) Surface along the ideal trajectory.

(e) Start the stroke without loss of momentum.

There is no doubt in my mind that David Thiele won his 1956 and 1960 Olympic gold medals for backstroke by executing the turn I am about to describe. At Rome, Thiele went into the turn 3 feet behind the leader and came out 3 feet in front. The American had executed an excellent turn but Thiele had performed a magnificent one.

As the swimmer approaches the wall he may, at about the 4 metre

Fig. 11. THE BACKSTROKE TURN

(a) As the leading hand approaches the wall, the head emerges

(b) The pressure of the finger-tips on the wall initiates the body roll

(c) The knees are now tucked toward the chin

(d) The feet are thrown over vigorously as the body changes its direction

(e) The body flattens out as the feet are placed on the wall, ready for the vigorous push

(f) The arms are stretched overhead as the knees straighten

mark, quickly glance over his shoulder in order to judge his relative position to the wall. This glance is just a quick one and no interference should be made to the stroke rate. Let us assume you prefer to turn on the left. When the head is about a metre from the wall, the recovering right arm reaches back and across the body, that is the right hand is placed on the wall directly behind where the left shoulder should be. Some swimmers hit the wall with a straight arm, some prefer the arm to be slightly bent. Just as the hand is about to touch the wall the left shoulder drops sharply and the upper half of the body does a quick half twist. The face is now facing into the wall and the chest is facing towards the bottom of the pool. The fingertips have been placed fairly deep, perhaps 12 inches below the surface. Care should be taken not to roll the body and especially the hips off the back position until the hand has touched the wall. The momentum of the body carries forward and is transferred into the half twist, causing the legs to flip over until the feet land on the wall with the toes pointing up. The feet should land at a point some 12 inches below the water line close to where the hand has been. The hands at this stage are tucked along the side of the face. The legs straighten, the toes push and the body is forced away from the wall with the arms extended out overhead. The body should aim to be completely streamlined, the head being tucked neatly between the arms and the toes pointed. As the body leaves the wall a narrow but rapid vigorous kick propels the swimmer to the surface. The swimmer should practise until he can surface and commence stroking at a point before his momentum starts to decrease.

Items worth including in this session of training should be:

(a) To be able to turn efficiently on either hand.

(b) To have your turns timed so that you may discover the turning procedure that suits you best.

(c) Whenever possible do your warm-up in your race lane and practise turns at race pace.

(d) Some swimmers find it advantageous to apply resin to their hands and feet in order to be certain of a better grip on the starts and turns.

17 Butterfly

A Few Thoughts

At the time of writing Australia is extremely short of top flight butterfly swimmers – with one exception, Lyn McClements of Perth, who won the Olympic title at Mexico. A few years ago we were either number one or number two nation in the world on this stroke. What has happened? The answer is very simple. Our butterfly exponents are not working hard enough. Certainly not as hard as they did in the years prior to 1960. I have seen Kevin Berry do this programme:

(a) 440 yards loosening up swim.

(b) 32 × 55 yards 'fly sprints at 90 per cent effort, with 10-second rest intervals.

(c) 440 yards dolphin kick for time.

(d) 16 efforts of 220 yards 'fly, one every 4 minutes, aiming for 2 minutes 50 seconds each.

(e) Finish off with 20 minutes non-stop butterfly arm action in a rubber harness fixed to the side of the pool.

This schedule was not an exception, it was an average work-out. I have seen Kevin so tired that he could hardly lift himself from the pool. Coach Don Talbot knew that this was the type of training needed to win an Olympic title – which he did in world record time. No one trains as hard as this on butterfly in Australia today, and this is where we are falling down.

By concentrating upon the principles outlined in this chapter and trying to recapture the work patterns set by Talbot, Hayes and Berry I have been seeing if this era of youngsters can take the work. They can. Jeffrey Van de Graaf, 8 years, covered 100 metres 'fly in 78 seconds. His 50 metres is 36 seconds. He leads a young school of butterfly swimmers in Melbourne who are not afraid to work.

Lyn McClements improved 4 seconds over 100 metres – a phenomenal amount, between her National win (February) to her Mexico win (October) simply because she worked harder than she had ever worked before. We must recapture that Kevin Berry attitude, failure is not falling down – it's staying down.

A Good Way to Start

Young butterflyers placed on kick boards with swim flippers and set 800 metres of dolphin kick to do twice a day will conquer the mysteries of the body wave and flutter very quickly. The major point is to keep the legs reasonably straight, so that the propulsion emanates from the hip and thigh area. Once the kick has become effective and automatic the pupil can devote all concentration to above the waist movements.

Body Position

If breaststroke demands a 'flat' body position butterfly demands it much more. Every effort must be made to keep the body high and flat during the stroke. Dragging legs or dropped hips will retard forward movement drastically. But as is usually the case a dropped rear end emanates from the shoulder and/or head position. Keep the centre of gravity well forward by keeping head and shoulders comfortably low on the water and the hips up. Actually the hip drop is too much emphasized by some coaches. The hips should be flat and later in the stroke (the downward kick movements) they should lift up. They do not drop at all.

The arm action (Recovery)

The arms leave the water at hip length when racing, but further back when training. They then recover along the water's surface, very straight and low, until they form a straight line with the shoulders. At this point the forearms bend slightly forward and the hands become cupped. The hands enter the water thumbs first directly in front of the shoulders, that is about 15 inches apart. The arms, especially the hands, are free of tension during recovery.

The pull

As soon as the hands enter the water they commence a definite sideways movement very similar to breaststroke. They are about 6 inches below the surface. This side movement is a balancing feature

of the stroke. Almost immediately the hands start to press downwards, there is a lifting of the elbows and the powerful shoulder
rotators take over. The arms have assumed a boomerang shape and
they describe what is commonly called the 'hour glass' or 'key hole'
pattern. The hands pull and then push directly under the body,
some 15 to 18 inches below the chest. The hands pass close to each
other, about 6 inches apart. Important things to watch are (a) keep
the elbows up (dropped elbows cause great loss of pulling power);
(b) the shoulders should be kept 'square' – do not drop them deep.

The push

From the moment the hands pass under the chest the pull
becomes a pushing action and great care must be taken to have the
palms and the flat underside of the forearm present as much pushing
area as possible. The hands continue their backward thrust staying
flat against the water as long as possible, until they become straight
and ready for recovery. Arms pulled through too wide will cause
upset in the 'timing' of the stroke, arms pulled through too close to
each other will give great power but only for a short period, the
shoulder girdle will fatigue, neck muscles 'tie up' and the swimmer
will have difficulty completing 100 metres let alone 200 metres.

The timing of the inhalation

When the arms are a little more than three-quarters way through
their underwater action, well into the push section, the face is
smoothly forced from the water. A lot of authorities advocate that
the pupil's chin should not leave the water. This is a good point in
training but during a race it is hard to control. Kok, McClements,
Robie and Berry all lift their chin about 2 inches above the water
line when sprinting hard.

As the face is lifted out, air is inhaled sharply through the gaping
mouth. The face stays out until the arms are in the recovery stage.
Just before the arms reach level with the shoulder line the face is
dropped into the water in advance of the recovering arms. The face
and head drop fairly low and this, plus the momentum of the
recovering arms, create a lunging movement which assists and
initiates the peculiar undulation body movement.

Exhalation does not commence immediately but as the hands are
passing under the chest. Remember it is the final hard thrust back

Fig. 12. THE BUTTERFLY

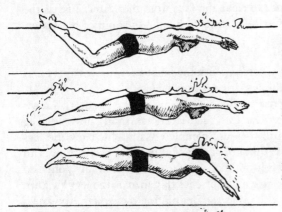

(a) This demonstrates the power that can be derived from the forceful downward action of the lower limbs

(b) The downward kick is amplified by the lifting of the hips

(c) As the arms take the pressure, the elbows are noticeably lifted

(d) As the arms pull underneath the stomach, the fingers almost touch

(e) This drawing demonstrates the tremendous propulsion that will be gained as the forearms push back and the legs drive down

(f) By co-ordinating the downward kick with the backward push of the forearms, the face is forced clear of the water and inhalation occurs

(g) It is important to drop the face back into the water well before the recovering arms reach the entry position

of the hands that tends to clear the face from the water. Just as the fast starting of a power boat tends to lift the bow out of the water.

The kicking action

From a straight leg position, with the heels a few inches apart and the hips held high, the leg drive commences.

The hips slightly rise as the knees bend down about 15 inches deep into the water. The legs then straighten and the lower leg drives down hard until they are completely straight. Now the legs are forced up towards the surface. Flexibility of the ankle joint is an advantage in this fish-tail-like action. The essential point to remember is that the hips and buttocks stay firm as the legs kick up. Conversely, the hips rise up in the undulating movement, the knees bend down and the straightening of the lower leg follows immediately. Some very fast 50 metre times are now being produced by swimmers who are minimizing the undulation of the lower body, that is swimming with a fairly straight leg dolphin kick.

More about the kick

Breaststroke kick is still allowable but is far too inefficient to be taken seriously by keen butterfly students. In dolphin the kick is usually the strongest but at speed the second kick should be emphasized to lift the lower body up into a more streamlined position. Attention should be paid to pupils who tend to trail legs during practice sessions. I have seen several stars completely lose form by having 'lazy legs' during training. These pupils revert to this poor habit during a race by becoming 'arms only' swimmers. They never do well.

The Arm and Leg Co-ordination

Beginners often experience some difficulty in dovetailing the kicking and arm actions. A fair amount of practice is necessary to 'fix' the stroke timing, but without proper timing no real speed can be obtained.

(a) As the hands enter the water and perform their sideways movement the legs execute the first vigorous downward kick and the hips rise.

(b) As the hands move under the stomach the heels rise to the surface. The knees are bent.

(c) When the hands are in the last part of the push, say 9 inches before the end of the stroke, the second downward leg drive is executed. This second leg drive tends to force the body forward, aids in the arm recovery and most important of all forces the face up clear of the water ready for inhalation.

Therefore remember one downward kick as the hands sink for the catch and the second downward kick as the hands are finishing the push.

Even Energy Distribution

Going too slow in butterfly can be nearly as bad as going too fast. The pupil, by repeated trials, should know his capabilities. The concluding stages of a butterfly race can be agonizing to swim and for the coach to watch, if the pace has been too fast, too early. For in no other stroke does one tend to 'go to pieces' as badly as in butterfly. In 1964 Kevin Berry swam 100 metres in 58 seconds. It was a flawless swim and it emphasizes even energy output. He covered the 50 metres in 28 seconds with 17 strokes, and the second 50 metres in 30 seconds with 20 strokes. His best times were usually made by 'sitting behind' in the early stages of a race.

Breathing Patterns

The world's fastest swims have been made by butterflyers breathing on every stroke, this includes the 100 yards and 100 metres. Some Australian and American authorities advocate breathing every two strokes. I personally feel that a better stroke cadence and a 'firmer' stroke can be obtained by breathing every stroke. Lyn McClements won her Olympic title by breathing 'as she liked' down the first 50 metres, which was: dive, 4 strokes, breathe, 4 strokes, then breathing on every stroke all the way.

Training Drills

(a) Arm actions can be technically improved and considerably strengthened by swimming with a kick board held between the thighs and working arms only.

(b) The undulating body movements can be improved by having students push off underwater and propel themselves forward with arms extended out in front. Although only 15 metres or so will be covered the 'feeling' of the movement will be quickly learnt.

(c) By harnessing the pupil to the side of the pool with a length of rubber rope and repeating the arm movements, greater endurance can be built up.

(d) Doing the leg action in a supine position without a kick board can aid in learning the kicking skill.

BUTTERFLY STARTS AND TURNS

'When touching at the turn or on finishing a race the touch shall be made with both hands simultaneously on the same level, with the shoulders in the horizontal position.'

'At the start and at the turn and also during a race when a swimmer is in the underwater position he may be allowed to make one or more leg kicks.' – *Australian Swimming Union Handbook.*

I have timed butterfly swimmers over short distances – say 10 or 15 metres – and found that the majority of them are faster if they dive fairly flat on to the surface of the water and commence the butterfly swimming action immediately, that is their bodies do not submerge or perform the body wave whilst surfacing. I have found the same applies to the breaststroke start and although this system has a high toll on the energy at the beginning of an event it is worth investigating further.

The butterfly stance on the starting block is identical to the freestyle. The take-off is similar but the entry is deeper than a freestyle but not as deep as breaststroke. Eighteen inches would be a reasonable depth to commence the body wave for races of 50 or 100 metres. A slightly deeper entry and a longer body wave action is permissible for races over 200 metres. Care should be taken to keep the head well down as the body projects through the water. A lifted head will cause the body to rise to the surface prematurely and usually at an awkward angle.

The correct number of body wave/dolphin kick combinations to be performed is a matter for individual testing, but usually two or three vigorous dolphin kicks are sufficient to force the head fairly close to the surface. Just before the head does break the surface the arms commence the pull and push action. This movement however should be extremely narrow. This coupled to a powerful leg drive propels the body up to the surface with great speed, the arms being then by the sides ready to perform the first over-the-water action.

Most swimmers do not take a breath upon surfacing but are content to take the advantage of the initial speed of the dive to get them balanced. Breathing patterns over the first 25 metres of a 100 metre race vary with individuals. I have seen world, Olympic and Australian records made with breathing patterns such as these:

Dive, 3, breath, 3, breath, 3, then regular breathing.

Dive, 4, breath, 4, breath, 2, breath, 2, then regular breathing.

Dive, 6, breath, 4, breath, 4, breath, 4, then regular breathing.

Which pattern set suits you best can only be ascertained by a series of tests against the stop-watch.

Turns

The correct approach to the wall needs fine adjustment, for the swimmer who can have his body in such a position that when he throws over his arms they reach the end of the pool in a straight and comfortable position will have a tremendous advantage over the competitor whose arms are foreshortened as they touch the wall, or whose hands miss the wall completely. Only by regular practice at racing speed and by adjusting the length of the last few strokes can the swimmer become consistent at this. For as important as it is at the turn it is doubly so at the finish. How many races have you seen where the swimmers' heads are level at the finish but A has thrown his arm forward in the normal rhythm of his stroke, but B is half a stroke away from the end of the pool?

As the hands touch the wall the knees are bent up under the stomach and the feet land on the wall about 18 inches below the surface (as in breaststroke). Just before the feet land on the wall, however, the swimmer drops one shoulder and the side of his face deeply into the water and at the same time throws his other arm over similar to the fall back turn of the freestyle. As the upper body submerges quickly it assumes a flat position with the hands placed by the side of the head. The toes have assumed a natural position on the wall, that is toes down and with a tremendous drive the knees are straightened and propel the body forward. At this moment the arms stretch forward. Usually only one major and one minor dolphin kick is executed before the arms are vigorously pulled back in the narrow butterfly movement. The head should now be surfaced and the arms ready to flick forward in their first over-the-water movement.

H

18 Breaststroke

The following rules apply to breaststroke. No doubt breaststroke swimming would be faster and more exciting if some of the rules could be modified or eliminated. For the purpose of this chapter the following descriptions fall within the rules as set out by the *Australian Swimming Union Handbook*. They are:

1. Both hands must be pushed forward together from the breast on or under the surface of the water and brought backward simultaneously and symmetrically with lateral extension.

2. The body must be kept perfectly on the breast and both shoulders in line with the surface of the water.

3. The feet shall be drawn together with knees bent and open. The movement shall be continued with a rounded and outward swing of the feet bringing the legs together. All movements of the legs and feet shall be simultaneous and symmetrical and in the same lateral plane.

Personal motivation

Prior to 1964 my pupils did not have much success as breaststrokers at National level. In 11 years of coaching (1953–1964) my pupils had won 62 National titles, but only four had been breaststroke. I disliked teaching the stroke and did not encourage it within my squad. I decided to study the stroke and plan a sensible work schedule for my breaststrokers. The plan was a success.

In 1965 my pupils won six National Breaststroke Titles and in 1966 we gained another four firsts, etc., etc.

The evolution of breaststroke has reached an exciting phase. The streamlining of the stroke mechanics introduced by Dr James Counsilman and Chester Jastremski have been the prime reason breaststroke has become a fast and interesting stroke. Only one

Australian, top flight swimmer Judy Playfair, so far has managed to include all of the Indiana principles in her stroke. She is the Australian record holder.

Former Olympic champion and world record holder, Ian O'Brien, has an almost faultless style and is a great example for Australian youngsters to copy.

Although I realize that certain body types are best suited to certain strokes, I do not limit my thoughts on the matter because I have seen all body shapes, except the endomorphs, perform well at championship level. One thing is evident, however, male breast-strokers of today have to be strong above the waist. O'Brien is a strong man, Jastremski, although not tall is very strong and compact, McKenzie is well proportioned and extremely strong. Today's breaststrokers obtain almost as much propulsion from above the waist movements as from the movements below. The Australian women breaststrokers at Mexico even though they were young; for example Joanne Barnes (13 years), Judy Playfair (14 years) and Sue McKenzie (17 years), were very compact and had great strength 'built in'. The Russian breaststrokers, both male and female, looked strong.

Here is a description of today's speedy breaststroke.

The Body Position

One should aim to keep the body very high in the water and very flat. This is where superior flotation is an advantage. Jastremski is a non-floater, and incidentally has poor flexibility. It therefore follows that his best efforts should be over the shorter distances where power is the major necessity.

The heels should be high enough so that on the thrust back they almost break the surface. You should aim for a level line through the shoulders, buttocks and heels. This position whilst giving the swimmer enough water to work in efficiently, reduces the resistance problem to a minimum when arms are fully extended the knuckles should be some 3 to 5 inches deep. During a sharp sprint the shoulders will ride up a little but at all times the chin is kept on the water line. During the forward glide the face drops into the water but the back of the head must be clear in order to avoid disqualification. Testing has shown that a horizontal body, with the face in the water has less drag or resistance when pulled through the water, than one in which the face rides clear of the water.

The Arm Stroke

From a fully extended arm position in which the shoulders are allowed to stretch forward, the hands glide for a short period with the palms facing down. At the end of the glide the hands immediately turn out so that they are back-to-back. There is a 'cocking' of the wrists providing firmness and power for the commencement of the pull. At this point the arms and hands are some 4 inches below the surface. A major fault can now develop if care is not taken. The hands on straight arms commence a downward and backward pull. But under no circumstances drop the elbows. Dropped elbows will cause a negative pull in which the water is not held but allowed to slip away.

The arms continue a backward and downward movement but start to bend and assume a boomerang shape. The hands are about 12 inches wide of the body and now at their deepest point, perhaps 2 feet deep. They should have executed a powerful movement in which the aim is to pull the body through the water, not over it. Too many students make the mistake of forcing their shoulders up out of the water causing the lower body to drop or an excessive arch of the back.

The elbows do go back beyond the shoulder line but the hands do not. They are tucked under the chin with the palms slightly facing up. Do not tuck the elbows on to the ribs, this causes round shoulders and stroke defects. The elbows clear the sides by a couple of inches.

From this point the hands roll over so that the palms now face down and they stretch forward in a streamlined recovery some 4 inches deep.

Points to remember are: (a) firm bent wrists to engage the water effectively and strongly; (b) do not drop the elbows, in fact slightly raise them; (c) do not take the hands back beyond the chin line; (d) do not tuck the elbows tightly on to rib-cage.

The Glide

At race pace over 100 metres there is little time for gliding but nevertheless there is a detectable glide. Over 200 metres the glide is definite. In women's breaststroke the glide is longer. Women usually rate about thirty strokes each 50 metres whereas men rate much higher in a 200 metre event.

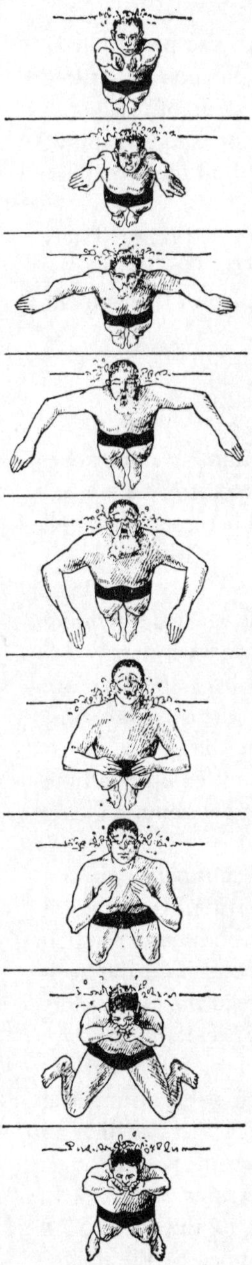

Fig. 13. THE BREASTSTROKE

(a) The hands commence their work from a back-to-back position. They should glide forward well below the surface. The stomach should be held up and the toes pointed

(b) By cocking the elbows and bending the wrists, the arms assume a very strong and efficient pulling position

(c) Coaches advocate a narrow pull, but underwater viewing proves that the pull is wider than generally imagined. Elbows are kept up

(d) You will notice that the legs have not commenced their movement as the arms continue their boomerang-shaped pull. Often this powerful pull tends to lift the hips and legs higher in the water

(e) When the hands are directly beneath the top of the chest, the face commences its smooth surfacing movement

(f) Note that the hands almost touch each other at the end of the pull. This swimmer has his elbows extended but I prefer the swimmer to tuck his elbows in quickly at the end of the stroke. The mouth is now ready for inhalation

(g) The heels have now commenced their rapid hinge movement up to the thigh. Note: do not bend the upper leg under the body

(h) Try to keep the knees relatively close together, certainly inside the line of the heels. As the feet whip back the hands commence recovery

(i) The legs are now in the position ready to squeeze together; there is also a backward flicking of the feet. The end of this backward flick coincides with the arms fully extended in front

The timing of the arms and the breathing

When the arms are three-quarter way through the pull, that is, when they are almost level with the chin, the face is smoothly tilted up out of the water until the gaping mouth is clear of the pool's surface and the inhalation commences. The chin should not be lifted from the water and it is important also not to lift the shoulders. The neck causes the head to be tilted.

The breath is taken sharply through the mouth and immediately the hands start to move forward into the recovery the face is dropped back into the water and exhalation commences, again through the mouth.

The Leg Action

Over the years, one feature in breaststroke swimming stands out. The narrower and quicker the leg drive becomes the faster we go. But there is a limit to how narrow the legs should become. Secondly, the narrow leg drive admirably suits most male swimmers but I have found that females make better time, and have less knee trouble with a slightly wider kicking action. At the Mexico Olympics this was borne out by observations on the respective winners.

The recovery commences from a position where the legs are trailing straight out behind with toes pointed and the heels are some 4 inches below the surface. Some swimmers cannot keep their heels together because they become unbalanced, this applies especially to those with poor flotation. The heels should be carried about 4 inches apart.

The heels now attempt to fold up on to the buttocks, without letting the knees drop too deep or spreading too wide. At this point the heels try to stay in a line with the knees, or perhaps a fraction outside the knee line, but under no circumstances should the heels be inside the knee line. In other words do not spread the knees wide. When the heels have folded up as far as practical the feet are suddenly turned out, that is the heels will be facing each other and the toes pointing outwards. The bottom of the foot has assumed a flat position ready for the sudden thrust back. The feet are only an inch or two below the surface. Of major importance is the knee position; do not tuck the knees forward, that is under the stomach. If this happens the buttocks tend to rise out of the water and tremendous resistance is caused by the water trapped by the thighs.

This also causes the body to move forward in a series of jerks and not smoothly.

The feet are now 'cocked' ready for the narrow and vigorous backward and slightly downward push. The feet push back and describe a slight arc, but at no stage do the heels spread more than 30 inches.

The propulsion from this movement comes from the pushing back of the flat surface of the bottom of the feet and the shins and the thighs. There is a noticeable squeezing together of the legs at the end of the leg drive. The final movement is the flicking back of the feet with the toes stretching. This final flick is very important. Make sure the heels come together in this final flick. I have observed it in the world's best breaststrokers. At the completion of the leg drive the feet are only about 12 inches deep. As the body moves forward the legs rise towards the surface and prepare for the recovery phase. From a side view O'Brien and his contemporaries appear to be doing a dolphin kick.

The Co-ordination – Arms and Legs

When the arms have completed their pull and the hands are about to tuck up under the chin, the heels start to move up towards the buttocks. Before the hands have extended out fully in front the feet have commenced the backward thrust. In other words the hard backward push of the shins and feet is synchronized with the hands being pushed out in front. Actually as the arms are completing the recovery, the legs are pushing. This timing allows the body to move forward smoothly. There being constant propulsion from either legs or arms.

Some top flight swimmers have a more delayed timing action. That is the arms are fully extended before the kick is completed. Prozumenschikova of Russia has this late timing.

Thigh Rise

At the completion of the leg drive, a little extra momentum can be gained by lifting the thighs a little. This gives the body a dolphin-like ripple. Ian O'Brien has this facet in his stroke.

Adjustments to the stroke should be made for women swimmers. Namely, a slightly wider leg action, a longer glide and more emphasis on developing the power of the leg drive and the whip finish to the kick.

I have listed a few training items that I consider important for the stroke development and to add interest to the training schedule.

(a) Repeat pulling (arms only) sprints from 50 to 200 metres.

(b) Repeat kick sprints of 50 or 100 metres.

(c) Kick without a board, lying on the back, trying to keep the knees fairly close together.

(d) Repeat short underwater sprints.

(e) Ankle flexibility exercises.

(f) Breaststroke arm movements on the dynastatic machine.

HOWARD FIRBY

Howard Firby, Canadian Coach at the Tokyo Olympics, is a fine stroke analyst. Here are his comments, mainly upon the Russian breaststroke scene:

'At Mexico the Russians had three finalists in the men's 100 metres and 200 metres breaststroke. In the women's events they had three in the 200 metres and two in the 100 metres breaststroke finals.

'Three of the six medals for breaststroke in the 1964 Olympic Games went to Russians. Five of the sixteen finalists, nearly one-third, were Russian. And at this time of writing, five of the eight world breaststroke records are held by Russians. Yet Russia holds only one other world record, the 440 yards medley relay for men, and breaststroke figures strongly in that event too. This brilliance of theirs in just the one branch of the sport, isolates technique as the clue to their success; if it were a matter of superior conditioning, their success would prevail throughout the full range of events.

'As coach of the Canadian swimming team in Tokyo, I had the freedom of the training pools and on several occasions I was able to study the techniques of Prokopenko (w.r. 100 metres and 220 yards), Babanina (w.r. 100 metres) and Prozumenschikova (w.r. 100 metres and 220 yards) at close range. What I saw was quite different from the breaststroke methods most commonly seen in North America.

'The two girls had very powerful kicks – Peter Daland, Head Coach of the U.S. Women's Team in Tokyo, referred to them as "three minute kickers", meaning that in his opinion they were capable of doing 200 metres in 3 minutes on a kick board. They did not use the knees-close-together "whip kick" so popular in North America; their's was a wide, knees-apart kick which featured a directing of the thighs upward as the propelling phase of kick happened. I mention this thighs-upward movement because it is so seldom seen in Australia. Here, the tendency is for the swimmer to hold his thighs in a semi-fixed position while the lower legs "whip" in a backward and downward direction. It is not until late in the kick, when the legs are almost fully extended, that the legs are lifted at all. (The deception of refraction can lull even an experienced coach into believing that his swimmers are almost level in the water when, in reality, they may be at angles of twenty or more degrees – "sinking by the stern", as it were.)

'The Russians use their thighs as propelling surfaces. (The thighs alone make good propelling surfaces; the author seeing a double amputee – both legs amputated just below the knee – make excellent time with a form of "thighs only" breaststroke.) Every part of their legs contributes to the effort.

'This "thigh rise", to coin a phrase, form of kick, was used by many of the top swimmers at the games; notably Ian O'Brien, the Olympic Champion and World Record Holder from Australia. The Russians were the most obvious in their use of it however.

'The thigh-rise feature, when allowed its full potential, affects the timing of the whole stroke to a very marked degree. There is a dolphin-like cadence which is aesthetically satisfying to both the swimmer and observer.

'As the after-parts of the swimmer are raised, the shoulders are driven lower into the water. The water line moves up the swimmer's face to the hairline during this phase of the stroke (care is taken not to allow the head to go under). At the conclusion of the kick, the swimmer is all but submerged in the manner of a submarine cruising with only its conning tower (in this case the swimmer's head) slicing through the surface. At no time is the swimmer stiffly posed in a "Look Ma . . . I'm gliding" way, yet there is a drifting continuity of momentum which gives the swimmer a "moving-with-the-current" appearance.

'I have mentioned that the thigh-rise style of kicking is not the Russians' exclusive. Something which is, very definitely, Russian is the arm action which will be dealt with now.

'The hands are brought together in a prayer-like way after the arm-pull phase is finished. From the "praying" position, the hands travel forward into the point position, the elbows rotating upward as the arms are straightened. The hands shift from the praying position to an overlapping position and then to a palms-turned-outward, thumbs-downward, wrists-overlapping position. All of the Russians did this to some degree and there is reasoning behind it; such positioning and shaping of the hands reduces any tendency for the swimmer to alter his angle in the water by using his hands as planes. The swimmer makes no attempt to lift himself with his hands. In fact, he strives to submerge up to the limit of the law. The breath comes late in the stroke cycle; i.e. when the arms have finished pulling and are shifting to the praying position, a breath is taken on each stroke; the cadence calls for a raising of the front end in each cycle so the swimmer might as well avail himself of a breath.

'The size of the arm pulls varied with the relative shoulder strengths of the individual swimmers. The girls were rather sturdy through the hips and the thighs – three minute kickers, remember, and tended to use abbreviated arm pull. The men used a more forceful and longer pull. Also, the men tended to get their arms into the next stroke before their legs came together; either the hands together with the feet still closing, or the feet together with the hands already separated and into the next pull, but not both ends pointed at the same time.

'The stroke with its rollicking rhythm is extremely efficient; I counted and observed that Prozumenshikova did an average of 22 strokes per length while cruising at 45 seconds a length (50 metre pool) during her training swims.

'I have no doubt that many who read this will wonder at the position of the hands – is it legal? The International Rule, F.I.N.A. Rule 66, reads as follows:

"Both hands must be pushed forward together from the breast on or under the surface and brought backward simultaneously and symmetrically with lateral extension."

'Now "together", according to the F.I.N.A. usage of the word, does not mean side by side – it means "at the same time". This becomes apparent when the butterfly rule is studied – butterfly swimmers bring their arms forward "together". Purists may relax. The Russian swimmers had their hands at the same depth before any pulling "backward" was started. The reasoning behind the peculiarly Russian hand positioning can be explained:

'(a) It is a natural position to strike after having passed one hand over the back of the other.

'(b) The hands, one above the other, are easier to start moving;

were they to be back to back then the decrease in pressure on the back of one would pull the other, and vice versa; by having the backs of the hands exposed to water flowing cleanly by (with little turbulence as is the case when the hands are close together and at the same depth) the swimmer is better able to sense the ideal moment for the commencing of the next arm pull. In any event, the shaping of the hands in exactly the Russian manner is not essential to the stroke; virtually any of the no-lift, late breathing arm actions can be blended into the thigh-rise rhythm.'

Galina Prozumenschikova's Training Programme
   ($1\frac{1}{2}$–$2\frac{1}{2}$ hours daily)
   'I never swim more than 60,000–80,000 metres per month, while my assignment in August was 104,000 metres – three stretches of 200 metres each, followed by four of 100 metres each, and eight more of 50 metres each, then repeat the whole thing again – all in a single work-out (about 2,800 metres for each daily work-out). And I had to do more than half this distance at full speed.'
   Height 5 feet 5 inches. Weight – just under 165 lb.
   Activities – gym, acrobatics, basketball and hand ball.

BREASTSTROKE START AND TURN

'Swimming under the surface of the water is prohibited except one arm pull and one leg kick after start and turn.'
   'When touching on a turn or finishing a race the touch shall be made with both hands simultaneously on the same level with shoulders in a horizontal position.'
   The stance on the starting block is a natural one, similar to the present accepted freestyle start. The entry into the water, however, is at a deeper angle because the momentum of the body will be carried forward more effectively if it glides through the water some 2 feet to 2 feet 6 inches below the surface. The second reason for the deeper entry is that the underwater pull and kick become much more effective at this depth. The swimmer will have to educate himself for that 'feel' which signals to him that the body is starting to lose momentum. At this point his hands turn out, pull and push backwards in a narrow but vigorous movement. This pull is underneath the body and not to the side as in the normal stroke. Some

swimmers whilst performing this movement, initiate a body wave. Minor body waves will normally be tolerated by the referee, but once the legs perform or even suggest a dolphin kick the swimmer will be disqualified. Therefore you can see how important it is not to influence the lower body when carrying out this pull.

The hands and arms are tucked neatly by the side of the body and the head is held down, thereby continuing the streamlined trajectory. Again when the swimmer 'feels' his speed is decreasing he commences to draw up his heels and cock his legs ready for a hard breaststroke kick. Simultaneously he has moved his hands up under his chest and as he drives backwards with his feet his arms extend out in front and his head breaks the surface.

Some faults to be avoided in the breaststroke start are:

1. 'Jack-knifing' on the entry.
2. The entry too shallow or the entry too deep.
3. The pull to be a wide one.
4. Lifting the head during the glide.

The Turn

The principles I have just outlined also apply to the breaststroke turn. The breaststroke turn should be the 'safest' of all turns. As the swimmer approaches the wall he should have no difficulty in adjusting his stroke so that as his arms stretch forward he touches the wall with fully extended arms. The momentum of his lower limbs carries forward and he bends his knees quickly up under his stomach at the same time pushing away from the wall with his hands in a sideways manner. There is a brief moment when the body has no contact with the wall. It is that fraction of time before the feet land on the wall but after the hands have left the wall. The legs are still bent and the feet are placed on the wall some 18 inches to 2 feet below the surface.

The legs straighten and the feet now push vigorously. The arms stretch forward in front and the body leaves the wall in a streamlined position. The underwater pull and kick is now executed the same as for the start.

THE FINISH

A modification to the racing stroke can be made towards the finish of a race. The arm and leg actions become narrower and consequently more rapid. Breathing is stopped, the face slightly tilted in the water and held in this position over the last 5 or 6 metres. This type of stroking is very demanding, especially upon a rapidly mounting oxygen debt, but if the swimmer has the will-power to carry it out a few precious inches can be gained. Needless to say that fully extended arms and stretched fingers will reach the wall before those in any other position. Finally, on the last stroke-lunge if the head is suddenly dropped and shoulders stretched forward the arms in turn can reach out further.

19 Medley Swimming in Australia

At the time of writing Australia has not produced a medley swimmer of note. Peter Reynolds and Diana Rickard have approached world times, but so markedly have the world medley records tumbled that Australia is in the doldrums in this event at present. The main reason for this is that we tend to think of medley swimming as a secondary stroke. To my knowledge there would not be more than three swimmers in Australia who are training with a long range view of becoming medley swimmers. Most Australian swimmers who swim medley do so as a secondary stroke and consequently we are second-rate. Also until this year associations and clubs have not included individual medleys in their programmes for the U/10, U/12, U/14 age groups. Finally we have no medley swimmer who is in world class in one of the strokes, as was Peter Reynolds, in backstroke.

All the above is being rectified. The new method of teaching swimmers to swim all the strokes correctly before they are ten years of age, plus the international prestige now associated with a medley performer are reasons why Australia will soon gain world records. There is much room for research into the training schedules best suited for medley performers. There is no doubt in my mind that a sensible programming of the strokes will tend to aid and not hinder each other. Every medley swimmer has experienced the dreaded few seconds when turning from breaststroke to freestyle (the changing from one set of swimming muscles to another) or the fatiguing effect on the legs in the breaststroke section when one is not a 'natural' breaststroker. Correct training can certainly minimize these effects and allow for a performance closer to 100 per cent effort.

Coaches do not seem to realize that one overriding principle controls a fine medley performance. It is superb conditioning, for in no other event does conditioning play such an important part as in the I.M. The reason for this is that as we pass through each stroke we leave specific areas of local fatigue, so that at the end of a race practically every muscle group is weary.

Educationalists tell us that the best way to learn a skill is to practise for a day or so then change to another subject for a few sessions and then complete the learning cycle by returning to the original subjects. It appears that the brain and muscles appreciate a rest in this manner. Some coaches have had success with a programme that sets out all backstroke and allied sections on the first day, all breaststroke and its components on the second day, freestyle with its kicks and pulls on the third day, butterfly only on the fourth day and on the fifth day medleys. Others prefer a system of a complete stroke each session, e.g. butterfly in the morning, backstroke in the afternoon, etc.

In preparing a medley swimmer I have found that it pays handsome dividends to set a weekly target of improving the swimmer's weakest stroke in (a) technique, (b) endurance, (c) speed. Secondly, training the medley swimmers with the distance freestylers is a decided asset. This is the method I used in preparing Forbes Carlile's pupil Diana Rickard for an attempt on the Australian record. In this attempt she lowered her time from 5·22·0 to 5·18·3.

(a) One session a day for a week working on breaststroke training with the breaststroke champions. A time trial at the end of the week revealed that she had reduced her best 100 metre breaststroke time from 1·31·0 to 1·26·8.

(b) The second week she trained one session per day on backstroke and since her backstroke is reasonable in technique I concentrated on superb conditioning in the stroke. At the end of the week Time Trial Diana was approaching a healthy 5 minutes 35 seconds for 400 metres backstroke.

(c) The third week emphasis was placed on reaching a level of fitness new to her. One session a day was devoted to training with Australia's Olympic 1,500 metres representatives.

A typical training session work-out was:

(i) 400 metres medley loosen up.

(ii) 2 × 800 metres efforts at 85 per cent.

(iii) 4 × 400 metres efforts at 90 per cent.

(iv) 8 × 200 metres sprints at 95 per cent.

A tough conditioning work-out indeed.

During the above three weeks the second session each day was devoted entirely to medley work.

A system such as this can have rewarding fringe benefits for in the season just concluded I was fortunate enough to produce an outstanding medley swimmer who also was rated No. 1 butterfly swimmer in the nation, No. 1 breaststroker, No. 3 backstroker, No. 4 freestyler for his age.

It must be realized the tremendous importance the breaststroke leg plays in the I.M. This section can be so demanding on those that are not accustomed to it that it often nullifies the freestyle leg.

The butterfly does not necessarily have to be the swimmer's best stroke. It is indeed rare that the leader of the butterfly wins the race, all other things being equal. It is good practice to control the butterfly in the 400 metre I.M. It will certainly pay dividends in the later stages of the event. The 200 metre I.M. is a completely different thing. It is a sprint. This is the reason why I train my 200 metre I.M. swimmers with the sprint team.

I cannot impress too strongly how vital it is to be super-conditioned for a medley. The swimmer must be able to swim 400 metres of each of the four strokes on par with the best stroke leaders of the squad.

Thought should be given to, and testing made on the turns of the I.M. To do the complete breaststroke turn or to surface without any underwater stroking is a matter for you to decide. Some swimmers find they have more energy in succeeding laps if they surface immediately. Likewise the preference to tumble from backstroke to breaststroke can be made after testing. When it is all boiled down it depends upon the magnitude of the oxygen debt, and the swimmer's determination to overcome it.

Many an inexperienced I.M. swimmer loses a race or records a poor time because he does not swim his own race. The I.M. is the one event in which you cannot pace the opposition. How foolish for a 70 seconds 'fly swimmer to pace a sub-60 seconds 'fly swimmer over the first leg. In Australia at least there are not enough competitive medley races to gain the valuable experience necessary for an even distribution of energy throughout the event. This experience can only be gained by frequent use of the stop-watch in 'repeat' medley swims during training sessions. To elaborate further on an even distribution of energy a good example is the system used by former world record holder Dick Roth, U.S.A., who alternates his energy output from below the waist and above the waist. For example, during the butterfly he works equally with his arms and legs. In the backstroke his arms play the major role. Conversely, in the breaststroke section his leg drive gives out 80 per cent of the power. His freestyle is a balanced stroke.

Most experts agree that a medley win, on the average, goes to the swimmer who has the better breaststroke, freestyle finish. Since it is rare for a breaststroker to be a good freestyler and vice versa, a true medley champion must have complete mastery over the technique of all the strokes.

20 Profiles on Youth

Sandra Bright

Sandra Bright, 15 years of age, lives in Brisbane, Australia. She is the best 'long-distance' butterfly swimmer yet produced in Australia. At 14 years she swam:

100 metres butterfly in 1·07·5
200 metres butterfly in 2·20·6 (national age record)
400 metres butterfly in 5·02·0
800 metres butterfly in 10·46·6

Sandra's weight is 7 stone 5 lbs and she is 5 feet 1 inch in height. She excels at water polo and tennis also. Sandra is one of those fine performers who can manage as much as 7,000 metres of butterfly in a session. Her stroke rate is rapid, low in recovery but very powerful. Her annual progression times are:

11 years	1·15·8	100 metres	2·40·0	200 metres
12 years	1·11·6	100 metres	2·31·3	200 metres
13 years	1·08·1	100 metres	2·23·6	200 metres
14 years	1·07·5	100 metres	2·20·6	200 metres

Sandra is a four stroke swimmer with a 400 metres individual medley time of 5 minutes 23 seconds. Her 800 metres freestyle time is 9·25·5. Her favourite workout is:

Morning

5 × 400 metres efforts, departing every 7 minutes, all on butterfly or 4 butterfly and 1 medley

20 × 100 metres 'legs tied' freestyle sprints, departing every 1 minute 45 seconds

10 × 200 metres medley departing every 3 minutes 15 seconds

1,000 metres fast dolphin kick with swim flippers

Total: 7,000 metres

Her butterfly arm action is almost ideal, the hands pull centrally along the mid-line, push to full extension and recover very fast and low. The hip lift is not exaggerated in the body wave and although the kick is not powerful, it is useful enough to give some momentum, and it does not hinder.

Whilst Australia is undergoing a swimming slump, Sandra Bright appears to be one of the individuals who will shine in the next few years. Her time of 2·20·6 seconds rates her in the top 10 of the world.

Coach: Harry Gallagher

Lisa Curry

Lisa Curry, 13 years of age, is brilliant at many sports, having the school record for running and high jump. She is the fastest swimmer over 50 metres freestyle (long course) yet produced in Australia at 12 years, as her Queensland schoolgirl record of 28·3 signifies. Her time eclipses the best in the U.S.A. for her year. Being tall and slim she closely resembles Australia's previous superstar, Shane Gould, at the same age. This body style certainly appears to be the ideal one for late-maturing sprinters. Lisa weighs 7 stone 10 lbs and her height is 5 feet 5 inches.

Lisa cannot yet carry a heavy load of swimming in daily training (she can manage 8,000-9,000 metres daily but this falls short of the 12,000 metres standard of her team mates). She exercises very little due to her heavy school commitment in athletics. She is an excellent student.

Her progression is:

10 years	35·5	50 metres	77·8	100 metres
11 years	31·6	50 metres	69·4	100 metres
12 years	28·3	50 metres	63·6	100 metres

Her favourite workout is:

Morning

3 × 10 × 50 metres freestyle sprints on the 60 seconds, 50 seconds, 45 seconds

20 × 50 metres kick sprints freestyle with or without swim flippers on the 60 seconds

500 metres breaststroke for style

500 metres backstroke for style

40 × 25 metres sprints in the medley order departing every 30 seconds

10 special 50 metres sprints from dive

Total: 5,000 metres

Lisa lives in the temperate Brisbane region of Australia and trains outdoors 10 months of the year.

Coach: Harry Gallagher

Nancy Garapick

Nancy Garapick is the brightest young swim star to emerge from Canada in years. She is just 13 years old and is the present world record holder for the 200 metres backstroke. Her time is 2·16·33 seconds. She is a member of the Halifax Trojan Aquatic Club. Nicknamed 'mighty mite' she is 5 feet 4 inches and weighs 8 stone 3 lbs.

Nancy has been training for 5 years and her long course progression times are:

10 years	1·25·8	100 metres	3·03·3	200 metres
11 years	1·16·4	100 metres	2·39·6	200 metres
12 years	1·07·9	100 metres	2·48·8	200 metres
13 years	1·04·3	100 metres	2·16·3	200 metres

A typical mid-season programme set by her coach is:

Morning
800 own choice of drills
24 × 50 I.M./F.S. pull on 50 seconds
5 × 100 kick on 2½ minutes
5 × 200 alternate 50s pace/fast on 3½ minutes
5 × 200 I.M. kick 25 swim 25 on 4 minutes
200 single arm free/fly
8 × 25 fly/free on 35 seconds
200 single arm back/free
12 × 25 back/breast on 35 seconds
200 F.S. easy
8 × 25 free on 35 seconds

Total: 5,800 metres

Afternoon
1,000 kick, pull, full
10 × 200 25 easy 25 fast on 3½ minutes
20 × 50 kick on 1·05 swim on 55
6 × 100 I.M. on 2 minutes descend 1–3, 4–6
500 pull, 5 seconds at 50
15 × 50 on 60 seconds, descend 1–3 etc.

Total: 5,850 metres

Nancy is an even pace swimmer. She prefers to go out steady and has a devastating finish. Physiologically she has an excellent maximum VO2 and very little body fat. She has a very positive attitude towards training.

Coach: Nigel Kemp

Tim Shaw

Tim Shaw is one of the super stars of the 'seventies. At 16 years he already holds the world records for 200, 400, 800 and 1,500 metres freestyle. He is only the second male to hold these records at the same time. He is also in world class as a backstroke swimmer. Tim started training at 8 years of age and is now a member of Phillips 66 Long Beach Club. He weighs 11 stone 11 lbs and is 6 feet 1 inch tall.

Here are his times:

Short Course Progression

Age	200 Free	500 Free	1,650 Free	200 Back
13 years	1·52·8	4·59·8		2·10·8
14 years	1·49·5	4·52·5	17·17·0	2·05·8
15 years	1·40·7	4·32·9	15·58·4	1·57·4
16 years	1·39·41	4·23·50	15·19·15	

Long Course Progression

Age	200 Free	400 Free	1,500 Free	200 Back
13 years	2·07·5	4·23·8		2·23·3
14 years	2·00·2	4·13·4	16·38·8	2·18·1
15 years	1·57·2	4·01·4	16·15·4	2·13·7
16 years	1·51·66	3·54·69	15·31·75	

Tim works at a tempo of 4,000 yards an hour. His work is of highest quality but he does not do the marathon schedules of some other distance stars. He averages 12,000 metres daily.

Coach: Dr Richard Jochums

INDEX

Figures in *italic* refer to line drawings in the text